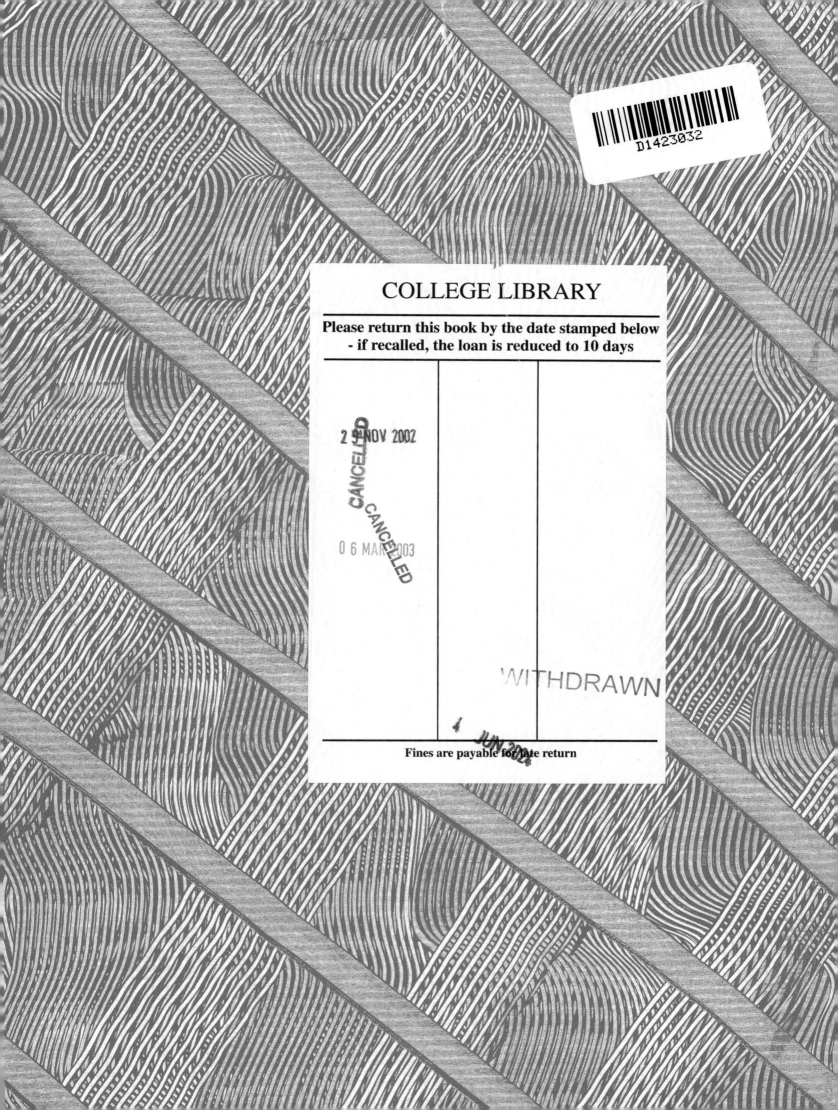

R 11
3490
3725
R 12
3726-3991
R 13
3992-4287
R 15
4578-4794
Y 13
4978 – 5250
Y-14
Y 15
5553 – 5835

the
ENGLISH
ARCHIVE
of Design and Decoration

with over 600 designs, patterns and settings
in colour and black-and-white.

STAFFORD CLIFF

THAMES · T&H · HUDSON

530.

531.

532.

22471
3422

22470
3402

22469
3410

22468
3418

22467
3403

22466
3419

22465
3405

22464
3404

22463
3416

22462
3420

22461
3409
8ᵗʰ 1905

22460
3406

22482
3407

22481
3412

22480
3400

22479
3414

22478
3413

22477
3408

22476
3423

22475
3411

22474
3426

22473
3424

22472
3421

8

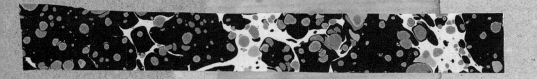

Author's
REFACE

This book is a celebration of the work of the named and unnamed artist-designers who made such an astonishing and original contribution to English domestic culture, craftsmanship and manufacture during the eighteenth, nineteenth and early twentieth centuries. Although it is formally divided into periods reflecting changes in the design and style concerns of the nation, it is neither a formal history nor a comprehensive directory of them. The brief introductions to each section are intended simply to provide the background against which the illustrations that follow can be seen and appreciated. Within each section I have grouped the designs visually, sometimes relating similar work by different artists, sometimes contrasting different solutions to similar problems, sometimes showing consecutive pages from the same documents, and elsewhere putting unrelated schemes side by side because of their visual rapport.

During my researches, some of the records I discovered could hardly have been expected to survive, being little more than scraps of paper, never intended for a client's eyes, let alone to be printed in a book. Other designs I found recorded in pattern books, swatch books, shape books, sometimes actually rendered in colour by the very craftsmen who had earlier made the finished artefact. Such records often showed the signs of constant use: the worn edges of pages marked with potters' clay or even singed by a glass-blower's flame; patterns annotated with later comments or artisans' instructions; bindings battered by constant handling. Yet, for the most part, the designs still reveal the remarkable skills of those who drew them, and a freshness and spontaneity as appealing today as when they were first created.

Half-title, Title and Contents Pages and Pages 6–7
The archive of the Spode pottery and porcelain factory in Stoke-on-Trent is a repository of English design genius from the 18th century to the present. Though one pattern record book from the time of the foundation of the company in 1776 by Josiah Spode I still exists, most of the well-worn volumes date from 1800, when the decorating department was established. Each page bears a hand-painted record of a pattern with its appropriate number. In spite of several changes in the ownership of the company, this extraordinary heirloom of design has remained intact.

These pages (pp. 6–7) from a master pattern book of 1804 record a sugar basin and cover, a coffee can and a 'Bute' shape teacup, decorated on-glaze in gold. Every pattern, when produced, was given a pattern number (there are 70,000 on record) which were sometimes stamped on the wares. The design of this coffee cup 531 was revived in 1950 in gold on dark blue and incorporated into the Arundel range.

opposite Early twentieth-century designs for bread knives from Elkington & Co., Birmingham.

INTRODUCTION

Between 1700 and 1939 England and English design held a pre-eminent position in the applied arts of the western world, creating a unique national heritage. Simply to mention some of the major names of this long and complex period – Kent, Chippendale, Hepplewhite, Adam, Sheraton, Pugin, Morris, Voysey, Liberty, Gimson – is to evoke a history and an achievement rarely equalled at any time in the decorative arts. The furniture and interiors of these designers have had world-wide influence; even when industrialization transformed and expanded the making of household materials and artefacts in the nineteenth century, the pattern books and catalogues of English firms remained the source of a multiplicity of elegant solutions to practical problems.

The names of Chippendale and Liberty could perhaps be taken as twin peaks of English achievement in design, one in the initial period and the other in the latter of the timespan covered by this book, both establishing their reputation by the dissemination of published matter about their creations. In 1754, Thomas Chippendale issued his *The Gentleman and Cabinet-maker's Director*. As well as being a record of contemporary style and taste, it was an advertisement for Chippendale's own work and a source-book for jobbing craftsmen throughout the world. At the end of the nineteenth century and the beginning of the twentieth the catalogues for furniture, textiles, pottery and glass of the London shop of Liberty established such a high reputation for the firm's products and retailing practices that the term 'Liberty' came to designate *fin-de-siècle* design in both France and Italy.

Yet, a nation's design heritage is made up of much more than a few well-known names. Behind the pattern books of nineteenth-century manufacturers lies the work of scores of anonymous draughtsmen and craftsmen responsible for thousands of original designs, whose uncredited work often displays great artistic flair and technical

ingenuity. Some of the names of designers whose work is included in the illustration pages of this book will be immediately recognizable as the taste-formers of their age. But many of the most interesting, imaginative and beautiful works are by those whose individuality remained unrecognized by the workshops and manufacturers which employed them.

The illustrations in this book have, therefore, been drawn from a variety of sources: design books, pattern books, shape books, swatch books, company archives, manufacturers' and retail catalogues. Many companies maintained comprehensive archives and design records until World War II, after which time some were lodged for safe keeping in public collections. These often consisted of books of original designs and sketches recording the used and unused motifs and forms over a given period and were therefore intended essentially for internal use. Such records provided a source and inspiration for further design and production years after their creation, especially in the case of those firms, notably in wallpaper, textile and pottery manufacture, whose reputation depended on the continuity of a certain English 'look'. A textile mill, for instance, would maintain a record of its production in the form of swatch books. These may contain the artist's original designs and sometimes trial impressions of printing on paper before application to a particular fabric. It is common, too, to find such books with actual cuttings from the cloth – swatches – as originally printed.

Clearly, such records were never intended for public use, and the beauty and extent of much of this material has only come to be appreciated since its appearance either on the open market at auction, in public archives, in exhibition and in publications such as *The World of Interiors*.

Much more directly accessible were manufacturers' catalogues, which contain records of a company's output and are therefore representations of post-production artefacts rather than pre-production design; these were intended for the use of sales representatives and the eventual customer or retailer. Late eighteenth-century sample books were rarely dated and bore no maker's name or title-page information. They were carried from town to town by itinerant agents who carefully guarded their own sources of manufacture and a network of contacts often built up over years. The cost and scarcity

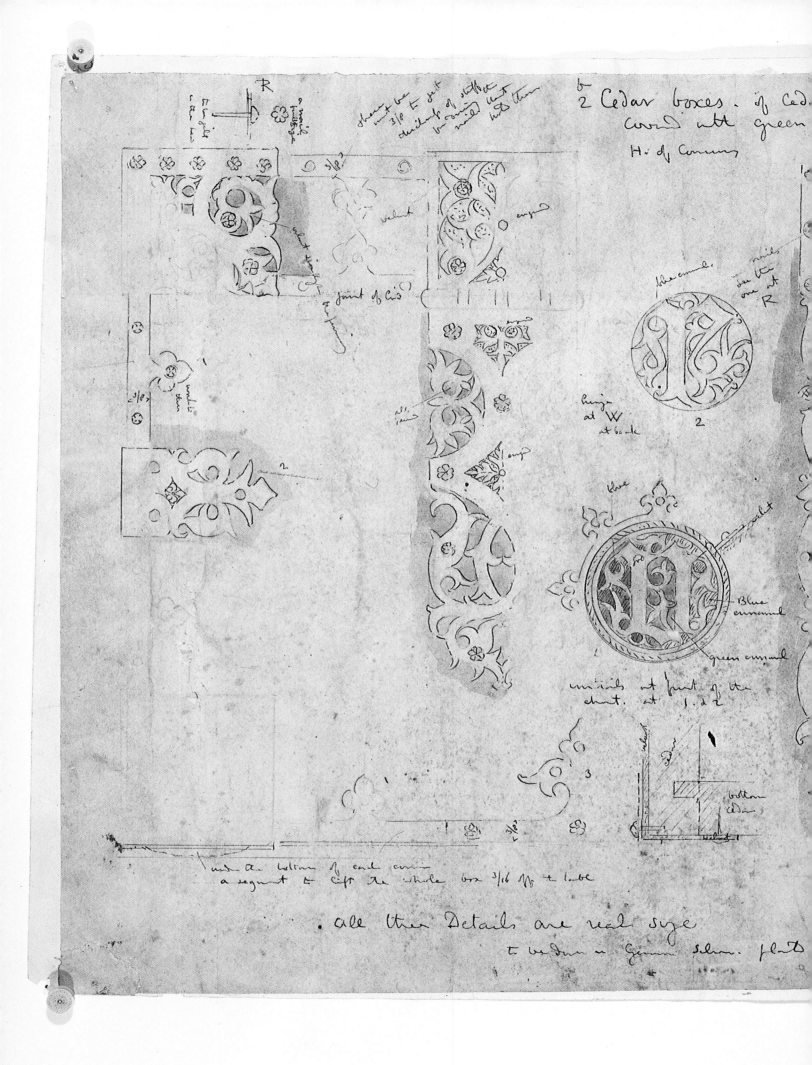

2 Cedar boxes . of Ced.
Covered with green

Ht of Corners

all these Details are real size
to be done in German silver plate

13

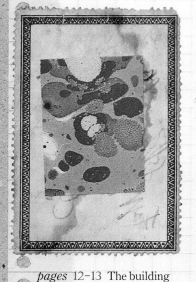

pages 12–13 The building of the Houses of Parliament in London was one of the great architectural feats of the mid nineteenth century. Much of the interior decoration was designed by Augustus Pugin (1812-52); these sketched designs are for two cedar boxes to be covered in green velvet.

of raw materials and poor state of the road network undoubtedly contributed to the growth of such secretive practices, but the anonymity of the books meant that clients found it hard to approach manufacturers directly and the lack of a date disguised to provincial eyes the fact that a style was out-dated.

In the early nineteenth century the customer may very well have been an architect-designer or 'upholsterer' (the equivalent of today's interior designer) who would employ craftsmen as well as purchasing furnishings and fittings, often for the new town and country houses of the burgeoning upper middle and middle classes. As industrialization grew in the production of domestic equipment and artefacts, so too did the production of catalogues aimed at suppliers to a mass market. These would often take the form of fragments of the finished object (wallpapers or textiles, for instance), rather than drawings or paintings.

A later development of such promotion of wares to both a specialized and general public was the issuing of store and shop catalogues. In the late nineteenth century and the early decades of the twentieth both Liberty and Heal's produced exciting anthologies of furniture, textiles and other objects, often specially created for the firm, which promoted a particular design ethos and helped to imprint a distinctly English look on the international design consciousness.

Another important category of pattern book, and one substantially represented here, is that of the publication intended both as a register of current fashion and also as an inspiration to the craftsman and the would-be decorator. In the early eighteenth century such books, containing engraved designs for ceilings, doorways and chimneypieces, were issued by architects and builders. The practice soon spread to the publication of designs for furniture, although it should be noted that some of the earliest examples of this were inspired by foreign craftsmen working in London, notably by the Italian Brunetti and the Frenchman De La Cour. Outstanding English pattern books of the period include Matthew Lock's *Six Sconces* of 1744 and his *Six Tables* of 1746, followed in 1752 by his *New Book of Ornaments*. Undoubtedly the finest eighteenth-century example of such publishing, however, is Thomas Chippendale's *Director*, which began a tradition to be followed by other famous English designers, decorators and furniture-makers: Thomas Johnson, George Hepplewhite and Thomas Sheraton.

In the nineteenth century, books, catalogues and journals devoted to the publication of styles, patterns and whole decorative schemes proliferated, which partly explains the wild eclecticism of much of early and mid Victorian domestic design. Robert Bridgens' *Furniture and Candelabra and Interior Decoration* of 1838, for instance, lists twenty-seven 'Elizabethan' designs, twenty-five 'Grecian', and seven 'Gothic'. Later examples of this type of publication do, however, show the influence of the great Victorian design reformers in the movement towards a more homogeneous approach to interior design and a greater respect for material and suitability of form. William Godwin, notably, created designs for an *Art Furniture* catalogue in 1877; in 1880, T. Knight and Sons published *Suggestions for Home Decoration*, which included whole room settings in a variety of styles. Later, the Arts and Crafts Movement was to take the concept of total domestic design much further, wherein every detail became a carefully considered part of a whole domestic environment. For these later periods, many of the original designs have survived and were, in any case, copiously reproduced, notably in the pages of *The Studio*.

The accumulation of design archives and the variety of publishing which accompanied the activities of designers, craftsmen and manufacturers throughout the eighteenth and nineteenth centuries were clearly not phenomena confined solely to the market in domestic artefacts. Such processes also aided the expansion of industrial, commercial and ecclesiastical design and knowledge. Yet, to have included so many different types of design in the present book would certainly have diluted our central concern: to demonstrate by comparative illustration the strength of the English domestic design tradition and the skills to record such design through nearly two and a half centuries. From whatever source they are taken – original sketchbook, pattern book, manufacturer's or retailer's catalogue, and even scraps of paper – the illustrations here have been chosen because they show exciting, occasionally very ingenious, solutions to design problems as perceived at a given time. They are all interesting, and frequently very beautiful. They have an immediacy, even to the contemporary eye, and are therefore equally relevant to the search for design inspiration today.

co cords N.º 8 & 11 — Ap.º 28:th 1721 — for Mr Alexander

Desines Simples —

16

CLASSICISM *and* ROCOCO

The development of the English applied arts in the eighteenth century is very much a history of alternating taste: classical simplicity, succeeded by the decorative exuberance of a native form of Rococo, and then back to a regard for stricter forms in Neoclassicism.

One name above all informed English attitudes to design in the early part of the century: that of Andrea Palladio, the Italian Renaissance architect. Two publications of 1715 helped underline his pre-eminent position as an exemplar of fine taste in the applied arts: Colin Campbell's *Vitruvius Britannicus*, which delineated the development of the large country house in England in a series of engravings, and an English translation of the Italian master's own *Four Books of Architecture*. This work had been a considerable source of inspiration to the earlier English architect, Inigo Jones, whose work had come to be much admired by both patrons and architects in the early eighteenth century.

Political and social factors also contributed to the vogue for a muted classicism in the early eighteenth century. Firstly, there was a Hanoverian, George I, on the throne and the Whig party supreme in Parliament—a combination which tended, expectedly, to promote a certain sobriety of taste. Secondly, the very architects who so admired the balanced proportions of Palladio began at this time to assume a much more prominent role in all fields of domestic design, taking over from guild-organized craftsmen; the latter, by and large, had not committed their designs to paper in any publishable form. In contrast, the new generation of architect-designers went out of their way to make sure that their plans, decorative schemes, details of ornaments and furniture were disseminated to a wider public in books of engravings published by themselves, usually with the sponsorship of a noble patron.

A new emphasis on formal entertaining began to emerge in the early part of the eighteenth century; this intensified the demand for integrated decorative schemes in the main rooms of great houses. Country house and town house visiting became a distinct social practice during the century; there are records, for instance, of Josiah Wedgwood visiting the London houses of the aristocracy and gentry as potential sources of new design ideas.

Typical of the new type of patron was the young Lord Burlington who spent much of the second decade of the century in Italy, studying the work of Palladio. He was also the patron of William Kent, the pre-eminent English architect-designer of the early eighteenth century, whose publication of *The Designs of Inigo Jones* in 1727 did much to reinforce the prevailing classical taste in all aspects of design. Ironically, Kent's own interior decoration and furniture design have a flamboyance and opulence which make more than a gesture towards the Baroque of the previous century.

The growing importance of pattern books in the forming of taste through the dissemination of 'fashionable' designs has already been remarked on in the general introduction to this book. And it is through pattern books that the development of mid-century taste for the lighter forms of Rococo can most readily be seen. Even as early as 1739, *The Gentlemen's or Builder's Companion*, published by the architect William Jones, contained some examples of carved furniture more suggestive of Louis Quinze than English Palladianism. But it was the publication of Chippendale's *The Gentleman and Cabinet-maker's Director* in 1754 which almost certainly ensured the widest possible dissemination of the new trends in taste. Almost all the 160 engraved plates are devoted to furniture designs, some incorporating Gothic and Oriental motifs (which also enjoyed renewed vogues in the middle of the century), but the main decorative repertoire is drawn from the sinuous curves, carved scrolls and flowers of Rococo.

More Rococo designs appeared in 1755 in *Twelve Gerandoles* by Thomas Johnson, which contained designs for wall lights in gilded wood – a form of ornament which lent itself particularly well to the swirling lines of the prevailing fashion. Johnson later published a second edition, entitled *One Hundred and Fifty New Designs*, which contained a wealth of exotic motifs in settings of scrolls and leafy branches. Another important publication of the time was Ince and Mayhew's *The Universal System*

of Household Furniture of 1762 which included a wide range of designs for cabinet-makers in the Rococo style.

 f all the designers who published their pattern books, it was Chippendale who seems to have had the most sensitive feel for changing tastes. When the third edition of his *Director* appeared in 1762 with 105 new plates, it was apparent that he had divined that a return to the classicism of the early part of the century was imminent and that the days of Rococo, however immediately charming, were numbered. In this ability to recognize shifts of taste, he must be accounted one of the central figures in the history of design and style of the eighteenth century.

The new Neoclassicism was taken up and disseminated widely by the Adam brothers, both in their work as domestic architects and decorators and in their folio volume of engravings published in 1777, *The Works in Architecture of Robert and James Adam*. Thousands of drawings by Robert are now preserved in the Soane Museum in London, providing a unique record of English style in the latter half of the eighteenth century. One notable contribution of Robert Adam to the development of design was his concern to provide artefacts which complemented his furniture and interiors. In his designs for Osterley Park, for instance, he provided for a complete range of meticulously detailed dining equipment.

The demand for the new style had extended well beyond London and the great houses by the penultimate decade of the century. Craftsmen and small firms of cabinet-makers in the provinces were well-served, however, in 1788 with the publication of *The Cabinet-maker and Upholsterer's Guide*, which made the elegant forms and motifs of English Neoclassicism available to a wide audience. Originally assembled by George Hepplewhite, who died in 1786, it was published posthumously by his widow. Although it was principally devoted to furniture design, it is easy to see that it could have served as a source-book for a wide range of domestic design in its display of Neoclassical ornament: husks, festoons, swags and grotesques.

The success of the Hepplewhite book probably inspired the publication of the last great design book of the century, *The Cabinet-maker and Upholsterer's Drawing Book* by Thomas Sheraton, published in four parts between 1791 and 1794. The cool elegance of the designs, the gentle emphases of flower and leaf patterns, the gracefully tapering legs provide a modulated but eminently satisfying finale to a century of fine English design.

page 16 A silk design by James Leman (*c.* 1688-1745) dated 1721; it is accompanied by the names of the mercer and the journeyman-weaver.

opposite Glass-blowers at work: an etching published in 1754 in *The Dictionary of Arts and Sciences.*

20

1
CLASSICISM
and
ROCOCO

pages 20–21

An interesting example of mid-century English Rococo, this design for a drawing room by John Linnell (1723-96) reflects the designer's knowledge of furniture-making; his father, William Linnell, had established a successful upholstery and cabinet-making business in Berkeley Square, London. Later furniture designs by Linnell were influenced by the prevailing taste for Chinoiserie (see p. 31).

page 25

The pre-eminent architect-designer of early eighteenth-century England was undoubtedly William Kent (1684-1748). His architectural work and drawings, like this front elevation and ground plan, did much to reinforce the classical taste of the time, although his interior design had an opulence which looked more, perhaps, towards the Baroque of the previous century.

pages 26–27

The alternation of preferences for the frivolity of Rococo or for the more sober lines of

Palladian classicism continued throughout the middle part of the eighteenth century. French artists, too, came to work in England when the more decorative style became less fashionable in France; these included Andien de Clermont who executed this ceiling design for Langley Park, Norfolk, *c.* 1750.

pages 28–29

The design of chair backs provides a wonderful barometer of taste through the century. This sketch by John Linnell (p. 28) has a wonderful mid-century exuberance and freshness and was probably executed as a preliminary design for pieces to be made by his father's company. The designs by Thomas Chippendale (1718-79) (p. 29 *above*) are the preliminary pencil sketches for the third edition of his *The Gentleman and Cabinet-maker's Director* (1762), which mixed the curves and scrolls of the first edition (1754) with designs which reflected a renewed classicism. This spirit continued in furniture to the refined Neoclassicism of the latter part of the century, notably in the graceful elegance of designs (p. 29 *below*) by Thomas Sheraton

(1751-1806), whose *The Cabinet-maker and Upholsterer's Drawing Book* was published between 1791 and 1794.

pages 30/32–33

Born in Sweden of Scottish parents, but educated in England, William Chambers (1723-96) travelled extensively in the Far East. His close acquaintanceship with Chinese architecture and design inspired his first published work, *Designs of Chinese Buildings, Furniture, Dresses, Machines, and Utensils* (1757), from which these pages are taken. The publication of the book was timely indeed, since it coincided with a period of intense interest among wealthy patrons in the Chinoiserie aspects of Rococo. At about the same time Chambers designed the Pagoda in Kew Gardens (see p. 51).

page 31

The taste for Chinoiserie reached its peak just as the mid-century fashion for the Rococo style was at its most intense, profoundly influencing design in furniture, textiles and porcelain. This little watercolour painting of an

armchair in the Chinese style by John Linnell, again probably for use in his father's workshops, dates from *c.* 1753.

pages 34–35

The spare classicism which characterized English design in the early part of the eighteenth century is marvellously expressed in two chimney-piece designs in pen, ink and wash by Christopher Cass (1678-1734). The first (p. 34) was intended for Vanbrugh's Blenheim Palace, the second for Hampton Court (p. 35).

pages 36–37

The eighteenth-century demand for complete decorative schemes in the main public rooms and spaces of great houses provided the impetus for many architects and artists to become, effectively, interior designers. Many of the original sketches have an engaging vigour and confidence, such as the design for the interior of a drawing room (p. 36 *above*), by Thomas Stothard (1755-1834), which demonstrates scale by the inclusion of sketched human figures. James Stuart's design for Wimbledon House (p. 36 *below*) makes greater use

1

CLASSICISM *and* ROCOCO

of classical motifs. Known as 'Athenian' Stuart, this architect (1713-88) exerted a strong influence on the maintenance of the classical ideal in England through his co-authorship of *The Antiquities of Athens* (1762-89) and his interiors in a Roman style for Spencer House, London. Some sense of the relationship between such architect- designers and their clients can be gained from Sir James Thornhill's (1676-1734) design for a staircase, probably for the house of his mentor, Thomas Highmore (p. 37); in the upper right-hand corner of the sketch, the painter has listed the proposed combinations of figures and events from mythology and classical history for approval. Thornhill was responsible for several grand illusionist painting schemes, notably at Chatsworth.

pages 38-39

The name of Gillow recurs repeatedly in the history of English furniture design and manufacture from the eighteenth century to the twentieth. Originally established *c.* 1730 in Lancaster by Robert Gillow (1703-73), the firm added a London branch *c.* 1765 on a site in Oxford Street occupied by their successors,

Waring & Gillow, until 1974. In their eighteenth-century heyday Gillow produced elegant, well-made furniture in the late Georgian style, typified by the sofa and writing-table designs illustrated on these pages. The company maintained, and jealously guarded, a comprehensive record of its production from 1734 to 1899, comprising some 20,000 designs; the extent and variety of this unique compilation contained in successive sketches only came to be properly appreciated in 1966, when it was acquired by the Westminster City Library.

pages 40-41

Matthew Darly (*fl.* 1741-80) was one of the most notable English furniture designers to be influenced by the fashionable French Rococo style. He was also influential in spreading the taste for Chinoiserie, especially by his 1751 pattern book, *A New Book of Chinese, Gothic and Modern Chairs*, from which these eight designs are taken. Darly was also an engraver and made most of the plates for Chippendale's 1754 *Director*. In that year, too, he published *A New Book of Chinese Designs*.

pages 42-43

This spare, classical design for a tallboy (p. 43) forms Plate 86 in the 1754 edition of Thomas Chippendale's *Director*, undoubtedly the seminal pattern book of the 18th century and the means of ensuring that Chippendale's name became a household word as England's most eminent furniture designer. The *Director* illustrated virtually every type of domestic furniture in a variety of styles, though mainly (unlike the piece illustrated here) Rococo and Chinoiserie, known as Chinese Chippendale. His sensitivity to changing taste was amply illustrated in the third edition of the *Director* which showed a shift to more Neoclassical sympathies. Another of the great eighteenth-century pattern books was George Hepplewhite's *The Cabinet-maker and Upholsterer's Guide*, published by the designer's widow in 1788, two years after her husband's death. The furniture epitomizes the Neoclassicism of the latter part of the 18th century. The designs, such as this one for a wardrobe (p. 42), have an elegant simplicity and must have been one of the principal sources of inspiration for

cabinet-makers throughout the country for the whole of the latter part of the century.

pages 44-45

The growth in importance of the architect-designer in eighteenth-century England could not be better illustrated than on these pages. A wealthy and well-travelled aristocracy and a powerful merchant class demanded new building, both in town and country, and with the building came the demand for complete integrated design, outside and inside. These anonymous sketches (p. 44) of Elton hall, Northamptonshire, show an extraordinary overlapping of plans and elevations for a complex of buildings, including an orangery, all drawn on a small scrap of sketchbook paper. The more finished treatments by Robert Adam (1728-92) for town-house elevations, front and back, in central London (p. 45) bespeak the Neoclassical influences which the architect absorbed during a four-year period spent in Rome. Adam was in many ways the complete designer, continuing the elegance of his architecture through to free-standing furniture, wall and ceiling decoration (see pp. 52-53).

1
CLASSICISM
and
ROCOCO

pages 46–47

The exchange and intermingling of highly ornate decorative styles and design of classical simplicity constitutes much of the history of eighteenth-century English design. This counterpointing is succinctly illustrated by the contrasting designs on these pages. Samuel Savill's sketched records (p. 47) have the sobriety of the classical models he clearly admired. Matthew Lock's original designs for free-standing and wall furniture (p. 46), on the other hand, have the exuberance and frivolity expected of a designer who played a leading part in introducing the Rococo style to England. His *A New Drawing Book of Ornaments* of 1740 was one of the first pattern books to promote this style in London. It was followed by *Six Sconces* (1744) and *Six Tables* (1746).

pages 48–49

Neoclassical elegance informs even these prosaically utilitarian artefacts of *c.* 1790. The Miles Patent Agitable Lamp came in several forms to suit both taste and position. Oil-burning, it was claimed to be free from spillage even when carried about. It was advertised as being 'cleaner, safer, and cheaper than candles' in the manufacturer's catalogue, which also showed one model which could be strapped to a horse-rider's calf.

pages 50–51

William Pain, the designer of the mouldings illustrated on p. 50, originally a carpenter by trade, commented on the vigorous state of English architecture in his *Practical Builder* (1774), presumably only too conscious that this was partly due to the influence exercised by such books as his. Indeed, the pattern books of English architects and builders began to have a transatlantic influence in the late 18th century. An American edition of Pain's own *Practical House Carpenter* was published in 1792, to become one of the most influential works for the classical architects of New England. A much more eminent contemporary of Pain's was William Chambers (see pp. 30/32-33) who became one of the most successful architects in England, designing – notably – Somerset House in London. Two years after his first book, *Designs of Chinese Buildings*, he produced his most influential published work, the *Treatise on Civil Architecture*, from which this illustration of mouldings is taken (p. 51). The book concentrated entirely on the decorative and design aspects of building and interior design, eventually reaching an expanded third edition in 1791 as *A Treatise on the Decorative Part of Civil Architecture*.

pages 52–53

These two sketches by Robert Adam (p. 52) for the wall decoration of 17 Hill Street, London, have a lightness, freshness and frivolity almost more in keeping with the spirit of the mid-century than with that of the later Neoclassicism. Festoons and scrolls distinguish him from the severity of his French contemporaries, as does the lightness of the palette he used for plasterwork. Note the precise instructions for colour contrast. A similar lightness of touch characterizes Adam's sketch for a balustrade 'for Lady Home' of 1777 (p. 53).

pages 54–55

Although the 18th century in English design ended on a distinctly classical note, it had overall been a time of eclecticism and marvellous design ingenuity and fantasy. The 1762 edition of Chippendale's *Director* still carried designs very much in the Rococo style (p. 54), while Thomas Johnson (1714-*c.* 1778) specifically devoted himself to designing the decorative elements known as 'carvers' pieces', which excluded larger pieces and chairs, concentrating on chimneypieces (p. 55), mirror frames, side tables and other decorative artefacts. His designs, strongly inspired by French models, were probably too intricate to have been fully realized by any carver, but his books went a long way to establishing the decorative style as a major theme in eighteenth-century English design. *Twelve Gerandoles* was published in 1755, with a further set following in parts during the next two years. These designs were eventually issued in volume form in 1758 and, slightly expanded, in 1761 as *One Hundred and Fifty New Designs*.

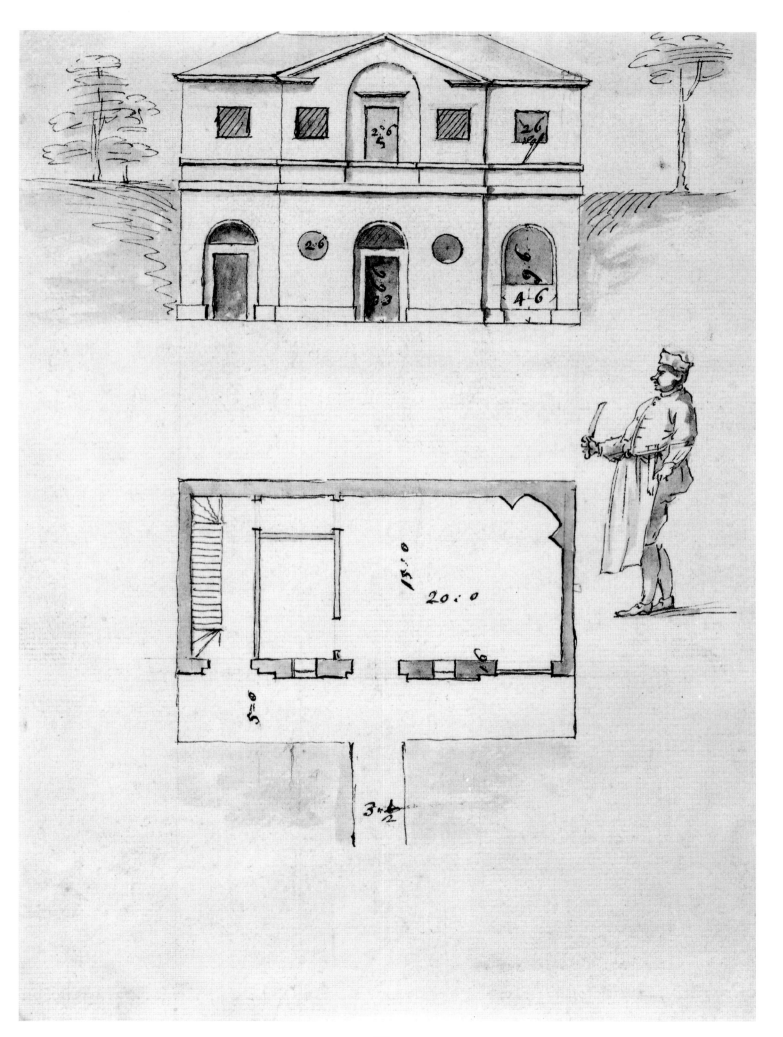

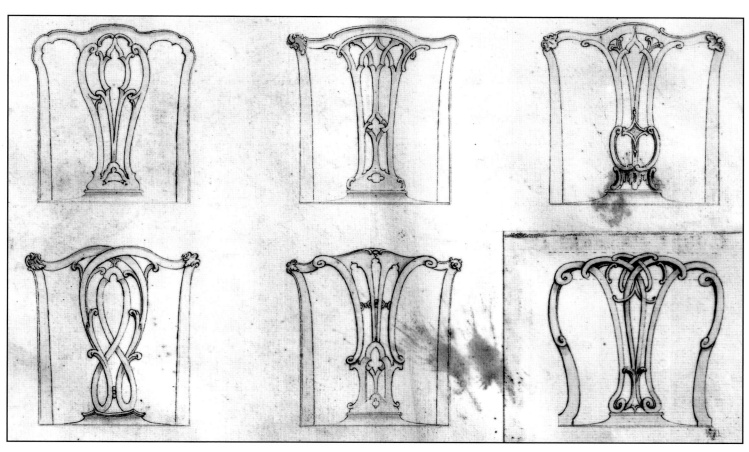

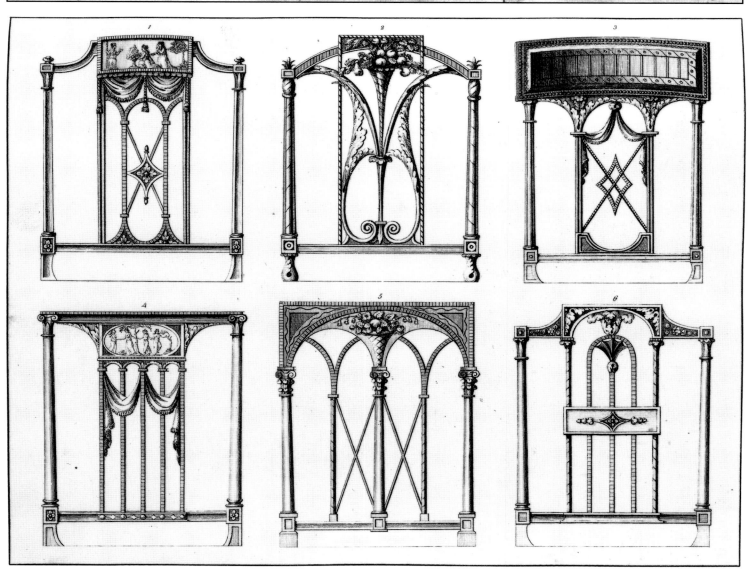

E 71-1929

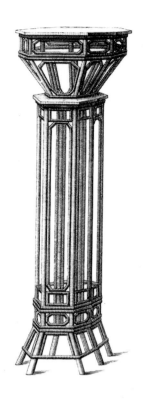
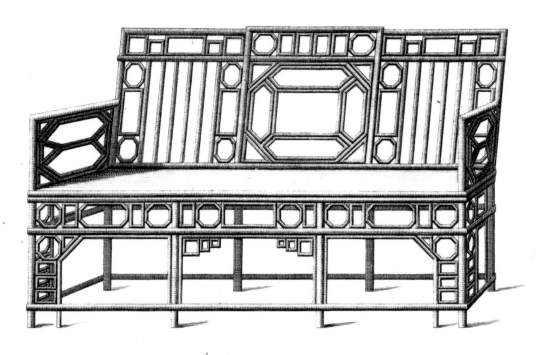

35

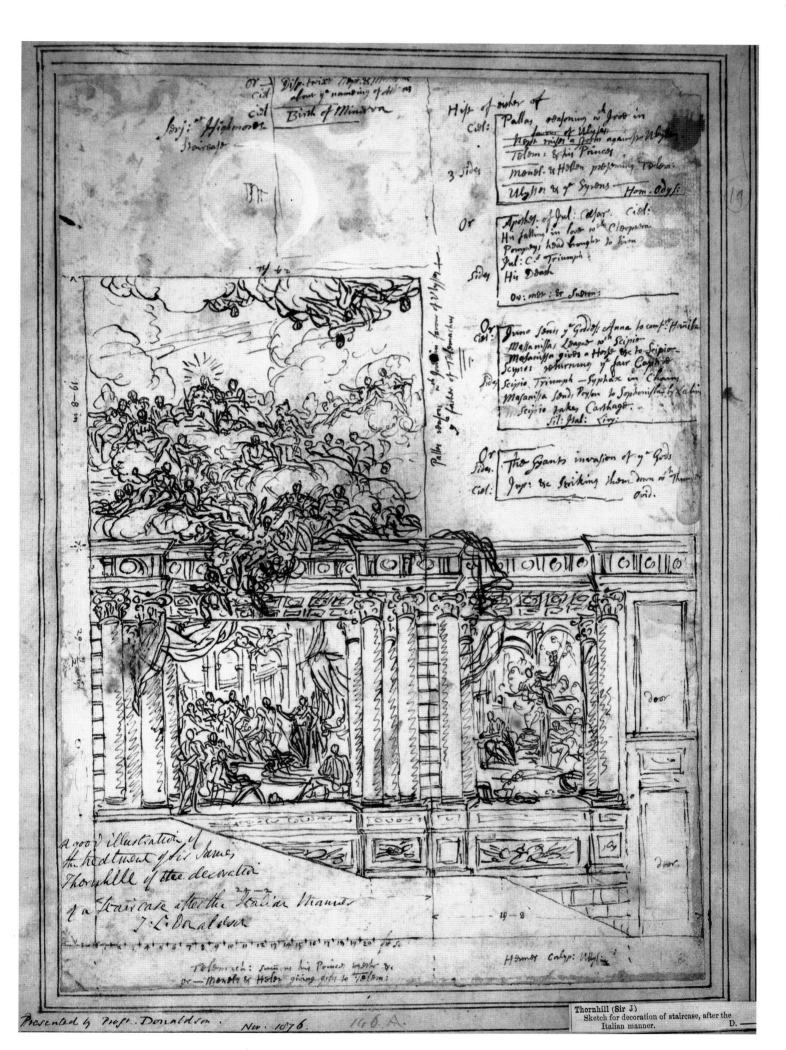

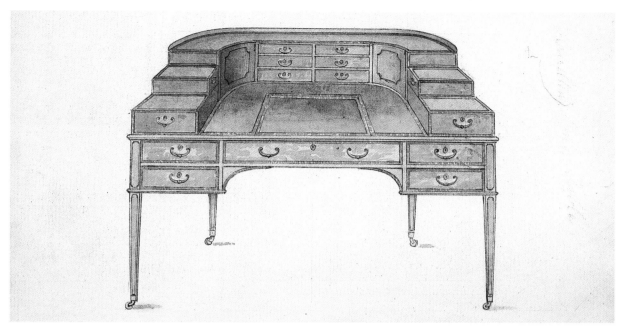

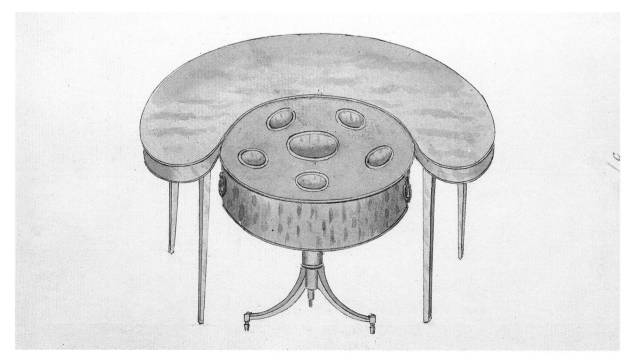

Publishd according to the Act

Wardrobe.

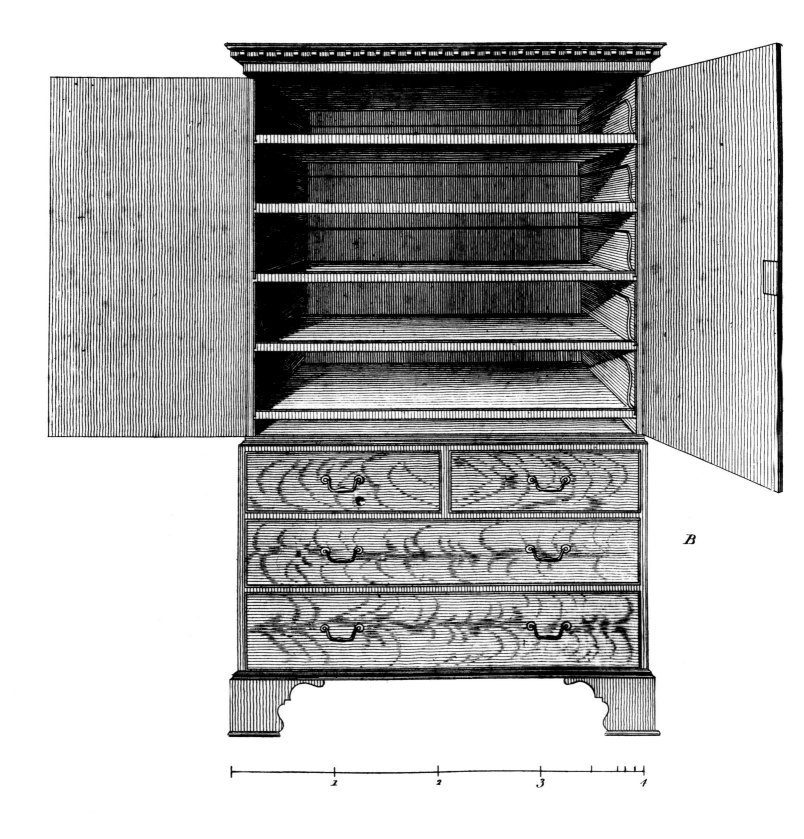

B

Chest of Drawers

Elevation of a House for Andrew Millar Esq.

Fronting to Pall Mall

two or three Drawings of frames
for Marble Slabs a comon Size
in Minature & at Large

A french Chimney with a piter over it
at Large

2 — 3

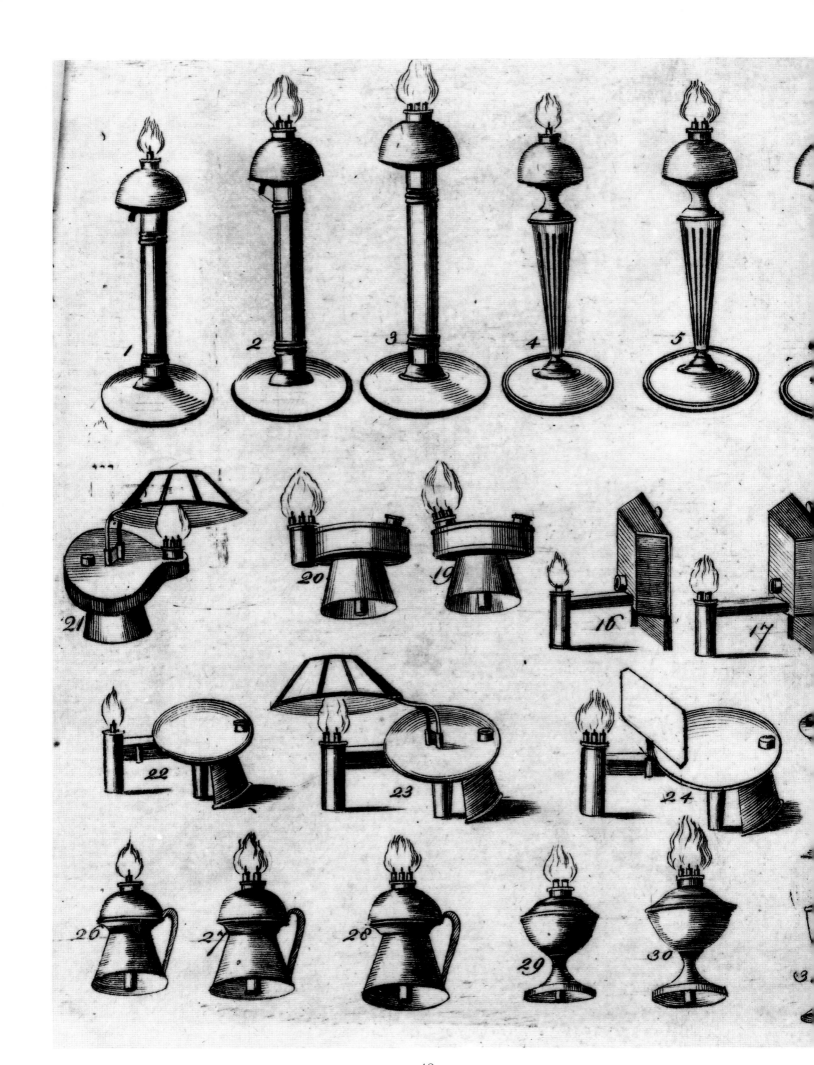

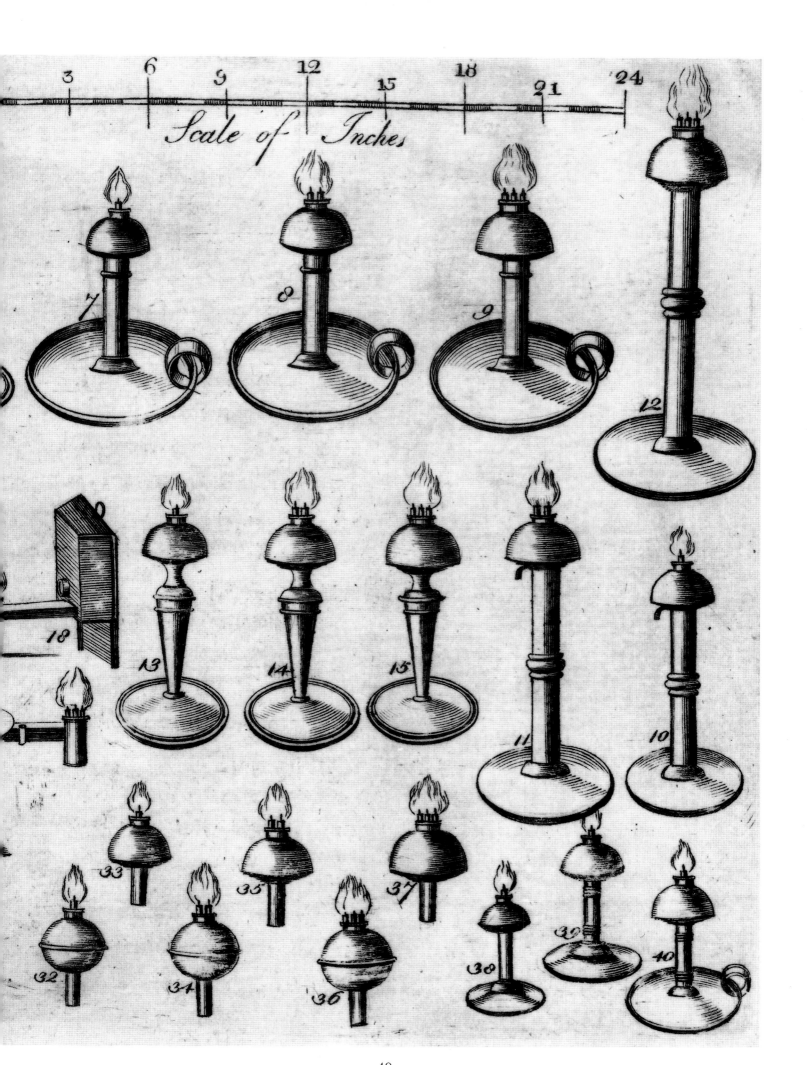

Scale of Inches

49

To proportion these Cornices with the frize & necking, give them ¾ of an Inch to a foot, including the frize &

Necking divide the whole into 12 parts give 5 to the Cornices & 6 to the frize 1 to the Neck moulding as Scale a,b.

any of these Cornices used without the frize in Rooms ⅜ of an Inch to a foot, outside ½ an Inch to a foot

W.& J. Pain del.   Published as the Act directs Jan.ʳ 1.ˢᵗ 1788, by I.& J.Taylor, N.°56, Holborn.   Woodman & Mutlow Sculp.ᵗ

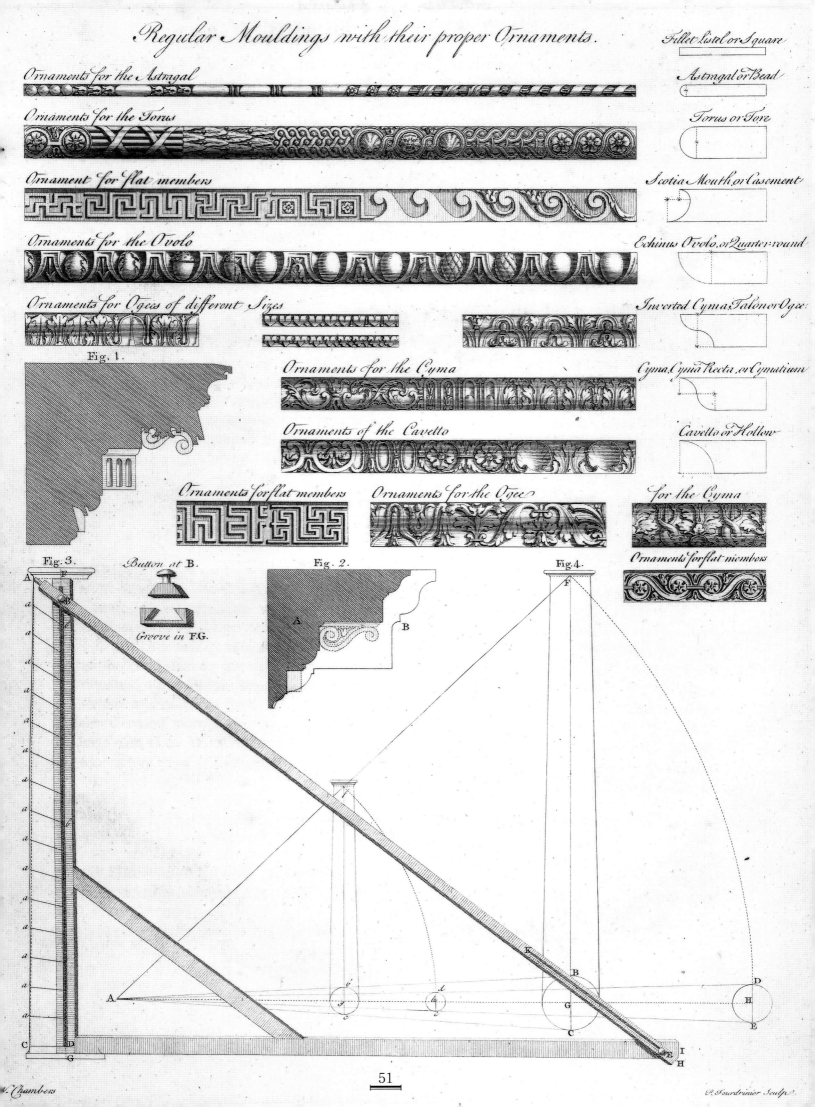

Regular Mouldings with their proper Ornaments.

Ornaments for the Astragal

Ornaments for the Torus

Ornament for flat members

Ornaments for the Ovolo

Ornaments for Ogees of different Sizes

Fig. 1.

Ornaments for the Cyma

Ornaments of the Cavetto

Ornaments for flat members   Ornaments for the Ogee   for the Cyma

Ornaments for flat members

Fillet Listel or Square

Astragal or Bead

Torus or Tore

Scotia Mouth or Casement

Echinus Ovolo, or Quarter-round

Inverted Cyma Talon or Ogee

Cyma, Cyma Recta, or Cymatium

Cavetto or Hollow

Fig. 3.

Button at B.

Groove in F.G.

Fig. 2.

Fig. 4.

Chambers   P. Fourdrinier Sculp.

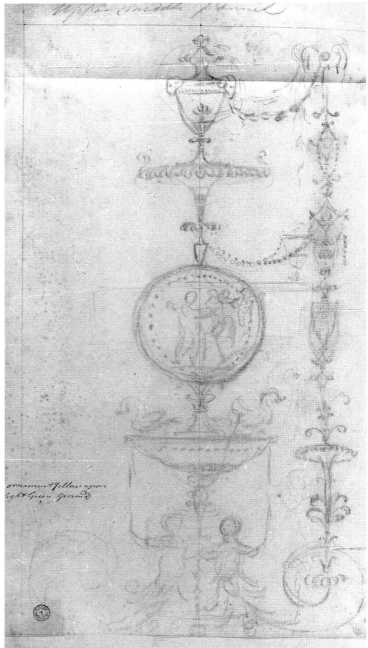

Design for a Toylet Table

T. Chippendale inv.t et delin.   Publish'd according to Act of Parliam.t 1761.   W. Foster Sculp.

2
Regency and After

REVIVAL and ECLECTICISM

The end of the eighteenth century, then, found English design and decoration very much as it had been during the whole of the century – characterized by a modulated classicism. From metropolitan cabinet-makers to provincial workshops, the dissemination of designs through pattern books had ensured a remarkable homogeneity of style and taste throughout the country. But this situation was not to last for long, as a new eclecticism began to appear. This mixing of styles, which became more noticeable as the new century advanced, has been termed 'the Picturesque'. Initially, it drew on an informed historicism, which grew steadily less authentic as the mid-century approached.

Some of the completed architectural/design schemes – although drawing on a new, exotic repertoire of forms – were remarkably successful. Wyatt's work at Fonthill Abbey, Nash's inspired plans for Brighton Pavilion, and the Sezincote of the Cockerells still displayed a sureness of touch which sprang from the good taste and refined scholarship of the previous generation. But already there was a growing tendency for architects and designers to seek to satisfy the often ill-informed whims of newly rich industrialists and the wealthy merchants and bankers of a rapidly growing middle class.

Yet the beginning of the nineteenth century in the applied arts in England did have a certain look of *status quo*. Sheraton published his *Cabinet Dictionary* in 1803, still expressing the classical ideals of the latter part of the previous century, but with a greater regard for historical authenticity. However, his *Cabinet-maker, Upholsterer and General Artists' Encyclopaedia*, published between 1804 and 1806, shows a number of designs which point to the coming proliferation of styles. He also illustrated several designs with 'Egyptian' motifs, a reflection of the nation's awakened interest in the eastern Mediterranean because of Napoleon's operations there.

It seems likely, though, that the majority of jobbing craftsmen and designers at the beginning of the nineteenth century still stuck to the well-established classicism of the preceding three decades. There is, for instance, an unassuming purity of line about the variety of patterns for wire fencing, illustrated on p. 69. A notable champion of this surviving classicism was Thomas Hope, who published his *Household Furniture and Interior Decoration* in 1807, essentially as a record of the interiors and furniture of his London house. Classical motifs of chimeras, sphinxes, acanthus leaves and wreaths proliferate in his designs. Hope's interpretation of the antique and its related motifs were taken up by George Smith in his 1808 publication, *Collection of Designs for Household Furniture*.

From about 1815, heavier, more florid forms begin to appear in English design. It is hard to know quite why this came about, but it is worth noting that the end of the Napoleonic wars offered greater travel opportunities to wealthy Englishmen who, in turn, developed a liking of the heavy French Empire style. In furniture making, brass inlay became popular, especially in floral and grotesque patterns which, in the worst cases, swamped whole areas of any piece. In other words, the Regency period saw a movement in English design from the supreme elegance of the Sheraton era to a coarseness which we normally associate with the Victorian period which follows. Furniture designs look over-ornate and even simple household objects begin to look too elaborate for their function.

page 56 The Spode factory flourished in the early nineteenth century under the founder's son Josiah II (1754-1827), producing a variety of transfer-printed wares with designs of classical and Oriental scenes. This page from a print record book of 1806 shows a variety of border patterns and Greek centres. These were printed from copper plates in black or brown in the record book, but were actually used on Spode china and porcelain in dark blue. The final pages of this book contain the record of the badges, crests and back stamps used on special orders or for individual customers.

right Hand-block printing of calico in an early nineteenth-century workshop; this illustration is taken from *The Book of English Trades Part III* (1805) by R. Phillips.

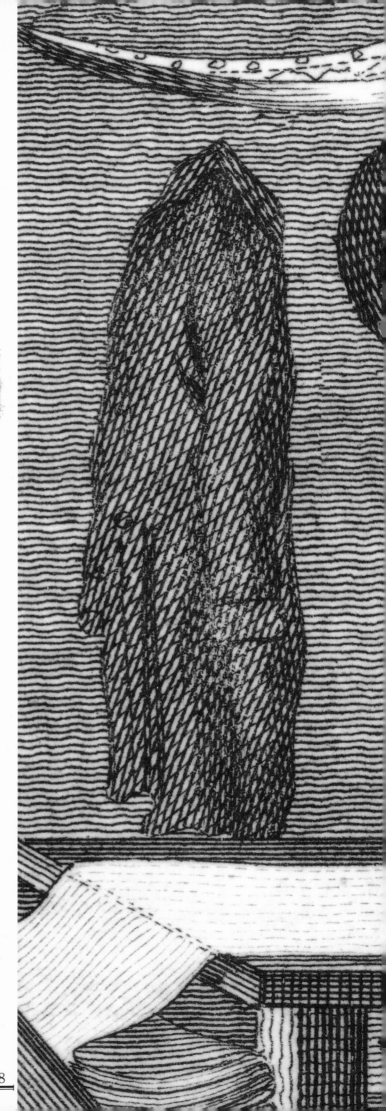

2
REVIVAL
and
ECLECTICISM

Thomas Hope (1769-1831) published his *Household Furniture and Interior Decoration* in 1807, chiefly as a record of the interiors of his London home. He designed furniture in the Greek and Egyptian styles to accompany his collections of antiquities. His Egyptian furniture (the 'Egyptian room' is illustrated here), especially, provided models for other cabinet-makers, already inspired by the nation's military and naval interests in the eastern Mediterranean. His influence on English furniture design was considerable, and sphinxes, lions and hieroglyphics now became part of the national design vocabulary.

The firm of Gillow (see pp. 38-39) was especially prolific in its designs during the late Georgian and Regency period. This design for a lady's dressing-table, for instance, is one of a series produced around the turn of the century. Other versions included one in the style of a desk and a rounded design with lift-up lid. These were entered as pencil

sketches in the company's record books, complete with dimensions.

This design for a *faux* bamboo sofa appears in a Gillow sketchbook of designs dating from the very end of the 18th century. It reflects the continuing taste for Oriental artefacts and would probably have been made from a local wood painted to resemble bamboo. A chair of similar design, made in beech, has been precisely dated to 1794. Gillow's continuing success was almost certainly due to the firm's policy of making attractive, affordable furniture in a wide range of forms which appealed to a burgeoning urban middle class.

Four pages from *The London Chairmakers' and Carvers' Book of Prices for Workmanship*; the prefatory pages of this volume, dated 1807, note that there is an introduction by R.J. Adam 'as regulated and agreed to by a committee of master chair manufacturers and journeymen, with methods

of computation adopted in the work, illustrated by reference to a variety of figures, engraved on sixteen copper plates.'

The persistence of classical inspiration in design in the early nineteenth century is abundantly evident in the architect L.N. Cottingham's *Smith and Founder's Director* of 1823 (2nd edition 1824) which illustrated a multiplicity of designs for railings and balconies; these would then have been copied by foundries at the request of builders and architects. The volume, indeed, was described as 'a director containing a series of designs and patterns for ornamental iron and brass work.' The introduction to the book concludes with the hope that the work will 'remove in some measure the severe and painful regret that has long been felt by ingenious workmen, for the want of a collection of good ornaments to select from, at a price within the compass of their limited means...' The 'several hundred specimens' are chosen from 'the choicest productions of the Grecian, Etruscan, Roman and Gothic schools...'

It was common practice for textile mills to maintain records of production in the form of swatch books, in which tiny samples of the printed fabric would be mounted after manufacture, occasionally juxtaposed with the original painted design. These pages are reproduced from a swatch book of the Rossendale Printing Company, whose factory was in the Rossendale valley, close to Manchester. The book covers the years 1815-20 and contains 216 pages with 24 printed cotton swatches on each side in a variety of plain and patterned designs printed in shades of rust, yellow, dark red, blue, pink and green.

Ever ingenious, the manufacturers of Sheffield plate and silver had, by the early nineteenth century, begun to offer a bewildering variety of household utensils to a gadget-conscious and status-seeking middle class. These designs of egg-cup holders are taken from an unidentified manufacturer's pattern book of *c.* 1825, offering candlesticks, candelabra, snuffers, epergnes,

2
REVIVAL
and
ECLECTICISM

cruet sets, ink stands, wine funnels, coasters, toast-racks, meat dishes and covers, and tea and coffee pots in 127 engraved plates.

pages 74–75

Founded by Josiah Wedgwood at Burslem, Staffordshire, in 1759, Wedgwood has remained one of the pre-eminent English potteries. Its first generations of wares closely reflected the prevailing Neoclassicism of the latter part of the 18th century, incorporating motifs from the statuary, plaques, urns and vases of antiquity. The pottery became especially famous for its jasperware which was characterized by white decorative motifs of classical inspiration on a blue or greenish ground. Even for the decoration of utilitarian wares, such as the teapots illustrated here, the pottery employed artists of note, including George Stubbs and John Flaxman. The range of wares produced by the factory – known as Etruria – was extensive, as the entries in the company records show. These teapot samples, drawn from the Shapes Number One Book, a

record book begun in the 18th century which catalogues both ornamental and utilitarian pieces, includes both late eighteenth- and nineteenth-century models.

pages 76–77

This illustration of a soup tureen is drawn from the same pattern book as that described in the caption to pp. 72-73. The manufacturer's concern to offer a multiplicity of choice to his customers is evident in the ingenious device of illustrating two different forms of decoration on one shape. The manufacturer further noted in his introductory remarks that the wares on offer had been drawn on a scale of six inches to the foot. The silver circles on some designs denote the placement for silver crests, while the figure of a hand indicates silver mountings.

pages 78–79

Carpet factories have existed in Kidderminster, south-west of Birmingham, since the early 17th century, but it was the first decades of the nineteenth century which saw

a major expansion of the industry in the town. Between 1807 and 1838 the number of looms in operation increased from one thousand to over two thousand. These designs are taken from the archive of Woodward Grosvenor, founded in 1790 and still in existence today. They all date from *c.* 1800, incorporating five or six colours in designs by anonymous artists.

page 80

These designs for lace are taken from a 106-page sketch book now in the possession of the Victoria & Albert Museum, London. The fly-leaf bears the name of Isabel Haddon Odiham, although there is no suggestion that she was the actual designer; the characteristics of the paper suggest that the book dates from between 1809 and 1820. The pages are filled with designs for borders and larger patterns, some of which are extended to fold-outs.

page 81

Another design from the archives of Woodward Grosvenor, Kidderminster;

prior to 1905, the company's designs were painted in miniature to half or a third scale to save expensive paper. This pattern for a hearth rug is in 13 colours and would have been mirrored in the other three quarters of the piece to complete the design.

page 82

Executed between 1809 and 1820, these designs for toast-racks are taken from three narrow pages of a pattern book recording the designs of Edward Barnard & Sons, manufacturing silversmiths. The first Edward Barnard set up a business partnership in 1808, after working for Thomas Chawner from 1773, becoming Edward Barnard & Sons in 1829 and moving to a new factory in the City of London in 1830. The company continues in existence as a subsidiary of Padgett & Braham Ltd. Now lodged in the collection of the Victoria & Albert Museum, London, the company archive comprises some 250 ledger volumes containing records from its inception to 1961. The production orders of the company record such eminent clients as Elkington & Co. and Garrard's.

2
REVIVAL
and
ECLECTICISM

This 5-colour 'Strawberries' design, half of a 27-inch pattern, among the many thousands in the archive of Woodward Grosvenor, is typical in its anonymity. Unsigned, only a code number enables dating to be done with any accuracy. But in this lies its significance: a national design archive consists of so much more than the well-publicized works of a few familiar names. Woodward Grosvenor undertakes special commissions to manufacture carpets to designs in its archve, which computerization has made immediately accessible.

These elegant designs, meticulously drawn in pen and ink by an anonymous hand, are the records for mugs and pots to be made as cream ware, lead-glazed pottery with a flint content which resulted in a cream-coloured body. The pottery producing these designs is no longer known, although each pattern has a production number. Geometric decoration would have been applied mechanically with an engine-powered lathe, the floral elements being added as transfers.

These leaves from an album of designs for ceramic wares lodged in the collection of the Victoria & Albert Museum, London, are further testimony to the vision of the anonymous craftsmen who created them. Utilitarian yet elegant, the designs are drawn directly on to the pages of well-worn calf-bound volumes, believed to be the record of the production of Messrs. Hartley Greens & Co. One of the volumes is stamped with the words 'New Teapot Book'.

Like the ceramic designs on the preceding pages, these textile designs provide even more evidence of the wealth of design talent employed in the workshops and factories of early nineteenth-century England. Reproduced from a 299-page volume now in the Victoria & Albert Museum, London; each page bears between eight and ten immaculately conceived and executed designs, each grouping positioned symmetrically on the page.

These pages are taken, like the illustrations on pp. 86-87, from the set of albums in the collection of the Victoria & Albert Museum, London, believed to be the production records of Messrs. Hartley Greens & Co. One album, containing the records of jugs and tureens (pp. 90-91), is made up of sheets of grid paper on which are pasted finely detailed pen and wash drawings. The date 18 February 1802 appears inside the front cover. Another album (pp. 92-95) bears the legend 'Original Drawing Book No. 1' on its glazed brown cardboard cover. The designs are either separately mounted or drawn directly on to the pages of bluish paper, accompanied with descriptive notes of range variations and code numbers.

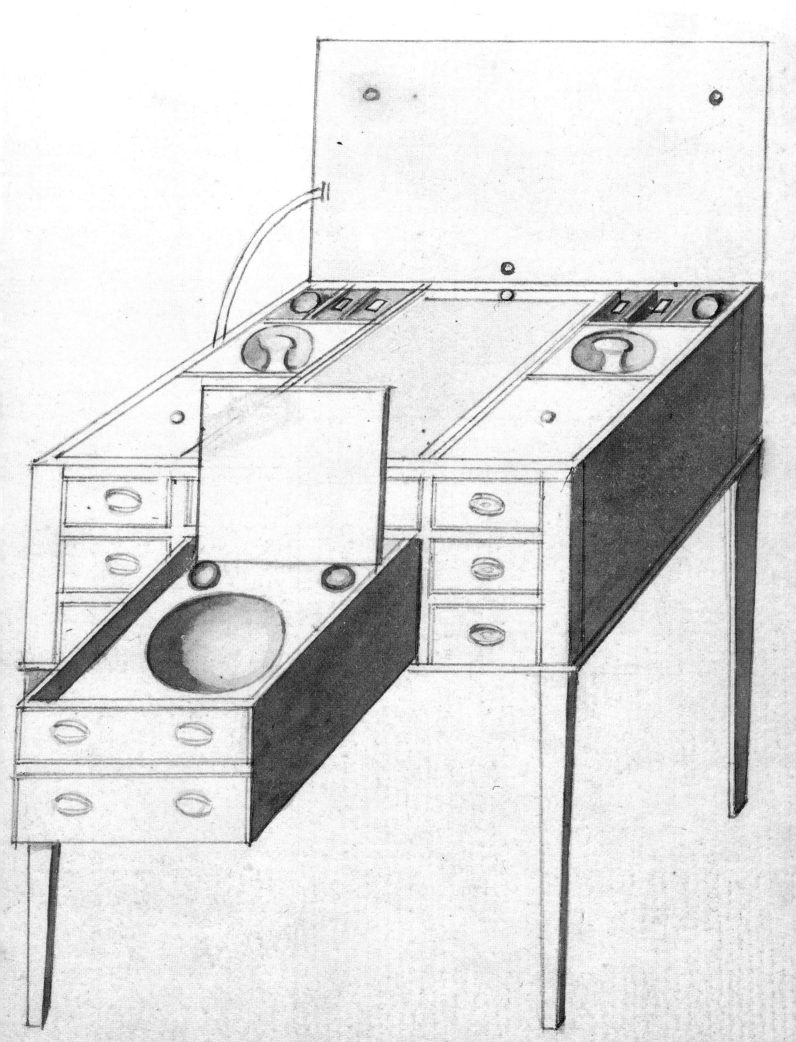

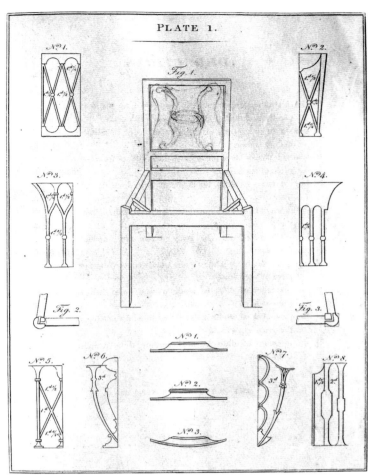

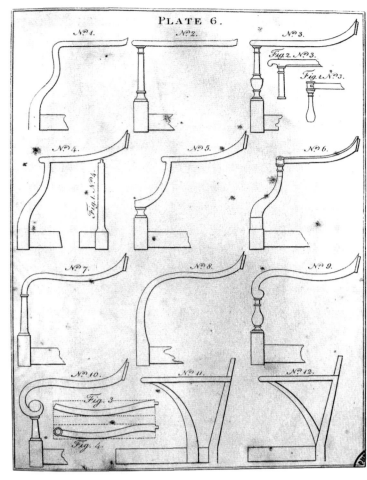

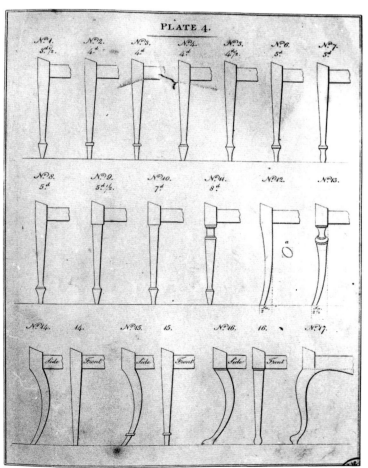

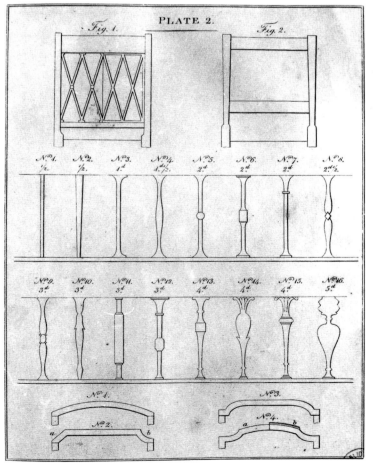

PLATE XVII

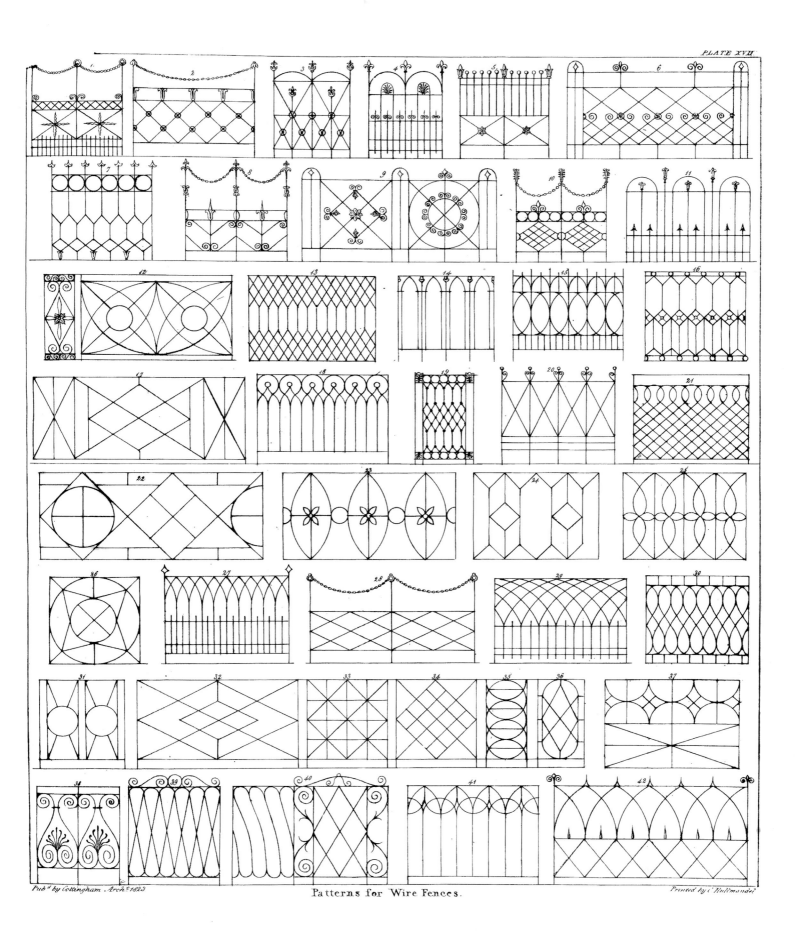

Pub.d by Cotingham Arch.t 1823

Patterns for Wire Fences.

Printed by C. Hullmandel.

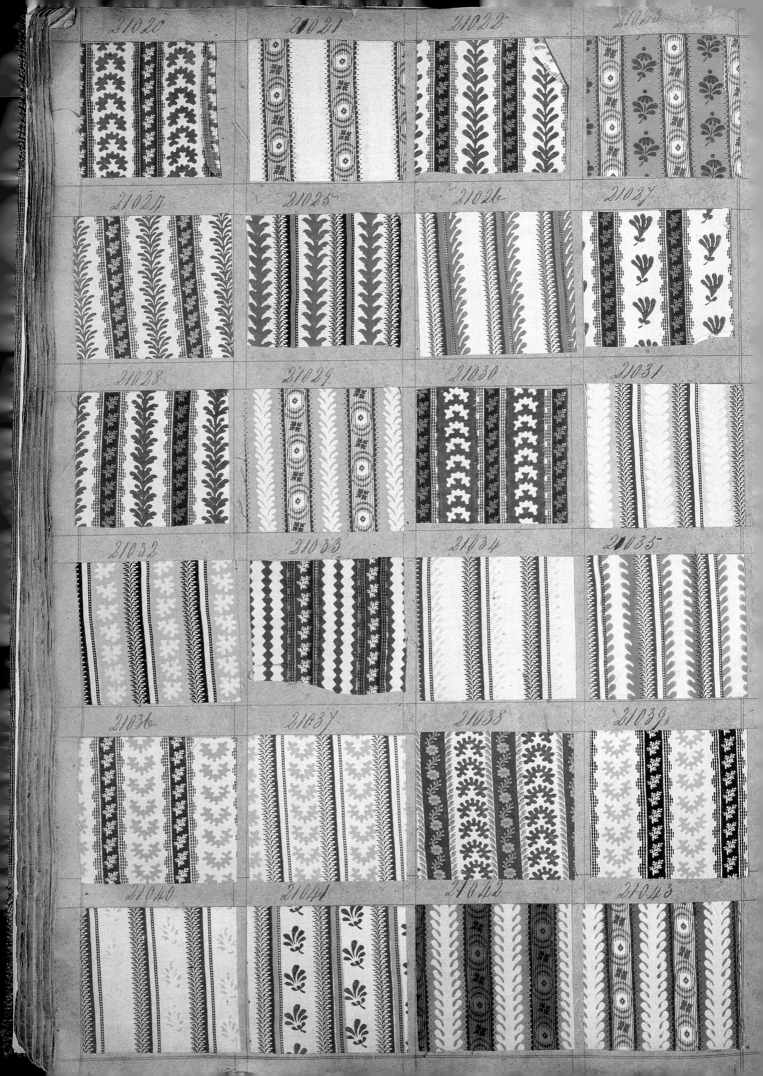

164

natch

163

130 Cords by 280 Lashes — to drop at 140 Lashes

Point d'hongrie 132 by 240

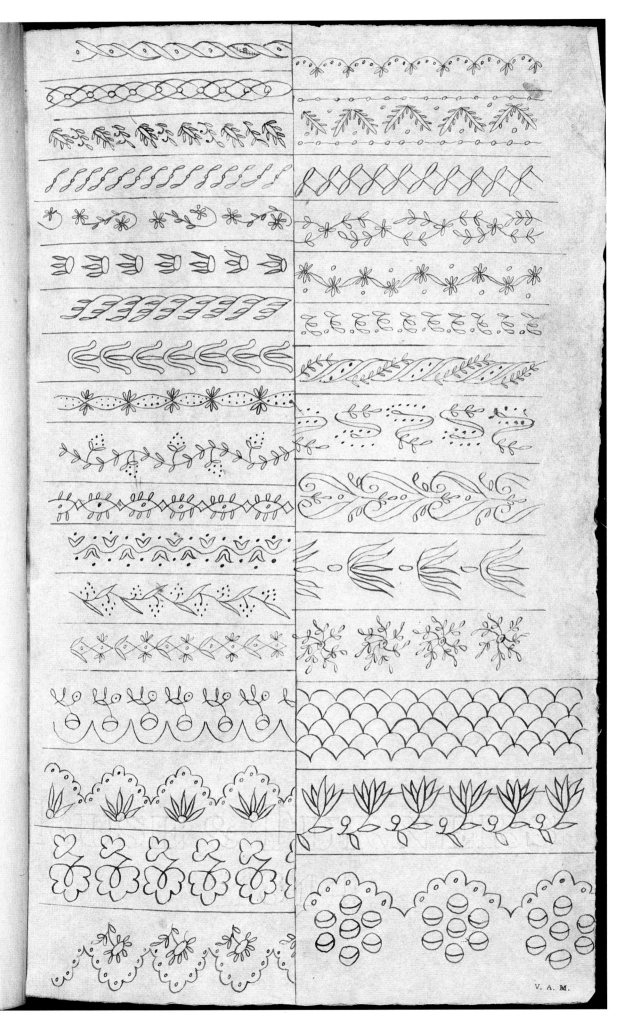

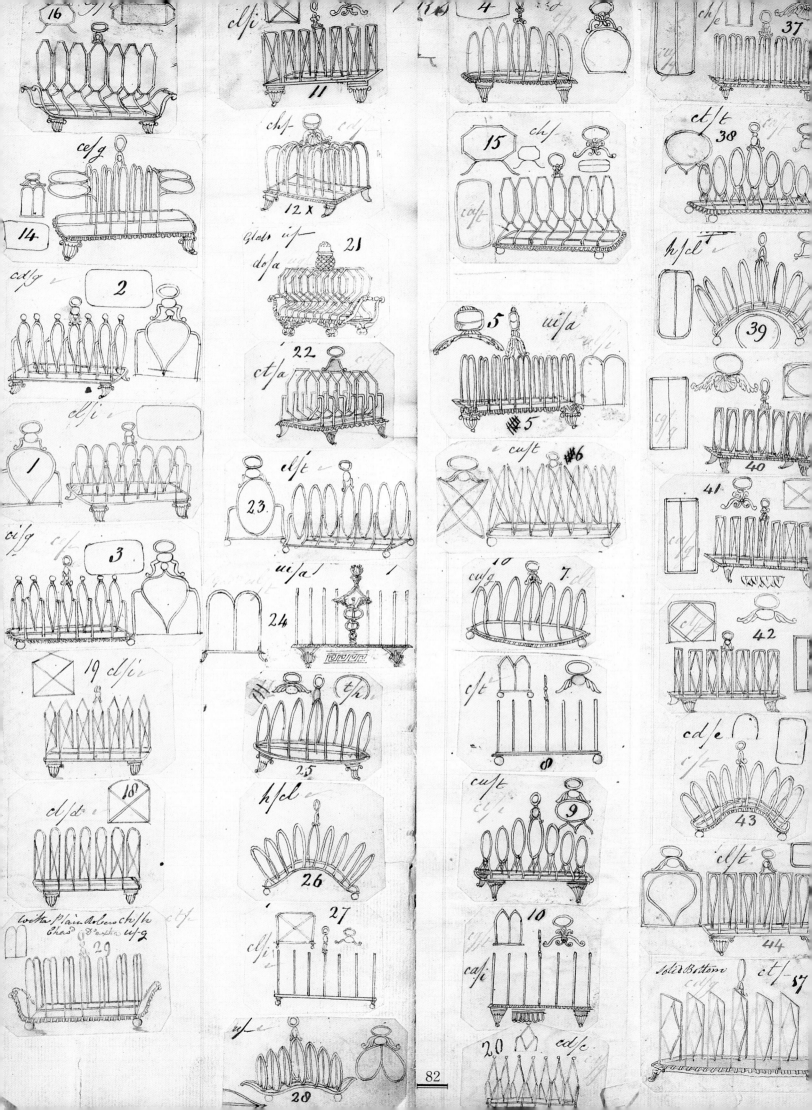

136 by 160 ___ 83 Bottom

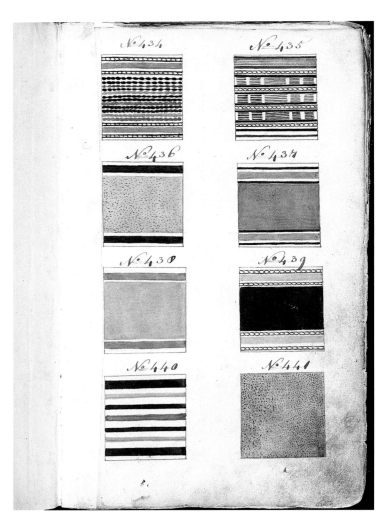

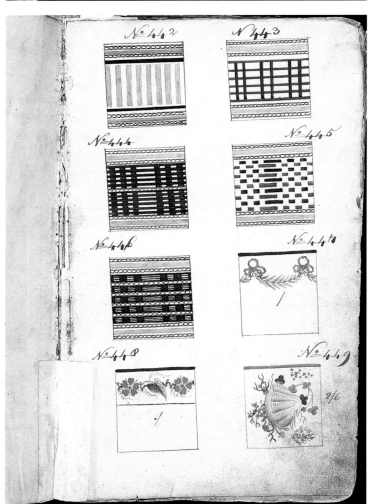

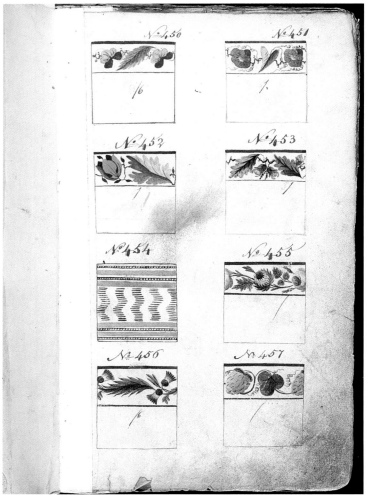

Diſp

347

Diſp

Cover'd Ware

No 376

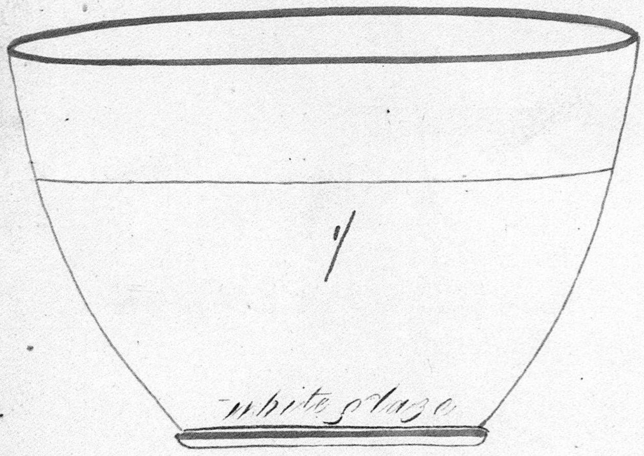
1/
white glaze

No 377

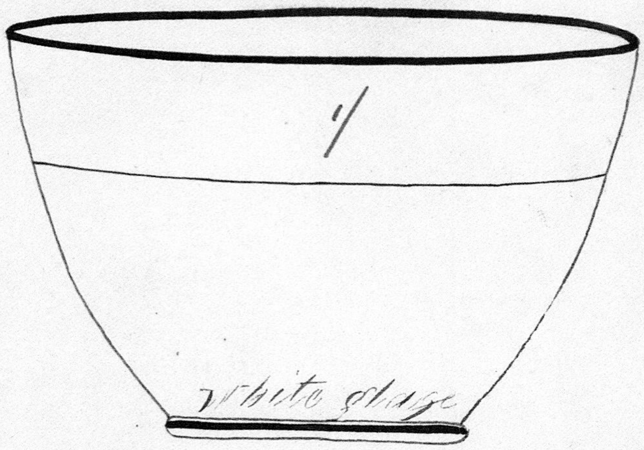
1/
White glaze

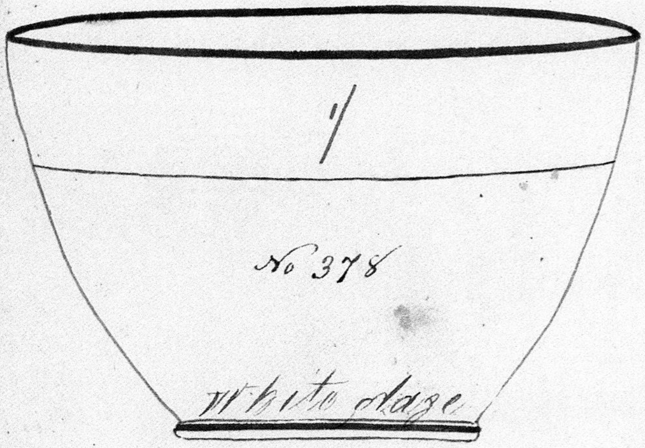
1/
No 378
White glaze

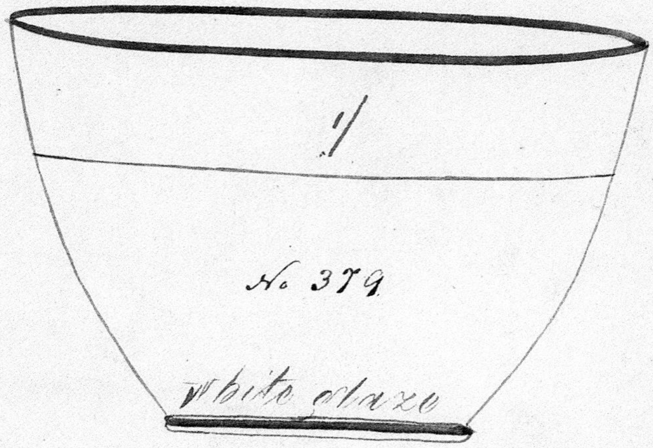
1/
No 379
White glaze

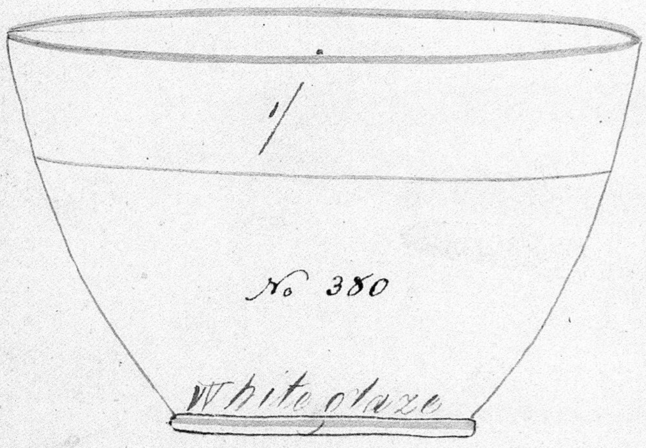
1/
No 380
White glaze

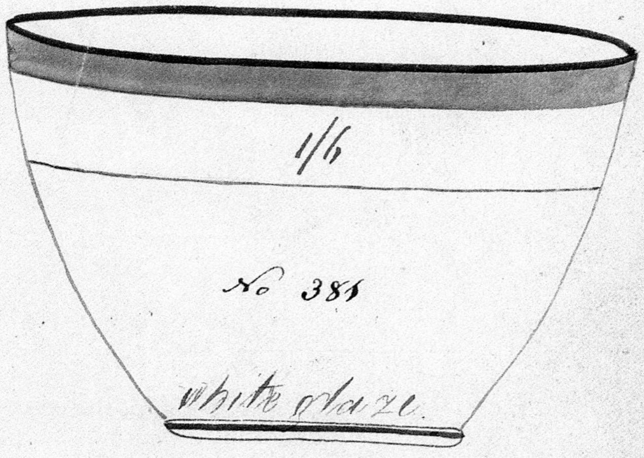
1/6
No 381
white glaze

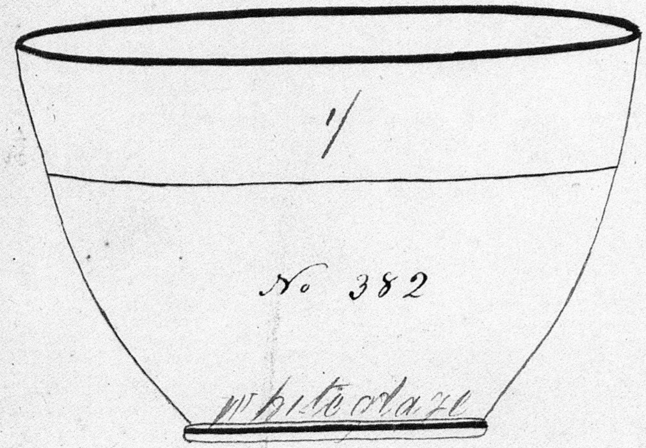
1/
No 382
White glaze

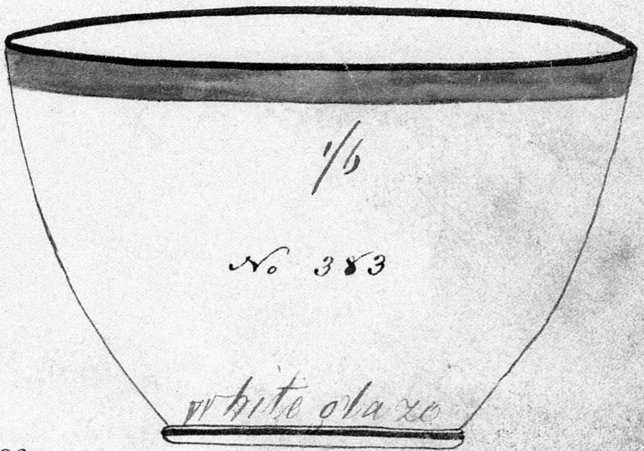
1/6
No 383
White glaze

No 384   1/6

white glaze

No 385   1/6

white glaze

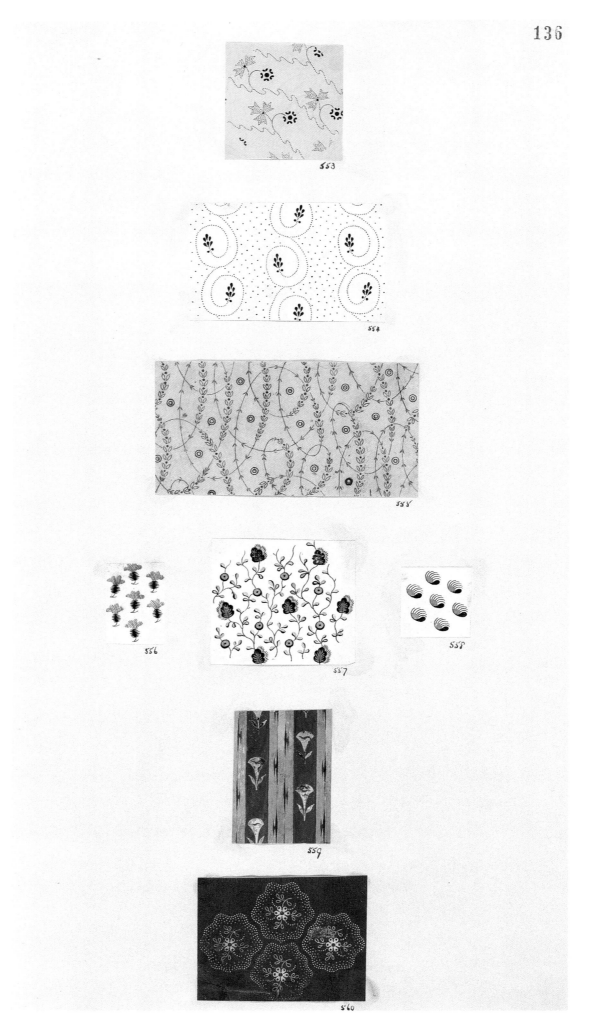

553

554

555

556

557

558

559

560

561

562

863

564

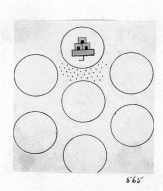

865

566

567

568

I.V.　18th Febry 1802

N.º 1.

N.º 2.　N.º 3.

N.º 4.　N.º 5.

N.º 6.　12 ⅞

N.º 7.

N.º 8.　14 ½

V.A.M.

No. 1.

Stand
of
No. 1.

No. 2.

Stand
of
No. 2. 3. 4.

No. 3.

by Letter 15 May 1827
No. 4.

Stand of No. 5.

No. 5.

. 12 . 11 . 10 . 9   Sauce
Cur: & Co. 1/6 . 1/3 1/ . 1/

HCC

A.

N°1

N 2

3 dois
Bew

A.

N°4

N°3.

SM
9bre 17 Aug 90

INN

Figures de diff.tes pièces de Fayance angloise
LAY 1784

a   b   c   e

f n:1   2   3   4   g   h   i

K   l   m   n   o

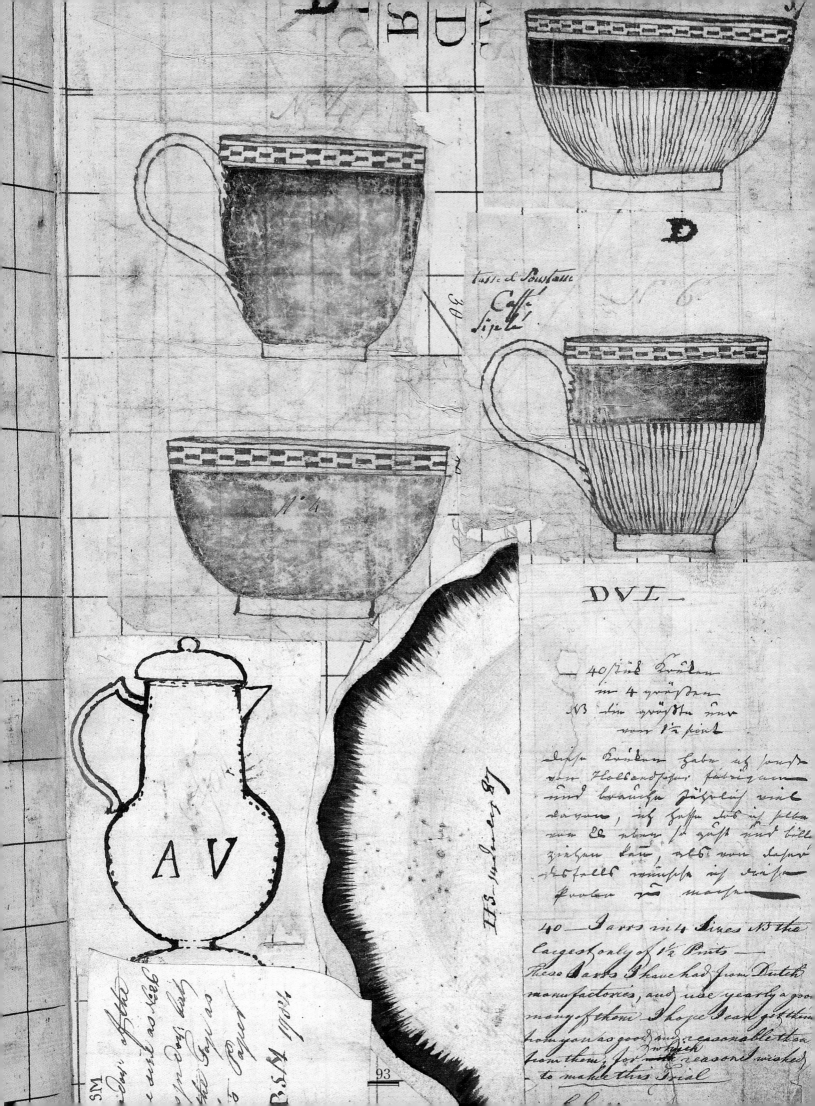

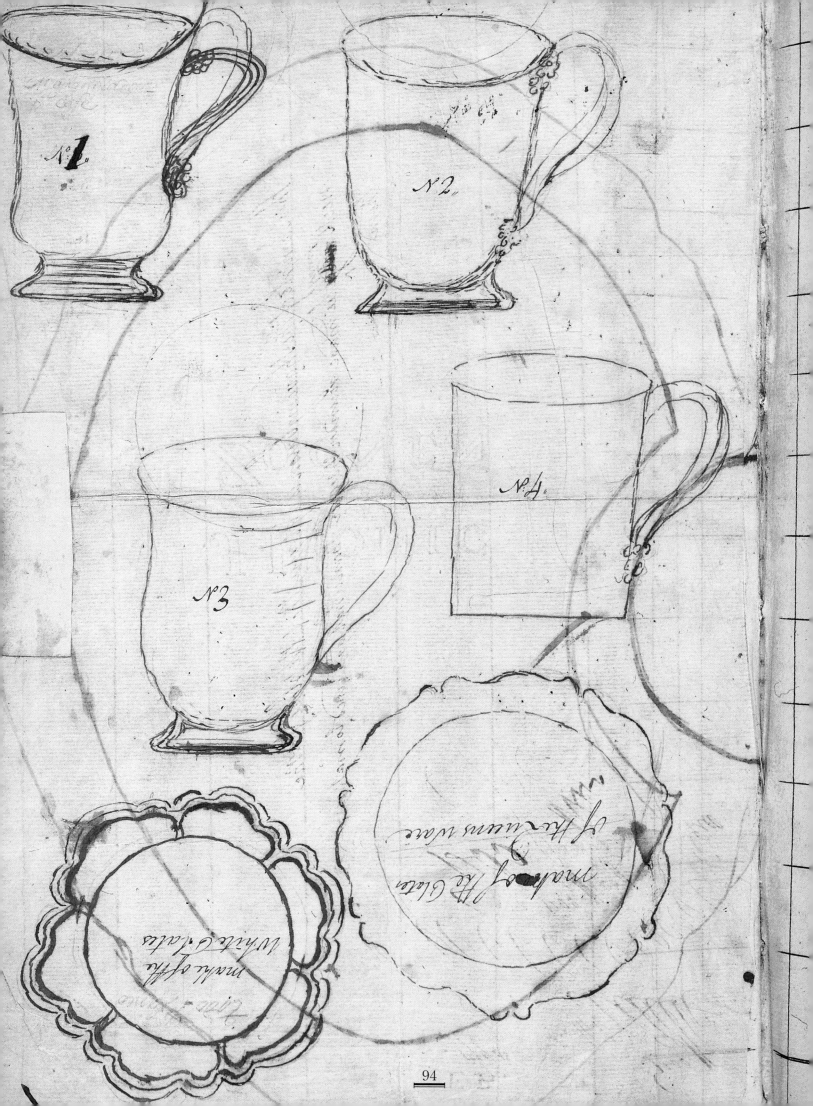

N.1

N.2

N.3

N.4

mark of the
White Glass

Mark of the Glass
of the brown ware

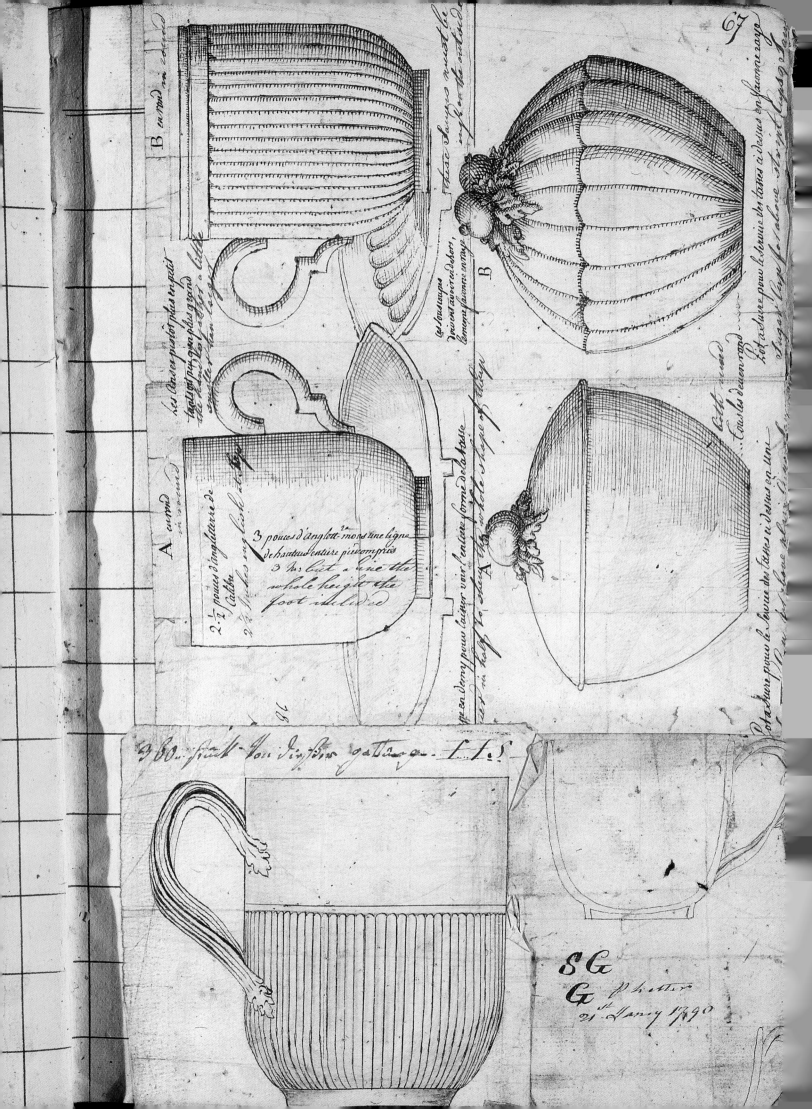

67

3 pouces d'anglett. mons une ligne
de hauteur entière pris compris
3 In: but a line the
whole height the
foot included

SG
G Potter
21st Jany 1790

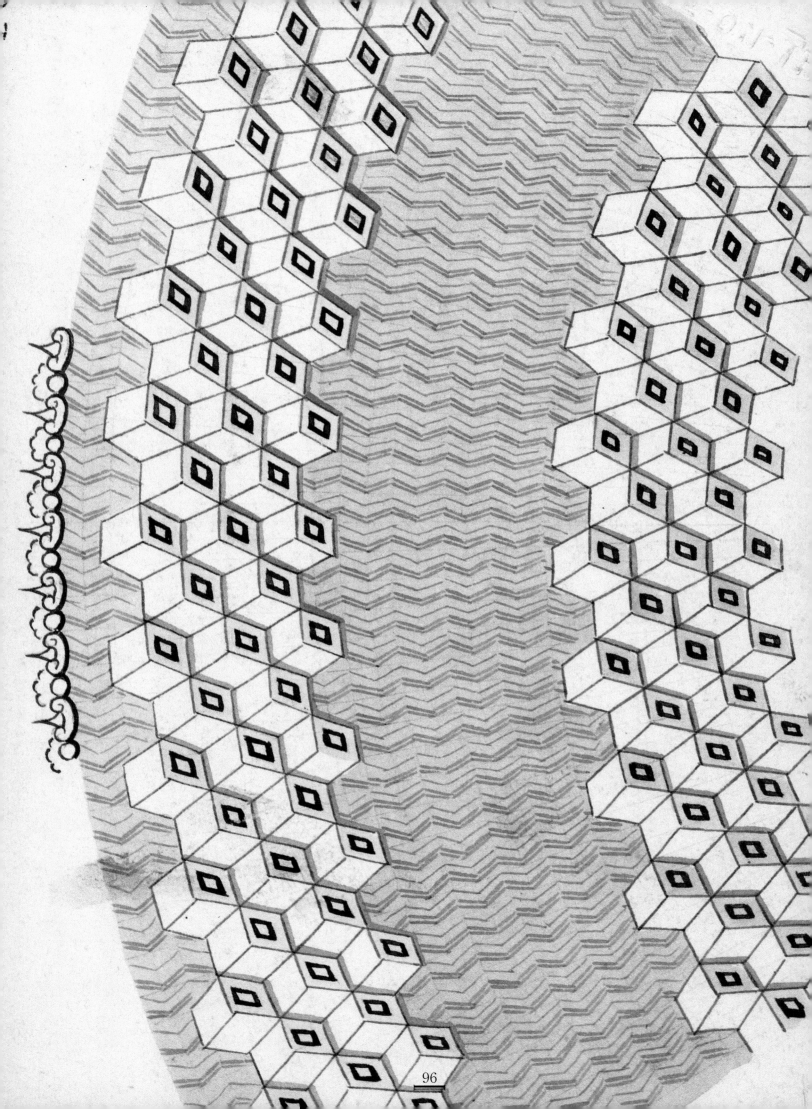

the
ORKSHOP
OF THE WORLD

The years between 1830 and 1851 saw England assume a position of apparent unassailability in world manufacturing and economic affairs. Yet the factors which ensured this pre-eminence – the growth of a factory culture and its related financial structure – also had an unfortunate effect on English design. The largely classical heritage which had survived reasonably intact into the early years of the century had been dissipated by 1830, as patronage passed from an informed and well-travelled aristocracy and upper middle class to a middle class whose taste was formed essentially by the manufacturers whose wares it bought in profusion. It was as though there was simply not enough good design to go round, as factories and workshops turned out goods in a bewildering variety of styles, often in inappropriately elaborate and exaggerated forms, perceived as the chief means of seeing off the competition.

The paucity of good English design in this period was made only too evident by the Great Exhibition of 1851, where far too many exhibits seemed preoccupied with the grotesque and vulgar detail of a half-understood traditionalism. After the exhibition, the tide of criticism of English design of the early and mid Victorian periods continued unabated until well into the twentieth century. The great Victorian reforming designers, from Burges and Morris to the major figures of the Arts and Crafts Movement, deliberately reacted against it; later critics, guided by an aesthetic formed by the precepts of the early Modern Movement, regarded its wild excesses almost as a manifestation of absolute evil. And we can see in the pages which follow that there is enough evidence of the tendency to disregard rightness of form for function in favour of crude visual effect: in wallpaper design, in interior design, in the styling of simple domestic artefacts.

The unsatisfactory appearance of much design of the period undoubtedly came from its eclecticism: there was virtually nothing in the way of new forms, just aspects of past styles, sometimes thrown together in the same artefact or pattern. Yet this same eclecticism, notably in furniture, did occasionally result in effective and pleasing pieces.

any of the stylistic devices of the time were undoubtedly affected by the prevailing mood of national self-confidence in their derivation from a specifically English past. 'Tudor', 'Elizabethan' and 'Jacobean' interiors were considered most appropriate to the many new country houses built in the first half of the nineteenth century. 'Elizabethan' was one of the styles considered by a Parliamentary Select Committee in 1835 for the design of the future Palace of Westminster. Again, printed pattern books were instrumental in the dissemination of styles, except that now such books would be used by mass-manufacturers as well as individual craftsmen. As we have noted in the general introduction, Robert Bridgens' *Furniture with Candelabra and Interior Decoration* of 1838 makes 'Elizabethan' its most extensive category of design.

lmost as important in Bridgens' book is the 'Grecian' category, which was effectively a continuation of Regency classicism. However, a new clumsiness had invaded the pure, elegant forms of the late eighteenth and early nineteenth centuries. Notable among the manufacturers of late 'Regency' was the firm of Gillow – a name which will recur throughout English nineteenth-century design as an indicator of popular taste.

The other style – eventually chosen – under consideration by the 1835 Committee on Westminster was 'Gothic'. Although it had still yielded pride of place to a gradually debased classicism in the early years of the century, in spite of isolated successful examples of Regency 'Gothick', Gothic was seen as another national, nordic style, as opposed to Mediterranean classicism. But typically of an age as contradictory and complex as the early Victorian, manufacturers and designers still frequently turned to Louis Quinze Rococo and to classical models for inspiration.

The Gothic style had an additional role, however, which gave it an importance well beyond its presence as part of the Regency and early Victorian design mix. It was also a vehicle for the first stirrings of design reform, providing a repertoire of motifs and forms which ran counter to the fussy, vulgar detailing of mainstream manufactured artefacts.

he first significant reformer to deploy this visual vocabulary and its related values was Augustus Welby Pugin whose two publications, *Gothic Furniture* and *The True Principles of Printed or Christian Architecture*, set forth new tenets of design responsibility in materials and form: '…there should be no features about a building which are not necessary for convenience, construction or propriety… all ornament should consist of enrichment of the essential construction of the building.' In his furniture, although by no means wholly consistent, Pugin veered away from the decorative tracery of Regency 'Gothick' towards an 'authentic', simplified style of Gothic which drew heavily on concepts of the medieval. The results have a toughness and honesty which point forward to the works of the later Victorian reformers.

ther voices were raised against the prevailing manufacturers' aesthetic, notably those of Henry Cole, Owen Jones and Matthew Digby Wyatt. In 1849 Cole launched on important publication, *The Journal of Design and Manufacture*, which based its editorial policy on the principle that, 'Ornament… must be secondary to the thing decorated.' But the century had a very long way to go before such principles could be applied to any significant degree in the manufacturing industry of Victorian England. Perhaps the most positive aspect of this period of English design is indeed its exuberance and energy, its sheer volume; and there are, in any case, many examples of intrinsic interest and great ingenuity, demonstrating a conscious effort by certain companies and individuals to apply a responsible design ethic to manufacture.

page 96 Pen and ink design of ceramic wares, for the Derby Crown Porcelain Company, from the originals now held in the Victoria & Albert Museum, London.

opposite Scenes from an early nineteenth-century pottery factory; the biscuit kiln would have been used for the production of an unglazed white porcelain, often used in the making of statuettes and other decorative objects.

Various Pottery Processes.

1. THE "THROWER."   2. THE "TURNER."

3. THE "BISCUIT OVEN."

4. PRINTING.   5. ORNAMENTING.

3

THE WORKSHOP
of the
WORLD

pages 100–101

Traditionalism and eclecticism: the library at Cassiobury, Essex, *c.* 1830, from an aquatint by F. Lewis based on a drawing by Augustus Pugin, published in 1837. The Fifth Earl of Essex, who succeeded to the title in 1799, commissioned James Wyatt to modify the Restoration house in the Gothick style.

page 105

The archive of Wycombe Museum, at the centre of England's traditional furniture-making region, contains fascinating material relating to the vernacular styles of the nineteenth century. These designs, in the form of small gouache paintings, appeared in a catalogue attributed to Walter Skull, furniture-maker. Each of the volume's 170 pages bears three separate designs, some with prices, as though this material was originally intended for the use of a salesman.

pages 106–107

The Whitefriars glassworks, originally located between Fleet Street and the river

Thames in London, had been in existence for well over a century when James Powell took over its management in 1835. It then became a leader in the revival of English hand-blown glass-making, promoting designs derived from Roman, Venetian, medieval and eighteenth-century models. The earliest Whitefriars pattern book, now in the Museum of London, contains 495 pages of hand-drawn designs, many of them dating from the 1830s. Most of these are for tableware, often annotated with prices and customer names. Shapes include claret jugs and bottles, some intricately engraved and with rope-ring finials, as well as glasses in all forms, such as those illustrated here.

page 108

In 1833 the Spode pottery and porcelain factory was taken over by W.T. Copeland, a partner since 1813 and in charge of the London showroom, and Thomas Garrett, who became the partner to manage the Staffordshire end of the business. The contemporary revival of interest in the art of Ancient Greece is reflected in this 1833 design for an

earthenware water ewer, decorated with whimsical Greek figures on a salmon-coloured ground. The ewer was part of a set which included a two-handled vase and a teacup which are illustrated on the opposite page of a master pattern book in the Spode Museum Trust.

page 109

This crowded sheet of designs for glassware *c.* 1840 by Leopold William Jones is a concentrated demonstration of how traditionalist and revivalist styles began to assume varied and exaggerated forms as the mid-century approached. Classical forms are here overblown in a disregard for rightness of form and a fondness for crude visual effect.

pages 110–111

Shoolbred, Loveridge & Shoolbred of Wolverhampton described themselves as makers of paper and Japan tea trays, general japanners, and iron and tin-plate workers. This company – located in one of England's industrial heartlands – was very much the epitome of the expansive Victorian business catering for

the ever-growing market in domestic products of variable design excellence. These designs for the company's jelly and blancmange moulds are taken from a catalogue of 1847, the introduction to which begs to remind customers that the wares on offer 'can only be shown as regards ornament, through the medium of patterns.'

pages 112–113

These two pages of teacup designs are taken from a master Spode pattern book containing, in all, 1,432 different patterns. Each of the designs is numbered and can be collated with the actual production records of the factory. All the cups illustrated here were to be made in bone china and date from the years just prior to the takeover of the factory by W.T. Copeland.

page 114

This selection of doorknobs and fastenings appears in a 340-page catalogue of engraved products manufactured by J. Rimmell & Sons. It is yet another demonstration of the colossal variety of forms and shapes available to the mid-Victorian market, when labour was cheap and the housing market in full expansion. The first page of the catalogue offers 'patterns priced etc. of Sheffield brass etc., furniture, fittings, domestic utensils.'

page 115

Another anonymous pattern book held by the Victoria & Albert Museum contains 145 pages of designs for light accessories and other metal fittings. These include candlesticks, as illustrated here, candelabra, hanging and standing lamps, as well as desk furniture, including letter-racks and ink-wells.

pages 116–117

During the 1840s the number of looms in the carpet-manufacturing centre of Kidderminster increased to more than 3,000 (see caption to pp. 78-79). For once anonymity seems to have been ignored and this original gouache painting is inscribed on the back, 'Edward Poole, designer of Kidderminster'. The design of banana leaves (p. 116) would have been woven on a Wilton loom *c*. 1830. The design on p.

117 was for a 27-inch half-drop pattern with a repeat at approximately 40 inches. The 11-colour design, painted in miniature, is dated 1830 on the back and would, again, have been woven on a Wilton loom.

pages 118–119

These designs, for the Derby Crown Porcelain Co. Ltd., are part of a book of ceramic patterns now held in the Victoria & Albert Museum, London. Each pattern, meticulously drawn in pen and ink, is accompanied by a company name and code number. The designs were clearly intended to be the original artwork for transfers. Porcelain factories had flourished in Derby from the mid 18th century; indeed, the town became known as 'the second Dresden'.

pages 120–121

Samples for wallpaper borders drawn from a precisely annotated album, dated 1840-41; again, the sheer variety of design on offer to the domestic decoration market of mid-Victorian England is astounding. It is perhaps small wonder that, given the sheer

volume of production, it sometimes seemed as though there was not enough good design to go round, and artists often worked for a number of different factories.

pages 122–123

Two further examples of design from the Rossendale Printing Co. (see pp. 70-71); the page illustrated on p. 122 dates from the early 1830s and shows samples of printed cottons. The complete book consists of 184 pages with engraved roller-printed and block print floral designs densely applied to each side. The swatch book of printed cottons, from which a page is reproduced on p. 123, is later in date (*c*. 1850). It consists of 234 pages with a variety of printed cotton swatches applied to each side in patterned, shaded and moiré-effect designs.

pages 124–125

The documentation accompanying this Rococo-inspired design for a Woodward Grosvenor carpet is more complete than is usually the case. Firstly, it is meticulously dated on the back: 18 September 1847. It is

also known that it was executed by the studio of the designer Anna Maria Garthwaite, who provided hundreds of designs for Woodward Grosvenor. It was sent, simply rolled and without protection, through the post (there is a Penny Red stamp on the back) to a Mrs Pardoe. The complex design uses 13 colours and would have been woven as a 27-inch Wilton.

page 126

Among the many pattern books in the Spode Museum Trust are six devoted to tile design. The Number Two Book, from which these designs are taken, contains 155 hand-painted patterns on paper, pasted down on to the actual pages of the book. Most of the designs are in a square format, although there are a very small number of rounded shapes.

page 127

A decorative adjunct to England's growing industrial might: a watercolour design for the ceiling of the refreshment room of Swindon station; this intricate pattern was designed in 1842 by F.&T. Grace.

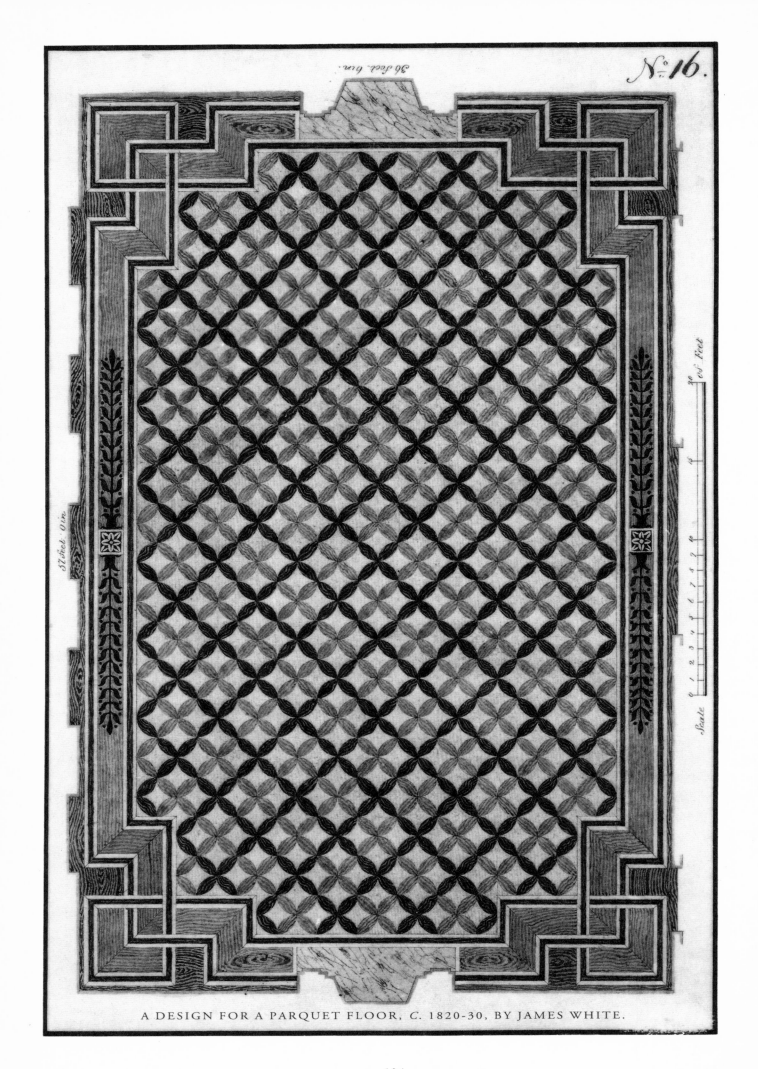

36 feet 6in.

37 feet 0 in.

20 feet

Scale

A DESIGN FOR A PARQUET FLOOR, *C.* 1820-30, BY JAMES WHITE.

N.º 481

15./ doz.ª

N.º 482

14./ doz.ª

N.º 483

17./ doz.ª

N.º 484

2/6 cts

N.º 485

21./ doz.ª

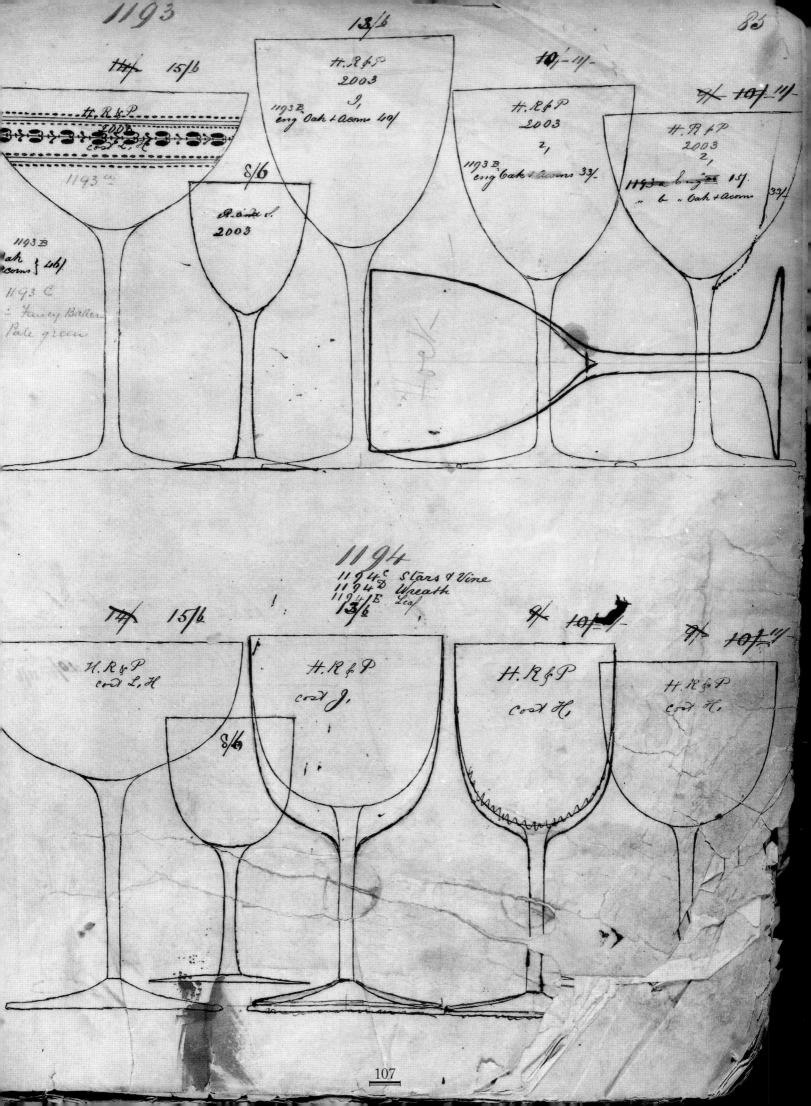

13/6

14/ 15/6

H. R. & P.
2003
9,
1193 B,
eng. Oak & Acorn 40/

10/- 14/-

H. R. & P
2003
2,
1193 B,
eng. Oak & acorn 33/

X 10/- 14/-

H. R. & P
2003
2,
1193 a eng. 15/
„ b „ Oak & acorn 33/

H. R. & P.
2003
cost L, H
1193 a

1193 B
Oak
acorns } 46/
1193 C
2 Fancy Balten
Pale green

8/6

R. and S.
2003

1194
1194 C Stars & Vine
1194 D Wreath
1194 E Leaf

14/ 15/6

13/6

9/ 10/- 11/-

9/ 10/- 14/-

H. R. & P.
cost L, H

H. R. & P
cost J,

H. R. & P
cost H,

H. R. & P
cost H,

8/6

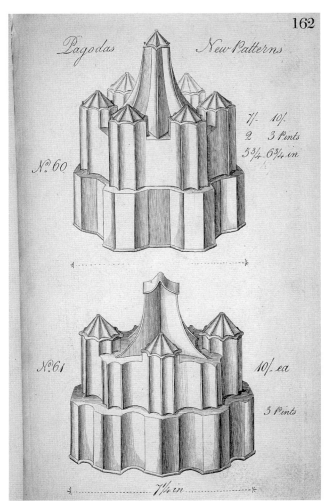

Pagodas   New Patterns

No. 60

7/- 10/-
2   3 Pints
5¾ 6¾ in

No. 61   10/. ea

3 Pints

7¼ in

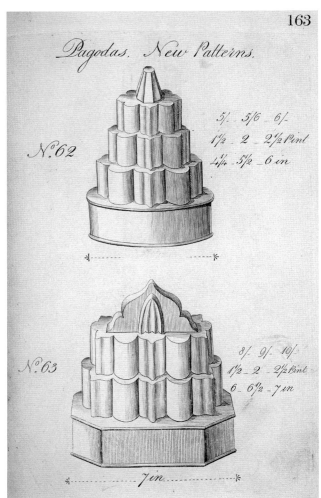

Pagodas. New Patterns.

No. 62

5/- 5/6 6/-
1½ 2 2½ Pint
4¼ 5½ 6 in

No. 63

8/- 9/- 10/-
1½ 2 2½ Pint
6 6½ 7 in

7 in

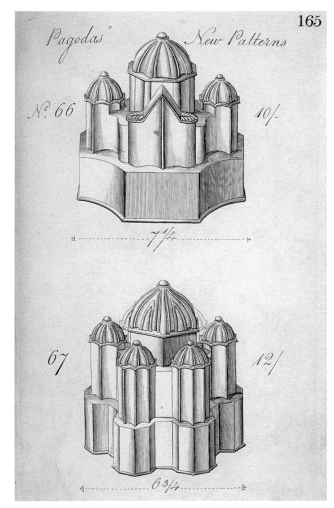

Pagodas   New Patterns

No. 66   10/-

7¼

67   12/-

6¾

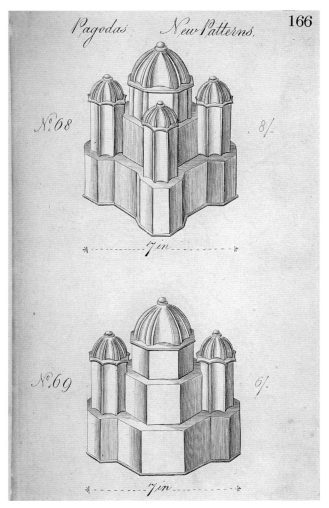

Pagodas   New Patterns.

No. 68   8/-

7 in

No. 69   6/-

7 in

Pie Moulds. ass.ᵈ Patterns.

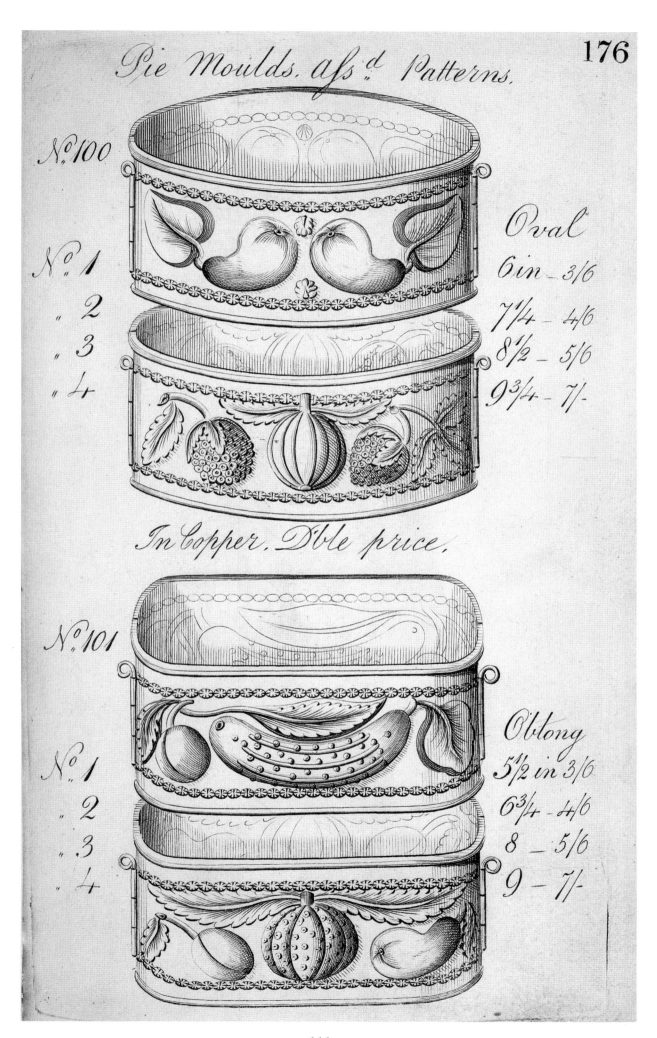

Nº 100

Nº 1
„ 2
„ 3
„ 4

Oval

6 in — 3/6

7¼ — 4/6
8½ — 5/6
9¾ — 7/-

In Copper. Dble price.

Nº 101

Nº 1
„ 2
„ 3
„ 4

Oblong

5½ in 3/6

6¾ — 4/6
8 — 5/6
9 — 7/-

Nᵒ 5223

Nᵒ 5224

Nᵒ 5225

Nᵒ 5226

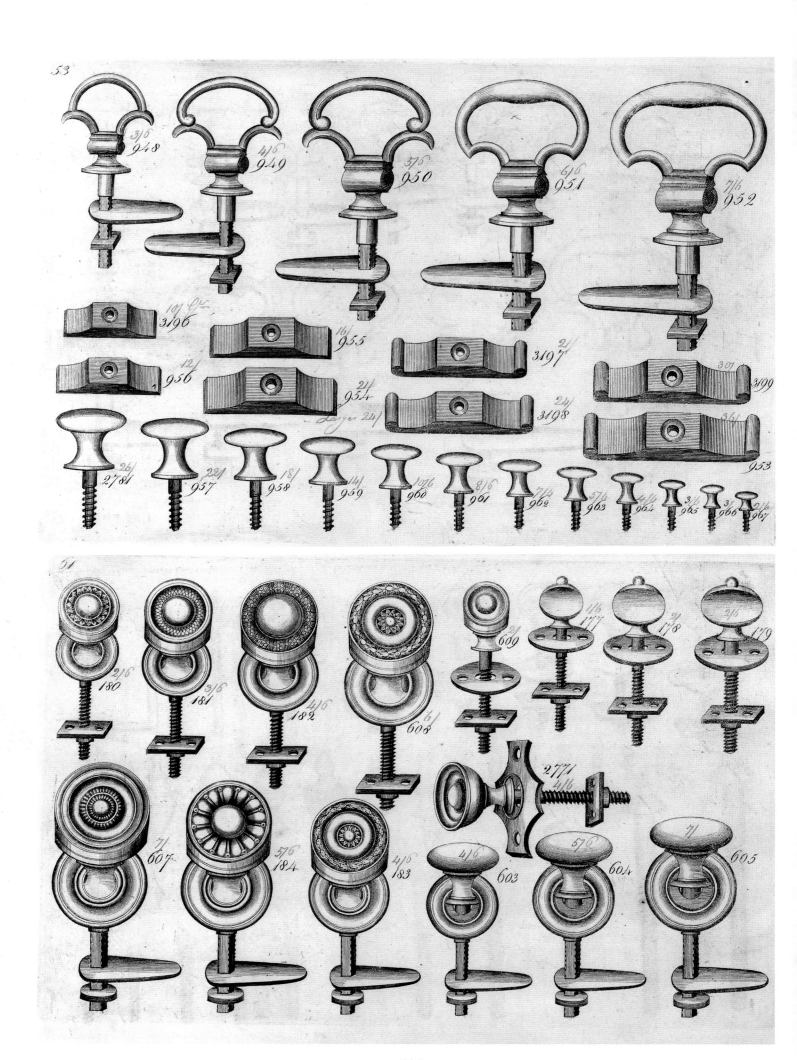

Glasses are   Charged Separately

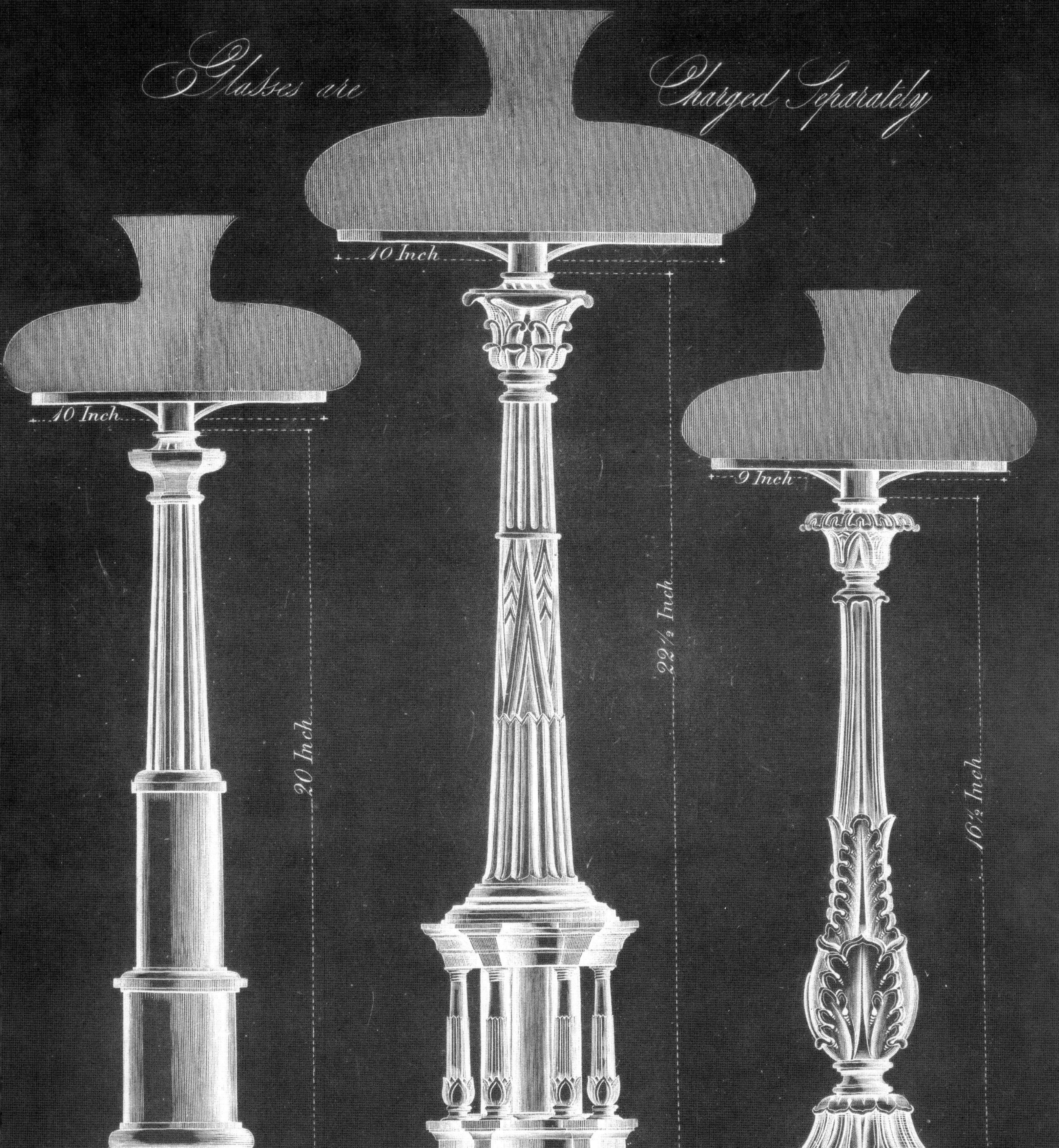

10 Inch

10 Inch

9 Inch

22½ Inch

20 Inch

16½ Inch

466...2/6...Each   429...45/...Each   467...22/...Each

118

January 1840

Heart Leaf 4 Prints Back 91 —

Walkers Cane 6 Prints Back 19 —

Scows Convolvulus 7 Prints Back 92 —

Sharps Rosette 6 prints Back 58 —

Talavera 3 prints Back 61 —

Salamanca Edge — 3 print Back 72 —

Heart & Daisy — 8 prints B14 Back

January 1841

Key Rosette   3 Prints   Rack 331

Rose & Lily 7 prints Rack 123

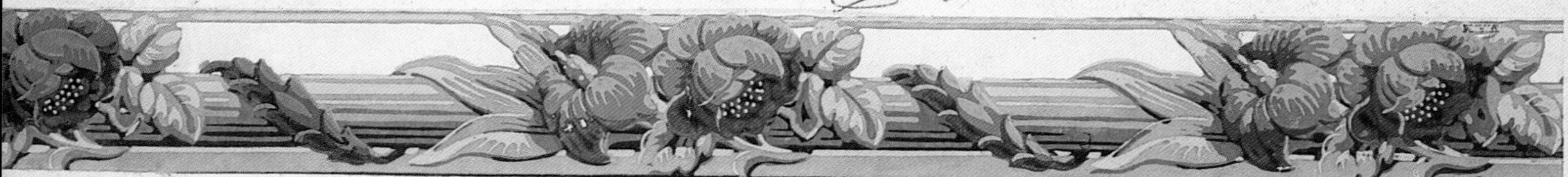

Walkers Rose Bud

Double Stock   7 prints Rack 121
Altered 1874

Reed & Ribband   8 prints Rack 16

Fruit Border 3 Prints   Rack 331

Anna Maria Garthwaite

Printed by Good & Son.

Anna Maria Garthwaite. N.º 8 and 9.

Printed by Good & Son, 63, Bishopsgate Without.

255
255

256
256

257
257

J. G. CRACE, Del. 1842.

High Victorian

4

FTER *the Great* EXHIBITION

The decorative excesses of the Early Victorian period did abate somewhat in the years following the Great Exhibition of 1851. Even commercial furniture of the type manufactured by the firm of Gillow began to display cleaner, sharper lines, although the most important advances in design and the decorative arts were undoubtedly those made by the great innovators of the period: Morris, Burges, Talbert, Eastlake and Godwin. But apart from such 'art' designers, English factories continued to pour out an incredible array of products: textiles, furniture, ironwork, pottery, glass and many apparently ingenious gadgets.

Manufacturers' catalogues of the time are remarkable for the sheer volume of goods on offer: varieties of plated cutlery; different patterns of wrought-iron balconies; rounded and square, decorated and plain marble chimneypieces; and an amazing collection of devices, some of dubious worth and efficiency, such as the Portable Vapour Bath offered by Shoolbred, Loveridge & Shoolbred (illustrated on p. 155). This was indeed the great age of the gadget, of the application of new processes on a massive scale. Anything and everything, it seemed, could be manufactured.

Against this background of the proliferation of goods and artefacts, the reforming zeal of a small body of designers took on a new importance. Versions of the Gothic style still continued to be the main idiom of the reformers after the Great Exhibition. Pugin mounted his Medieval Court at the exhibition itself. In 1853 John Ruskin published his *Stones of Venice*, with its famous chapter on the nature of Gothic. The new Houses of Parliament by Barry and Pugin were completed in the 1860s in the Gothic style. But undoubtedly the dominant figure of the time was William Morris.

nlike the majority of his contemporaries, Morris did not accept machine manufacture as a necessary good. Realizing that the very organization of Victorian industrial society, in the workplace and in the home, militated against good design, Morris decided to go to the very roots of the design process by turning artist-craftsman, teaching himself various disciplines which gave him a real respect for the nature of materials and an understanding of the ways in which they could be worked. He was a designer of genius; his chintzes and wallpapers, although often based on historical or exotic models, have a fresh, incisive quality which set them quite apart from the fussy, confused historicism of pre-Exhibition and Exhibition designs. Tradition and originality are constantly combined in a beautifully balanced handling of the fundamentals of decoration and design. His furniture, too, has a fineness and simplicity which are in stark contrast to the befuddled elaboration of the eclectic mix which characterized the pieces of earlier decades. It wasn't that Morris eschewed historical models – far from it – but he always seemed to be able to select those elements, notably from traditional English country styles, which he could then combine in entirely convincing and contemporary designs.

he founding of William Morris's own firm in 1861 meant that the teachings of the master designer could be disseminated more effectively among like-minded spirits. Philip Webb and J.P. Seddon were directly associated with the Morris concern and both designed furniture which first appeared in the company catalogue for 1862. Much of the inspiration for their work was overtly medieval.

Painted furniture is surely one of the most distinctive and freshly innovative categories of design of the period. The most striking examples must be the secretaires and cabinets of William Burges (see pp. 152–153), whose virtuosity in combining monumental forms and painted planes in a roughly Gothic format sets him apart as one of the truly adventurous designers of the latter half of the nineteenth century. Other influential reforming figures – largely through the wide dissemination of their designs – include Bruce Talbert, whose *Gothic Forms Applied to Furniture* appeared in 1867-68, and Charles Lock Eastlake. The latter's *Hints on Household Taste* of 1868 was reprinted many times and had a profound influence on design, mainly because the author focused his attention on the domestic interior, producing simple but stylish designs for whole room settings and sturdy, uncomplicated furniture.

Other design influences joined the reform movement, notably the taste for *japonisme*, the cult of things Japanese,

with special attention to the swirling lines of the Japanese print-makers. Their work had been included in the London 1862 Exhibition and was already being collected by leading aesthetes, notably by E.W. Godwin, who later became a design consultant to the firm of Liberty. He was also a friend of the painter Whistler for whom he designed the White House in Tite Street, Chelsea, in 1878. Godwin's design ethos introduced a lighter touch in the midst of the sturdy Gothic of other reformers. His furniture is distinctly Anglo-Japanese, often in ebonised wood, and once again publication ensured the dissemination of the style – in William Watt's *Art Furniture* catalogue of 1877, and in *Decoration and Furniture of Town Houses* of 1881 by Robert Edis. Godwin's extensive sketch-books are now held in the Department of Prints and Drawings of the Victoria & Albert Museum, London.

t would be misleading, though, to see the whole of English design of the post-Exhibition years as being informed by reforming zeal. Historicism was still a powerful force, notably in interior decoration and complete room settings, which therefore affected the design of individual elements, notably furniture, textiles and wallpaper. In architecture, too, a new nostalgia for a classical past began to emerge, typified by the so-called Queen Anne Revival associated with the architects Norman Shaw and Eden Nesfield. 'Renaissance' styles began to be more in evidence from 1870 onwards; significantly, Walter Pater published his *Studies in the History of the Renaissance* in 1873. This new classicism, though, is characterized by a heavy, ponderous quality, far removed from the delicacy and lightness of eighteenth-century Neoclassicism. One design element typical of the period was the massive, almost architectural, overmantel, complete with pediment and niches for the display of decorative objects.

uch revivalism was to continue well into the Edwardian era. But, from the Great Exhibition onwards, the debate as to what constitutes good design had been fully engaged, in the swatch books, catalogues and pattern books of the era. It was a debate that was shortly to lead to one of the most magnificent flowerings of English design – the Arts and Crafts Movement.

page 128 This fragment of wallpaper, printed from wooden blocks in the third quarter of the nineteenth century, was recovered from Lanhydrock House, Cornwall.

opposite An early Victorian power-loom for weaving tufted pile carpets.

4
AFTER
the Great
EXHIBITION

A 'modern dining room' from a drawing of 1872 by H.W. Batley; Batley later published a *Series of Studies for Furniture, Decoration etc.* in 1883.

The first stirrings of the reforming spirit in English design which culminated in the finest achievements of the Arts and Crafts Movement began to show themselves during the third quarter of the nineteenth century. William Morris began business in the 1860s, while William De Morgan (1839-1917), undoubtedly the Movement's greatest potter, began to produce pottery and tiles to designs such as these in London in 1869, later moving to Morris's Merton Abbey in 1882.

Whether in mainstream furniture production, ecclesiastical furnishings, or as a vocabulary for the great designers of the age, versions of the Gothic style played a dominant role in the design history of mid to late nineteenth-century England.

Pugin and Ruskin urged its claims to pre-eminence after the Great Exhibition of 1851, and the greatest building project of the age – the new Houses of Parliament – turned out to be a Gothic masterpiece. These two designs for Gothic-style chairs are by Turner & Sons; they are reproduced from a folder of etchings of hundreds of variations by anonymous craftsmen and designers now held in the Victoria & Albert Museum, London. A simpler form of Gothic eventually became the style of design reform.

Although there was undoubtedly much increased attention to the need for good design after the recognized failures of the Great Exhibition, historicism and eclecticism nevertheless remained powerful forces for decades to come. Albums of complete room settings, such as these published by T. Knight & Sons in varieties of historical styles, were a staple of the interior decorating business. And the demand for such settings clearly affected the design of individual elements, especially furniture, textiles and wallpaper.

Catalogues of virtually every type of household product abounded in late Victorian England, a reflection of the country's increasing economic might and the accompanying growth of the domestic market. Compared to the standardization which has characterized much of twentieth-century domestic design, the individuality of the variety of beds offered on this page is striking. Many of them hint at the Gothic in their pavilion-like forms, suggesting the medieval themes so beloved by Morris and his followers.

Ironwork in the form of railings and balconies decorated the façades of even the humblest terraced house in Victorian London. Catalogues offered standard designs to the builders of the massed houses of the inner city. Grander projects, however, such as this design for the Green Park façade of no. 20 Arlington Street, would attract an individual touch. This design, by L.W. Collmann, is executed in pen and ink, pencil and watercolour.

Like Morris and De Morgan, Christopher Dresser (1834-1904) was active as a designer throughout the latter part of the nineteenth century, from the 1860s until the full flowering of the Arts and Crafts Movement. He designed for a wide variety of media, including pottery, textiles, wallpapers, furniture, metalwork and glass. An enthusiastic botanist, his early designs (those reproduced here date from 1861) show a preoccupation with adapting and transforming natural forms to decorative ornament. Always active in promoting good design, Dresser was later editor of *The Furniture Gazette*.

The productions of Shoolbred, Loveridge & Shoolbred (see p. 155) typified the High Victorian fascination with the gadget. New ideas – some sound, some unsound – were applied in profusion to the production of household wares, and nowhere more so than to those for the bathroom. Presumably the shower-head of the Oval Pillar Bath (p. 147) could be raised or lowered by the winding mechanism.

In common with a number of English and Continental potteries, in the 1850s and 1860s Wedgwood introduced a number of designs derived from the Italian painted *maiolica* of the sixteenth century. 'Majolica', as it was termed, was shown extensively by Minton's at the Great Exhibition and in the following decades coloured glaze coupled with relief decoration was applied to all manner of domestic objects, including umbrella stands and *jardinières*. Wedgwood's reaction to this market opportunity was to revive production of their eighteenth-century green-glaze ware, with decorations of botanical forms. These designs are taken from one of three 'majolica' pattern books in the Wedgwood archive: 'Apple Blossom flower pot' (p. 148) and 'Shell Oyster tray' (p. 149) (see p. 203).

Best known as a painter, Sir Edward Burne-Jones (1833-98) also had a close association with William Morris as a designer, notably of tapestries and stained-glass windows. This sketch, inspired by Chaucer's *The Legend of Good Women*, is a preliminary study for embroidered wall-hangings which were to have graced the house of John Ruskin. The project was never completed, although the needlework may have been begun. The figures represented include Cleopatra, Dido, Medea, Ariadne and Philomene, all martyrs to love; the names of the proposed seamstresses were written above the figure on which it was intended they should eventually work.

The furniture which William Burges (1827-81) designed in his entirely distinctive manner was either intended for his own house or for the major decorative schemes he undertook for the Marquess of Bute at Cardiff Castle and Castle Coch. Gothic in overall style, the forms of his furniture are relatively simple, as these designs for a cupboard and secretaire, but the brilliant surface decoration places it among the most innovative achievements of nineteenth-century design. The painting drew on a variety of figurative subjects, including birds and flowers and scenes from the Bible and pagan mythology.

Artists commissioned by Burges included Burne-Jones, H. Stacy Marks, Albert Moore, E.J. Poynter and Simeon Solomon.

Providing as much choice as possible for the customer – probably a jobbing builder – was clearly an underlying principle of the activities of Henry Greene & Co., manufacturers of fireplace surrounds in a variety of materials. This page is reproduced from one of their trade catalogues of *c.* 1880-90, part of the archive now held in the Geffrye Museum, London.

Another example of ingenious Victorian gadgetry: the Portable Vapour Bath was offered in two models by Shoolbred, Loveridge & Shoolbred at 30 shillings. It purported to allow sufferers of rheumatism to undergo beneficial treatment in the home, presumably clad in dressing-gown and slippers. Based in Wolverhampton, the company epitomized the spirit of late Victorian manufacture in the ambitious range of its trade catalogues, which also offered slipper and shower baths and basins, coffee pots and urns, seamless cooking vessels, tea and coffee pots.

The fresh, incisive wallpaper designs of the William Morris firm – revolutionary when compared with the fussy historicism of Great Exhibition design – were among the first successful examples of the reforming spirit in design which began to show itself in England during the 1860s. Traditional subject-matter is rendered new and exciting by the boldness of the design. These samples, part of the record of the Morris firm's output maintained by Jeffrey & Co., are pasted into an old account book, accompanied by code numbers, pattern names and other annotations. Each published colouring of every pattern was recorded, since new ones were added after the original publication of the design. These records are now in the archive of Arthur Sanderson & Sons Ltd.

The firm of Elkington & Co. Ltd., now a subsidiary of the

4
AFTER
the Great
EXHIBITION

Delta Metal Co. Ltd., had its origins in the early part of the nineteenth century, when George Richard Elkington (1801-65) and his cousin Henry Elkington (*c.* 1812-52) patented their methods of gilding base metal in 1836 and 1837. By 1840 they had perfected their technique of electroplating, and the company's first factories were established in London, Birmingham, Liverpool and Dublin, with a showroom in London. The company records for the nineteenth century and for the first part of the twentieth (now held in the Victoria & Albert Museum, London) contain a large number of original drawings, with annotation. These pages of ornate candelabra designs are taken from the record book for 1840-73, one of 26 similar volumes in the archive.

pages 160–161

One fascinating aspect of Morris's preserved designs is the sense they give of the designer's activity still continuing. The archive pattern 'Daisy' (p. 160), printed as a wallpaper in 1864, bears traces of layers of pencil lines, as the artist changed the position of the leaves and then used wash to conceal the changes. Only the birds appear to be in final form, unlike those in the 'Bird' pattern (p. 161) which seem to be independent of the background.

pages 162–163

Philip Webb (1831-1915) was yet another relatively long-lived designer who worked successfully during the final decades of the Victorian era and into the full flowering of Arts and Crafts at the turn of the century. He was closely associated with Morris, for whom he designed the Red House at Bexleyheath in 1860, where he seemed deliberately to eschew classical features in favour of an English rustic vernacular with some dashing touches of modernism. From 1861 Webb worked exclusively with Morris, designing furniture, metalwork and glass, until 1875 when he resigned his partnership in the firm. These elegant designs for champagne glasses were manufactured by the Whitefriars glass factory and may have been created as early as 1859.

pages 164–165

The design of flat patterns, for whatever medium, was dominated in this period by William Morris. His equivalent in ceramics, specifically earthenware, was William De Morgan (see p. 137). After a period at Merton Abbey he set up a factory in Fulham in 1888, where his output was characterized by patterns derived from Persian, Greek and fifteenth-century southern Spanish wares. His decorative plates in lustre painted earthenware display stylized yet vibrant designs in colours which De Morgan referred to as 'Persian' – green, black and turquoise.

pages 166–167

This double-page of designs for butter knives is taken from the exhaustive production records of Elkington & Co. Ltd. The designs are meticulously hand-drawn in black ink on cartridge paper; the pages of the pattern books are indexed. This, the first of the 26, also contains designs for butter boats, butter coolers, candelabra, claret jugs, cups and tankards. In the same archive are 10 volumes of company history, administrative papers, press cuttings, company deeds, account books and general correspondence.

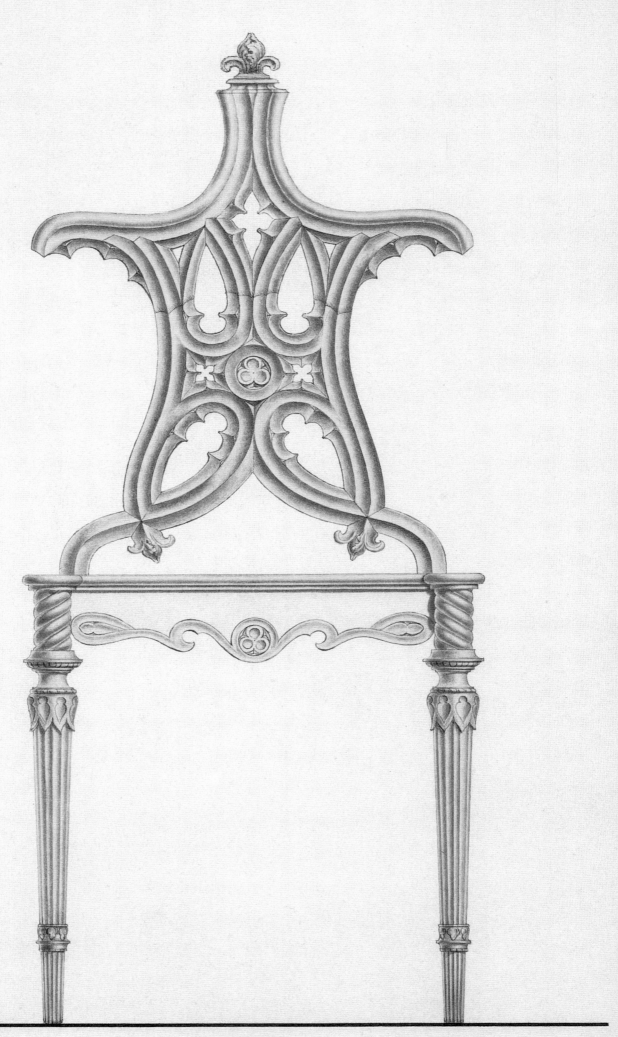

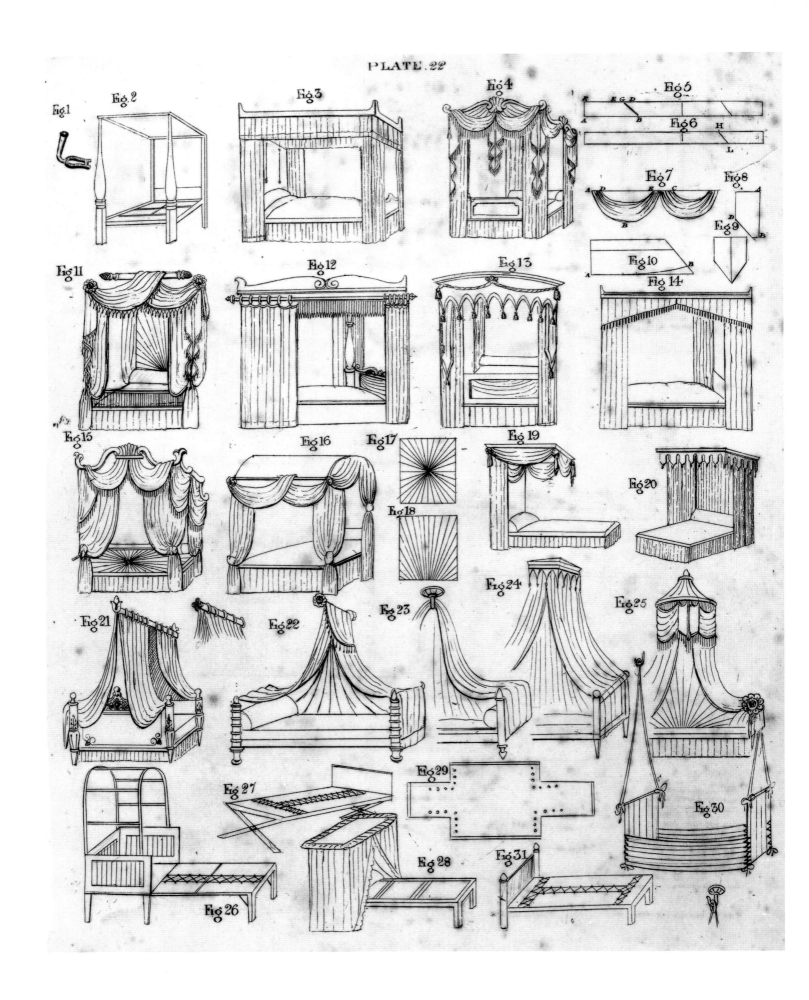

PLATE 22

Fig 1 Fig 2 Fig 3 Fig 4 Fig 5 Fig 6 Fig 7 Fig 8 Fig 9 Fig 10 Fig 11 Fig 12 Fig 13 Fig 14 Fig 15 Fig 16 Fig 17 Fig 18 Fig 19 Fig 20 Fig 21 Fig 22 Fig 23 Fig 24 Fig 25 Fig 26 Fig 27 Fig 28 Fig 29 Fig 30 Fig 31

20 ARLINGTON STREET.
IRON WORK TO PARK FRONT.
Scale ½ in. = 1 ft.

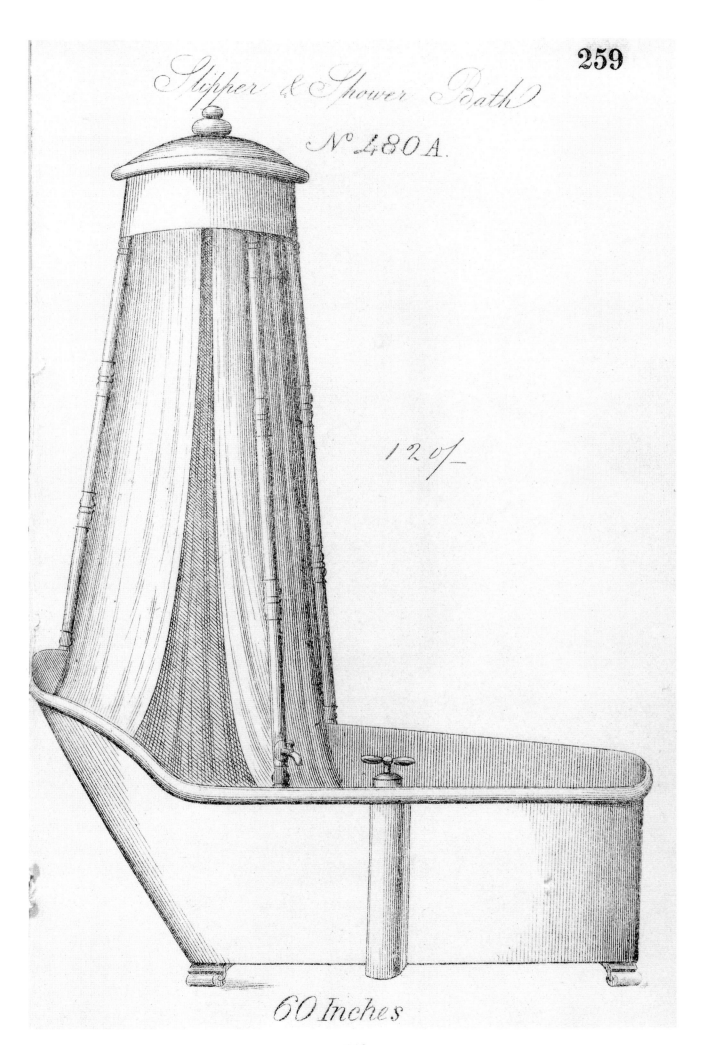

Slipper & Shower Bath

N.º 480 A.

1201

60 Inches

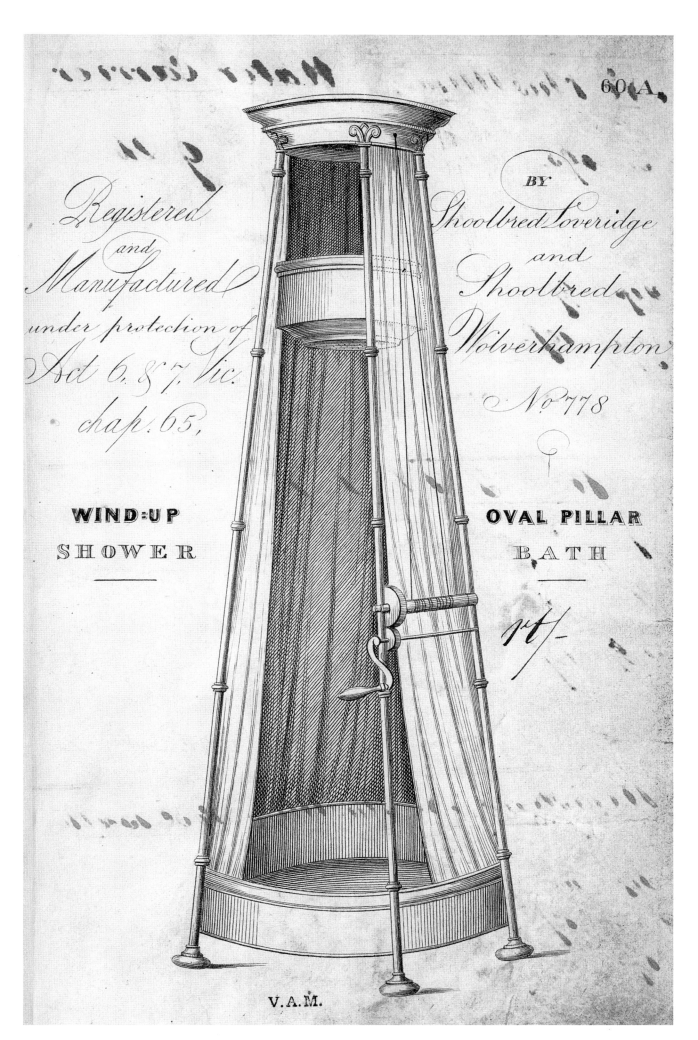

Registered

and

Manufactured

under protection of

Act 6. & 7. Vic.

chap. 65,

WIND=UP

SHOWER

BY

Shoolbred Loveridge

and

Shoolbred

Wolverhampton

No. 778

OVAL PILLAR

BATH

V.A.M.

2947 Shell Oyster Tray See pattern

White
Olive Green
Crimson
Shaded in
Crimson & Lavender
Shaded in Dk Brown
Crimson
Green
Yellow
Palid in Yellow
White Foam
White
Crimson
Shaded in Pink
Lavender Ground
Dk Brown Ground

2948 Shell Oyster Tray See pattern

White Foam
Mottled in Pink Yellow Brown & Gray
White Foam
Yellow Ground
Olive Green
Shaded in Dk Yellow
Gray
White
Crimson
Ivory

Burges archt
15 Buckingham St Strand Oct 17/188

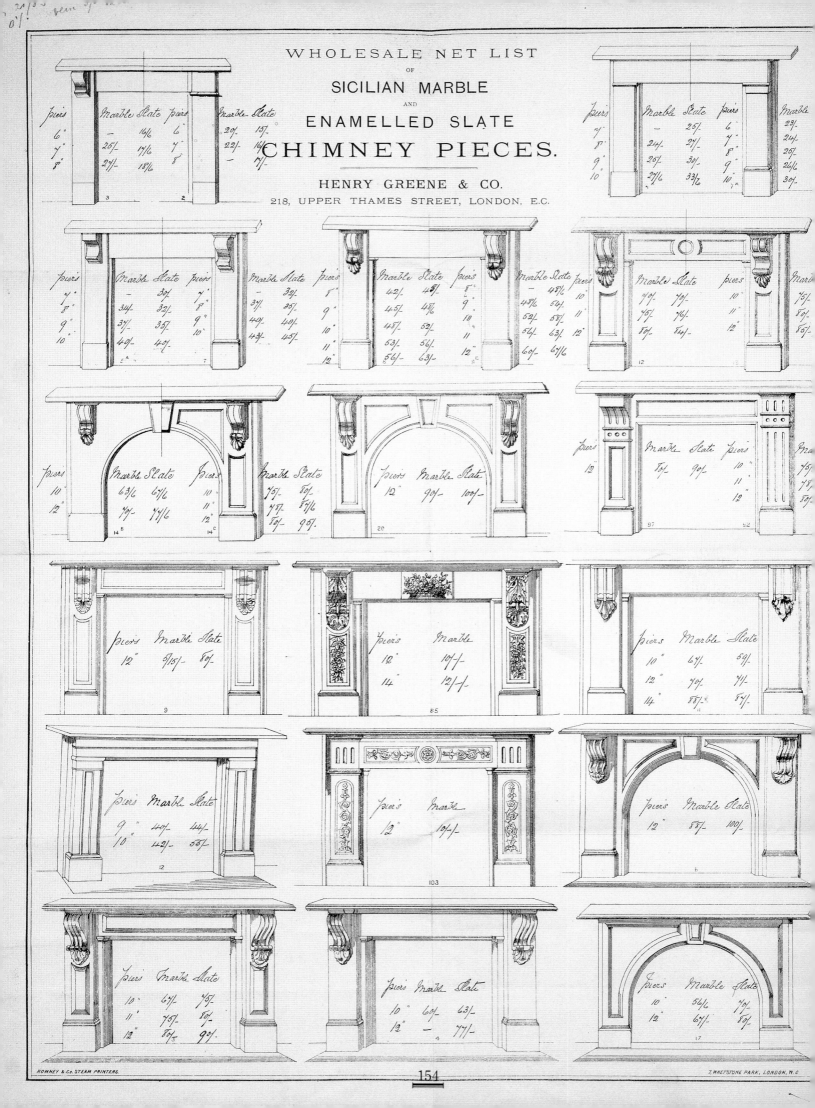

WHOLESALE NET LIST
OF
SICILIAN MARBLE
AND
ENAMELLED SLATE
CHIMNEY PIECES.

HENRY GREENE & CO.
218, UPPER THAMES STREET, LONDON, E.C.

ROWNEY & Co. STEAM PRINTERS.

7, WHETSTONE PARK, LONDON, W.C.

Nº 691

30/-

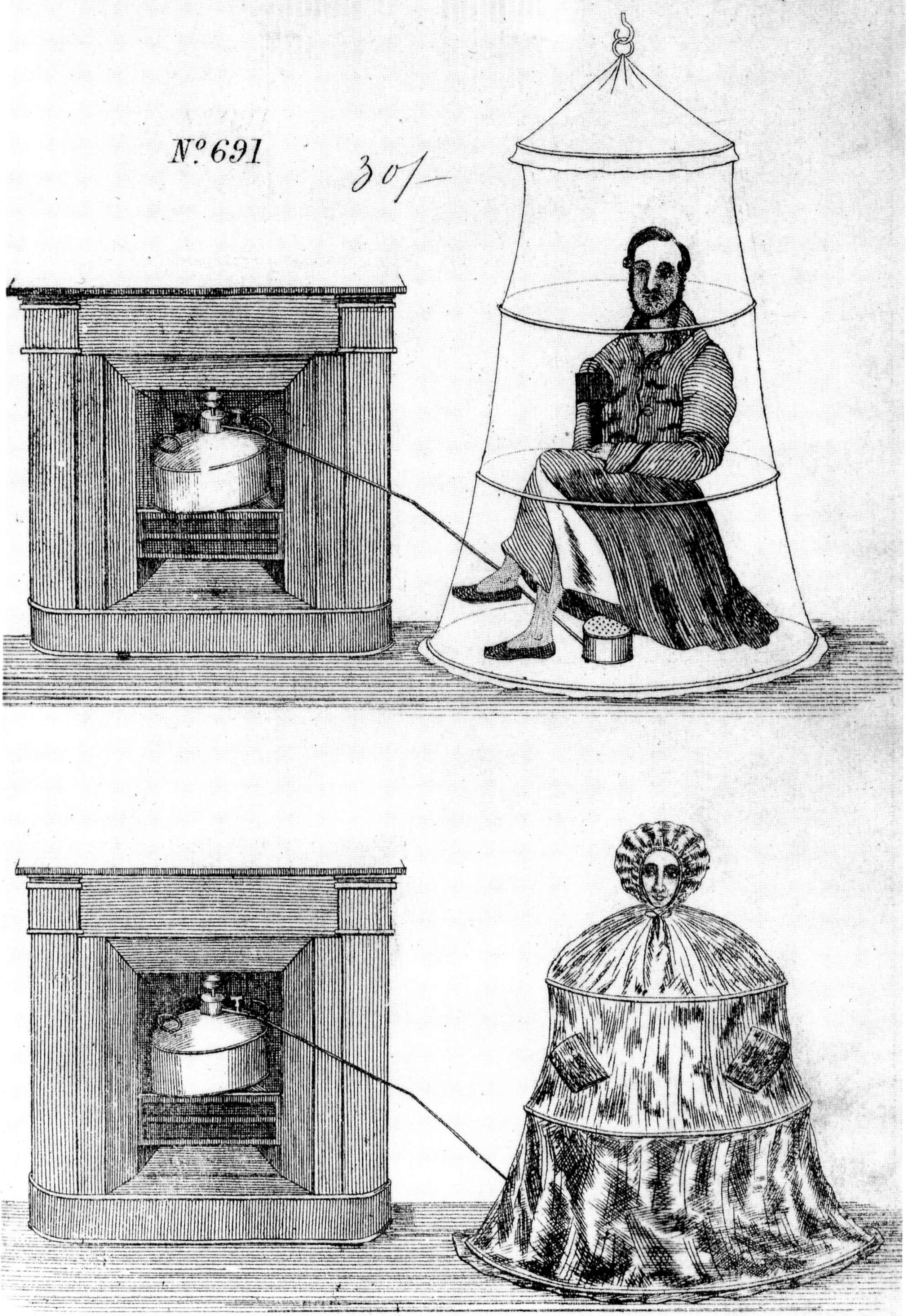

Either with Hood, or Suspension Cloth.

Oct 1875 W. Cranes decoration   1875—6

7 Blocks Lilly Dado
15 . x 26 . 0098
1 extra for   } 12
2nd. Backgm

Back 133

6 Blocks Margaret
21 x 15 002324   8

Back 128

2 extra Blocks   3
002667   Alaster

Barratt
24–24" Blocks   36
002295

Back 117

Dove Freize 8 Blocks   11

Barratt
116010
one Border   4
3 Blocks
Paper 2¾   5
short do
Freize   8 Blocks   6
Dado   5
3 — 15°0

Barratt
6 Blocks   12
21
Back 114

Barratt 00125
Back 189
Tulip
2 print Safe

Barratt
00110
12 . 21 .   20
Back 100

Resulting 1 Block Barrah	002234	
3 – 15"	6	0
61874 Destroyed Dwarf	Rack	

£ 6
Barrah

Champatt Safe
(4 col.)

Barrack
de Colr
62012   Feb 2.
Rus.

	7	10
	Rack	

Beirrah
61592
3 – 12"
Gowan

002316	
5	✓
Rack 138	
Bord	

62050 Cranes Iris   001207   Rack.   1. drawn
washed   62155 Rushes   Rack   11. Blocks   135   –17
140   2 –   140   –4.   10.
140   3. 002673   140
140   3.   126   –3   5

Ceiling Sign 62140+
"   Border 60+0+002655

Rack 132–133
Lisk Drawer 00378/Blocks – Barrah   Irs 7   0
153   Boat press 60228   8 4h. Blocks   Swan   21.   0
001107   6 12. do   Dado
51 002441   Rack 15+14
001269
Rack 001286   60200   8 3/4. Block Boat
158   Swan dado   Lisk   17   10
Rack 15+158 +14 B. 152 ×13

all Parts Safe

Elder see back ←

Plum   61415 Barrah Rack 143
Mango & Border 60334   Plum –18
5 Blocks   Laurel   7
1 Bird Frieze 60306 Marigold –6   10
5 Block   002289
002343   Pine   6
Laurel Dado 61390
5 Blocks

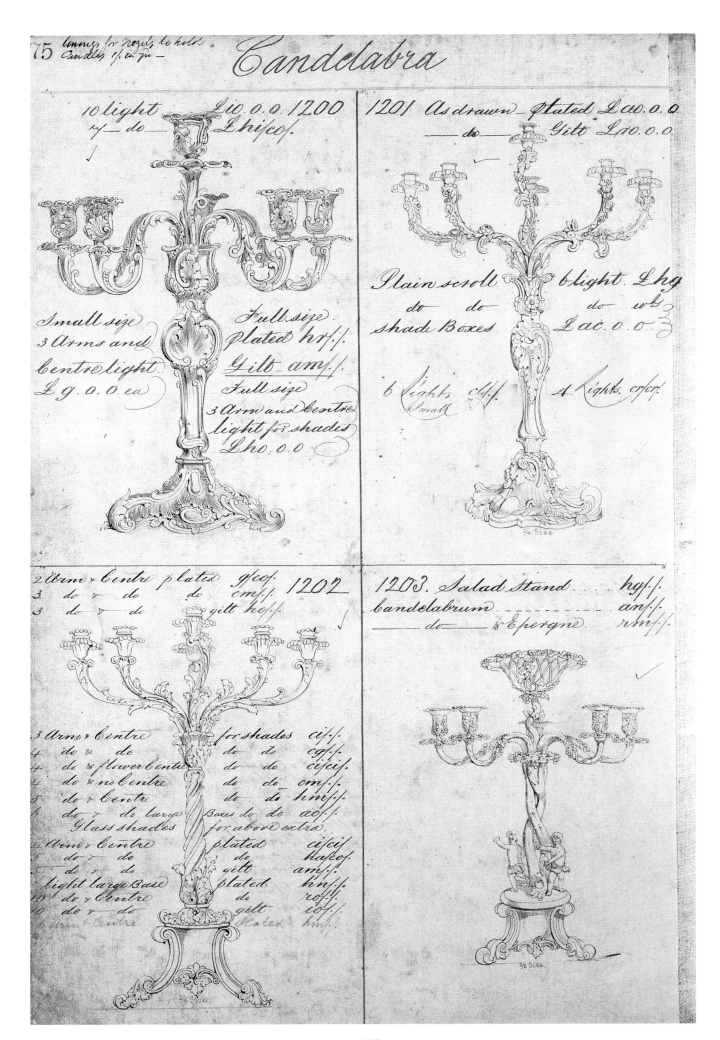

75 _Linings for nozels to hold_
Candles 1/ in ...

10 light   £10.0.0. 1200
3/ — do —   £ hi/co/.

1201 As drawn — Plated £ 10.0.0
— do —   Gilt £ 10.0.0

Small size   Full size.
3 Arms and   Plated hr/./.
Centre light.   Gilt — am/./.
£ 9.0.0. ea   Full size
                  3 Arm and Centre
                  light for shades
                  £ 10.0.0

Plain scroll   6 light. £ hg
do   do   do   10/.
shade Boxes   £ ac.0.0

6 Lights c4/./   4 Lights cr/co/.
Small

3/4 Size

2 Arm & Centre plated g/co/.   1202
3   do & do   do   cm/./.
3   do & do   gilt ho/./.

3 Arm & Centre   for shades ci/./.
4 do & do   do   do   cg/./.
4 do & flower centre do   do   ci/ci/.
4 do & no Centre   do   do   cm/./.
5 do & Centre   do   do   hm/./.
5 do & do large   Boxes do do a o/./.
   Glass shades   for above extra.
4 Arm & Centre   plated   ci/ci/.
5 do & do   do   ha/co/.
5 do & do   gilt   am/./.
7 light large Base   plated   hn/./.
10 do & Centre   do   ro/./.
10 do & do   gilt   ro/./.
   Arm & Centre   Plated   hn/./.

1203. Salad Stand ...... hg/./.
Candelabrum ....   an/./.
— do — & Epergne   rm/./.

1/6 Size.

2/4 Size.

2466   Candelabrum & Epergne — rn/./
_____ do _____ & _____ do __ gilt — ig/./

ndelabrum   10 light
Epergne w.   Candel rn
ucers for   only — rn/./
pergne.   W. Basket.
mi/./   mm/./
andel rn only — ag/./   Salad Stand only — h.../

andelabrum only,   With Basket and
ilt   mi/./   glass as 2458.
P.I.W.987). Cand rn   Epergne.
Epergne   mh/co/.
mplete, but w.   With nozels
Boys and.   io/. extra.
igher in   Centre light
roportion   only — ao/
o/./

andelabrum and   Boys only — 10/. ea.
pergne no boys   Wire Net — co/. gros...
ra/./   Double do — ci/. ...do
and rn only, no
oys — av/./

1159 Size.

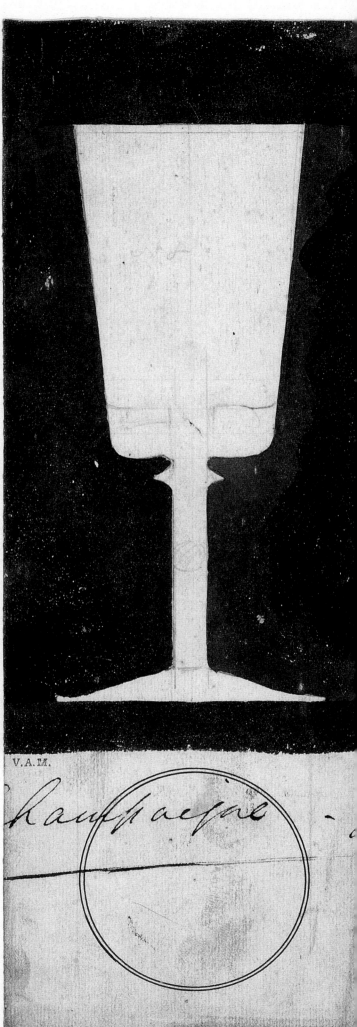

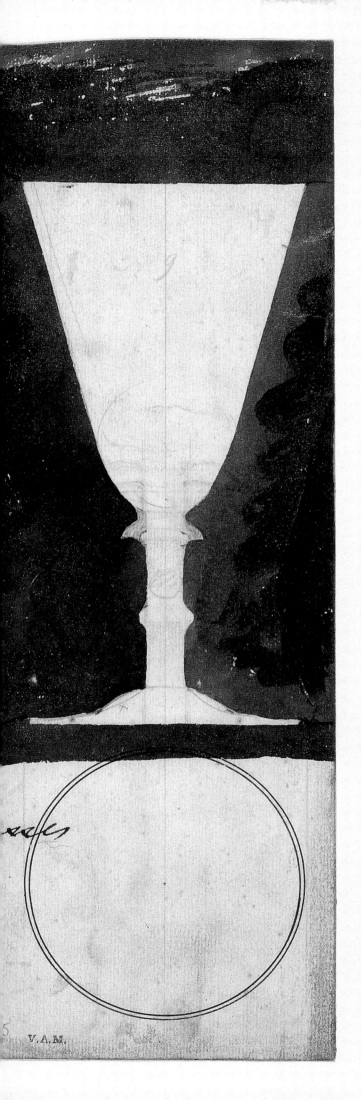
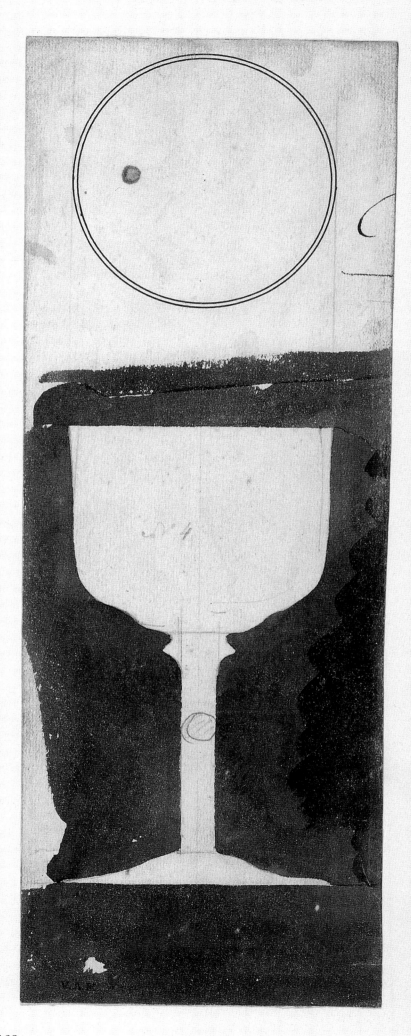

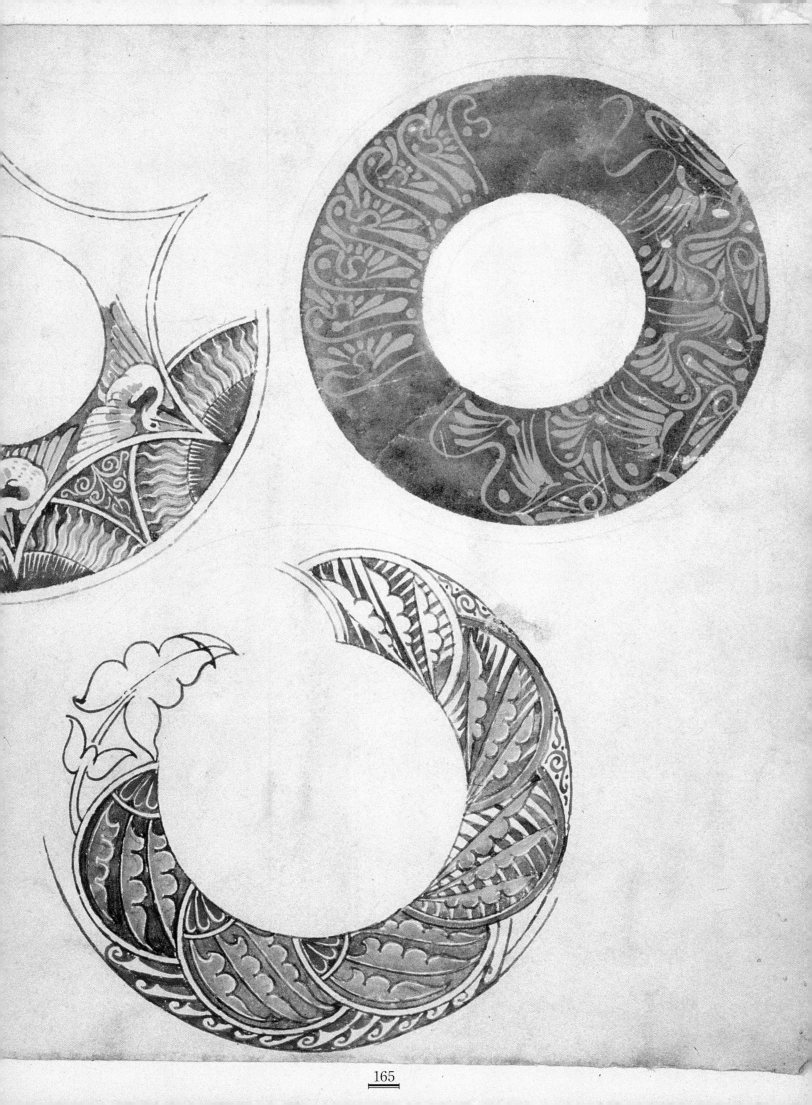

4380

4381

4382

444

Error

See Pickle Forks

Pearl.
Eng cop

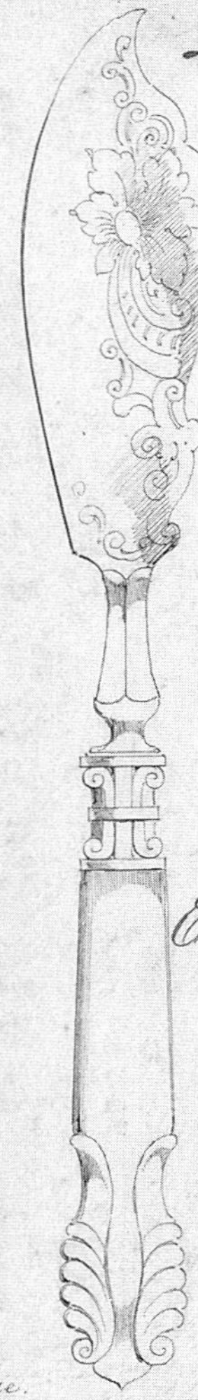

Ivory
Eng cop

9/i

Full Size.

Full Size.

Full Size.

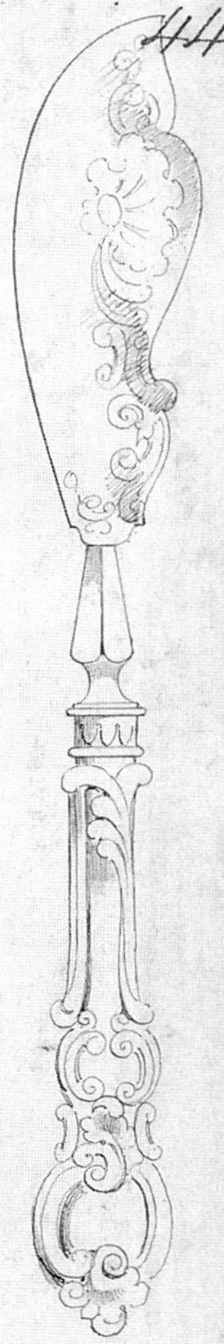

4421

4422

4423

444

Ivory cop

Pearl cop

Eng? Pearl plain 9/i
Yi Ivory
9/ Ivory Yi

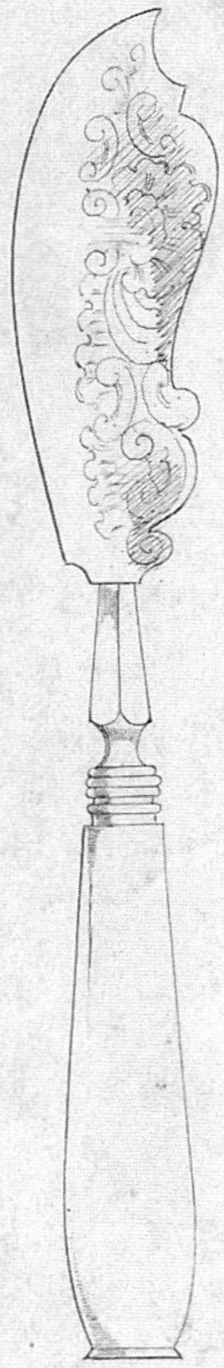

Full Size

Full Size

Full Size

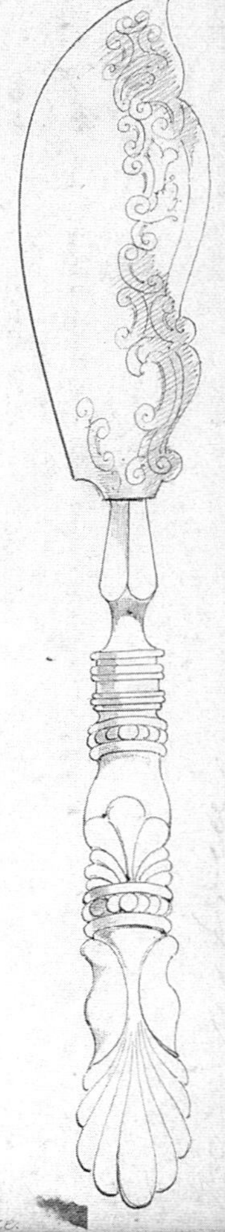

Full Size

25. | 4426. | 4427 | 4428.

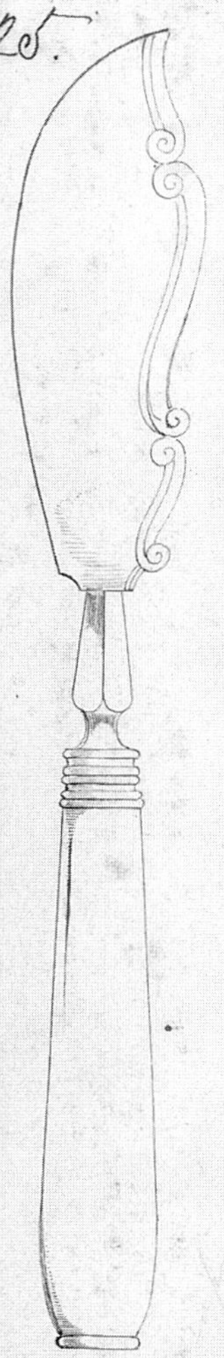

Plain 4/- Eng.ᵗ 9/-

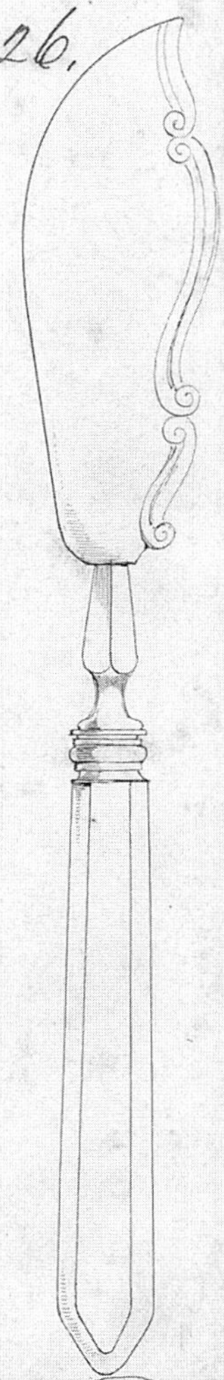

Plain 4/. Eng.ᵗ 4/6

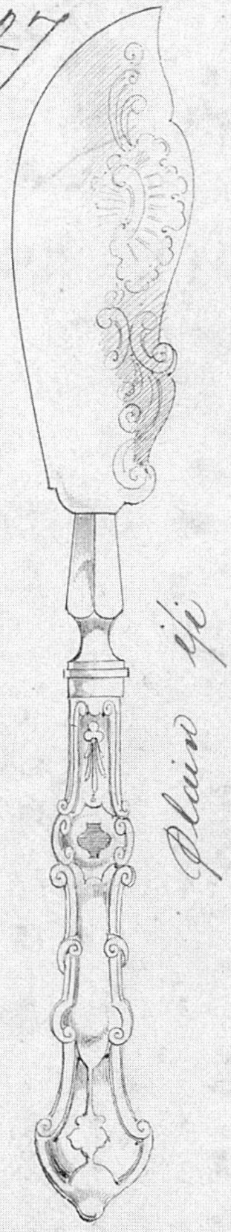

29 | 4430 | 4431 | 4432

Ivory Eng.ᵗ 9/6 | Ivory Eng.ᵗ 9/6 | Lily handle chased Blade 1/-

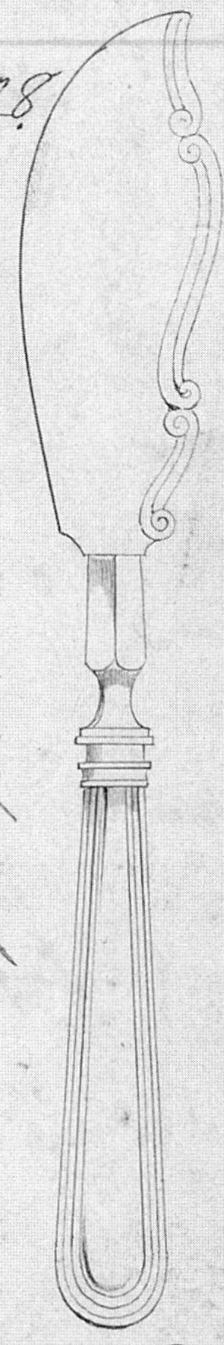

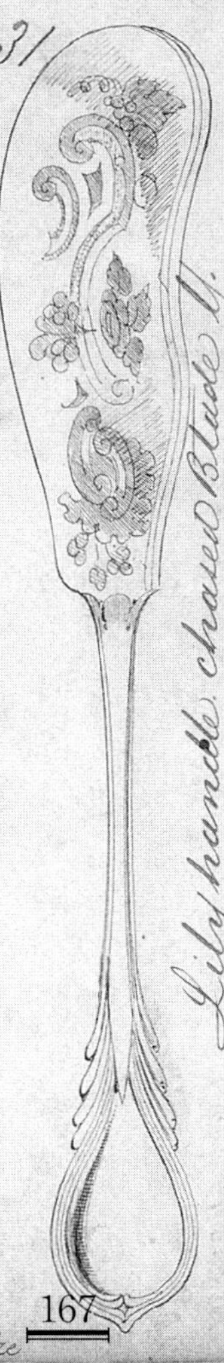

Full Size. Full Size. Full Size. Full Size.
Full Size. Full Size. Full Size.

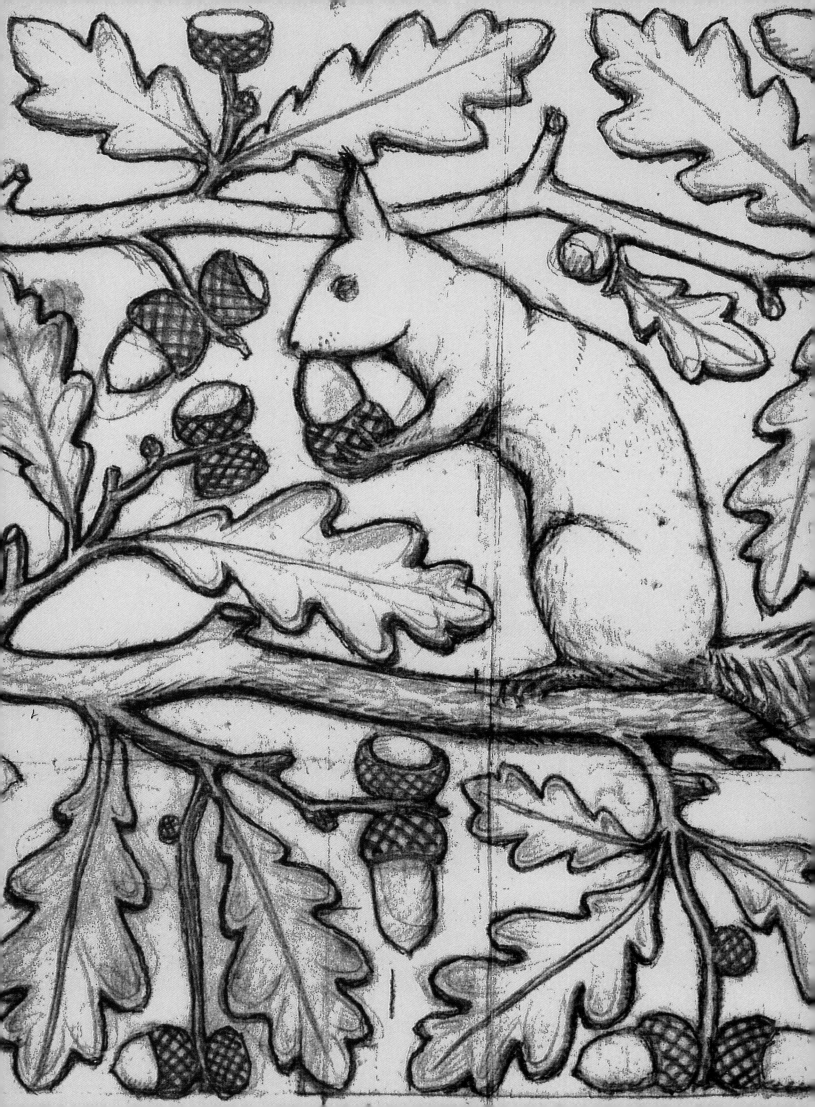

INTO

A RTS *and* CRAFTS

The emergence of a distinctly new, yet emphatically
English aesthetic in the latter part of the nineteenth
century is one of the most fascinating chapters in the
history of design. However, the chronology of the Arts
and Crafts Movement, as the new design came to be
known, is not straightforward; generations of firms
and individuals overlapped from the eighteen-seventies
onwards. Even as late as 1890 William Morris had still
to establish his last great enterprise, the Kelmscott Press
(a major factor in elevating the status of English printing
and typographical design throughout the western
world). But there were a number of unifying aspects
in the works and writings of most of the leading
practitioners of the style: a belief in the dignity of the
craftsman as an essential concomitant to good design,
and an acknowledgment of the seminal influence of
William Morris and John Ruskin.

   Central to the teachings of Ruskin was the demolition
of the distinction between the fine and applied arts;
from now on, the design of interiors and related artefacts
was to be as important as the creation of painting
and sculpture – just as the decoration of ecclesiastical
buildings had been at the time of the Renaissance. At a
lecture in Bradford in 1859, he adduced Correggio's work
in Parma churches and Tintoretto's decoration of the

Great School of San Rocco in Venice as examples of the successful combination of the fine and decorative arts. He was also concerned that the latter and, especially, architecture should reflect the permanent underlying forms of nature, although this part of Ruskin's teaching was often much more literally interpreted by *fin-de-siècle* designers on the Continent than by their English counterparts. Nevertheless, integrity and congruity of materials and form were major concerns of the English designer-craftsmen of the period.

In the last two decades of the nineteenth century a number of guilds and societies were established which reflected the new respectability of the applied arts and the pre-eminence of the artist-craftsman. There is more than a note of medievalist nostalgia in some of their names: A.H. Mackmurdo's Century Guild of 1882, the Art Workers' Guild of 1884, C.R. Ashbee's Guild of Handicraft of 1888, the Arts and Crafts Exhibition Society of the same year, and the Birmingham Guild of Handicraft of 1900.

Many of the designers affiliated to these guilds were of a generation younger than Morris (1834-96), but two of the most interesting (whose original work is represented in the illustration pages which follow) were virtual contemporaries: William De Morgan (1839-1917) and Christopher Dresser (1834-1904).

De Morgan was undoubtedly the great English potter of the late nineteenth century and, as a designer, close to Morris. He began production in London in the early eighteen-seventies, turning out decorated pots and tiles in earthenware. His role, though, was very much that of artist-designer rather than craftsman-potter, since he generally left the actual application of his largely blue and green palette to others. His sketches and watercolours show a lively appreciation of the relationship between form and pattern, often in a 'Persian' style, another instance of the late-century fascination with exotic design.

Christopher Dresser was, effectively, one of the first professional designers for industrial production. He taught design at South Kensington and published a number of significant books on the relationship of design and ornament. He travelled extensively in Japan and the Far East during 1877 and returned with a large collection of Oriental works of art; his book *Japan* was published in 1882. Like De Morgan, Dresser designed pottery, mainly decorative earthenware for the Linthorpe Pottery near Middlesbrough. He was also an ardent botanist, and his work certainly shows a preoccupation with adapting natural forms to decorative ornament. His Clutha glass vases, designed for James Couper of Glasgow, are richly curvilinear, almost organic in shape. In his *Principles of Decorative Design* (1873), Dresser wrote: 'I have sought to embody the one idea of power, energy, force, or vigour...

I have employed such lines as we see in the bursting buds of spring, when the energy of growth is at its maximum....'.

English furniture design of the period, especially in interiors conceived as coordinated schemes of related artefacts, produced work of great craftsmanship and elegance. The names of the men who turned their hands to it form a catalogue of the highest achievement in European terms: A.H. Mackmurdo, C.F.A. Voysey, C.R. Ashbee, W.R. Lethaby, W.H. Baillie Scott, whose most stylish furniture was made for the New Palace at Darmstadt, without forgetting the innovations taking place to the north in the revolutionary designs of C.R. Mackintosh and the Glasgow School.

Yet, the English craft tradition, as it was interpreted by the Arts and Crafts Movement, was perhaps best expressed by the designers and cabinet-makers who came to be known collectively as the Cotswold School. Kenton & Co. had originally been established in 1890 by a group of architects, including Ernest Gimson, W.R. Lethaby and Sidney Barnsley. In 1891 the group held a first exhibition at Barnard's Inn, Holborn, but in 1893 Gimson and Barnsley started to look outside London for a suitable place to establish a workshop, finally settling in specially built premises at Sapperton.

The designs of the group drew heavily on English country furniture traditions: ladder-back chairs, capacious cupboards and refectory tables. Both Gimson and Barnsley had immense respect for the materials they used, and most pieces show fine workmanship in the use of the wood. Much of the work was carried out by local craftsmen; any metal parts, such as handles, were made by the local blacksmith. In this linking of designer and workman, the work of the Cotswold School was one of the purest expressions of Arts and Crafts ideals.

One relatively unsung hero of this particularly fecund period of English design is Archibald Knox, Liberty's most prolific designer of metalware. Knox had come to London from his native Isle of Man in the 1890s when, it has been suggested, he worked in the design studio of Christopher Dresser. The drawings reproduced on pp. 170 and 190–191 show a consummate mastery of the intricate tracery of traditional Celtic ornament, combined with a pure sense of overall line and form. In the bold originality of his handling of technical problems and in his appreciation of the importance of elegant designs which properly serve a purpose, Knox could stand as one of the purest practitioners of the Arts and Crafts ideal.

page 168 An undated pencil design by Ernest Gimson for a plasterwork frieze.

opposite The workshop of the Charles Knowles & Co. factory, London *c.* 1904; established in 1852, the firm produced high-quality block-printed wallpapers.

5

INTO ARTS
and
CRAFTS

pages 172–173

A drawing by T. Raffles Davison, executed in 1890, of the drawing room at Bullers Wood, Chislehurst; the interior decoration had been completed by Morris & Co. in 1889.

page 177

Perhaps more than any other group of designers, the furniture-makers of the Cotswold School – Ernest Gimson and Sidney Barnsley – were responsible for reinterpreting the English vernacular craft tradition in the context of the Arts and Crafts Movement. After beginnings in London as Kenton & Co., the group finally settled in the Cotswolds, where their designs strongly reflected English country furniture traditions, concentrating on solid, well-made pieces like ladder-back chairs, cupboards, chests-of-drawers, and refectory tables. Most of the drawings of the group, from the establishment of Kenton & Co. until the deaths of the principal designers, are now held by Cheltenham Art Gallery and Museums. These undated sketches for two writing cabinets are by Ernest Gimson.

pages 178–179

Metalwork became one of the major areas of English design achievement in the latter part of the nineteenth century, notably in the hands of C.R. Ashbee and his Guild of Handicraft. Another successful figure in helping to spread appreciation of design for metalwork and enamelling was Alexander Fisher who began to teach from his studio in 1887 and later became head of the enamelling department at the Central School of Arts and Crafts in 1896. One of his most notable pupils was Nelson Dawson (1859-1942), whose 1906 design for a candlestick is reproduced on p. 178. In common with other Arts and Crafts designers, Dawson was fascinated by the idea of the craft guild, and founded the Artificers' Guild in 1901 in his Chiswick workshop. His original watercolour, pen and pencil sketches are held in the Victoria & Albert Museum, London.

Archibald Knox brought an altogether more elegant touch to his designs for Liberty, transforming the swirls of 'Celtic' iconography into refined and elegant realizations of Arts and Crafts ideals in metal. This candlestick design (p. 179), probably for the Cymric range, has an engaging stylishness, yet is thoroughly modern and functional in its rectilinear central column and broad foot.

pages 180–181

These watercolour and pencil designs by William De Morgan (see pp. 137 and 164-165) for vases date from 1880-84, roughly the period when the most eminent ceramist of the Arts and Crafts Movement was in closest contact with William Morris at Merton Abbey. Like Morris, De Morgan drew much of his decorative vocabulary directly from nature – leaves, animals and birds – and then deployed it with a vigour and clarity which sometimes rival the imaginative power of Morris's own designs. De Morgan was particularly adept at suiting motif to the form of any vessel, as in the case of the lizard designs here. In this, De Morgan was more designer than potter, often employing assistants to apply his designs to the wares.

page 182

In many ways, Christopher Dresser (see pp. 144-145) could be considered as one of the first professional designers in the modern sense. Unlike Morris and many of the Arts and Crafts designers and craftsmen associated with the guild movement, Dresser directly addressed the problems of providing good design for manufacture in industrial conditions. As early as the 1870s he was designing domestic artefacts in metal which seem to prefigure the modernist aesthetic of the Bauhaus. In 1879 he became the art director of the Linthorpe Pottery near Middlesbrough, producing designs for a variety of vessels and ornamental pieces. The bold, simple lines of his designs of this period, a page of which is reproduced here, reflect his admiration for the elegant minimalism of Japanese applied arts.

page 183

Unlike many of the great English retail businesses which burgeoned during the latter part of the nineteenth century to serve the needs of an increasingly wealthy middle class, the firm of Liberty was devoted to the purveying of fine design from its inception in 1875.

5

INTO ARTS
and
CRAFTS

Founded by Arthur Lasenby Liberty (1843-1917), its first trade was in fine artefacts from the East, but by the end of the century it was playing a central role in the dissemination of Arts and Crafts and Art Nouveau design, often in association with the leading designers of the day, including C.F.A. Voysey, Rex Silver and Archibald Knox. Both of the latter provided the firm with numerous designs for its 'Cymric' range of silverware and its 'Tudric' range of pewter, decorated with interpretations of 'Celtic' forms and floral and plant motifs. Attribution of the designs (like those for the silver wares reproduced here) is difficult, since Liberty's guarded the identity of their designers, several of whom worked in similar styles. The actual manufacture of the metalwork was undertaken by the firm of W.H. Haseler in Birmingham, but the Liberty catalogues simply note that it was made to 'Original Designs by Liberty & Co.' These pages are reproduced from a 350-page hand-bound volume containing drawings of a substantial amount of the Liberty product range, including bowls, clocks, dishes, decanters, mirrors, trays, tea sets and tankards.

pages 184–185

The Spode factory (see pp. 108, 112-113 and 126) continued to flourish throughout the latter half of the nineteenth century under the name of W.T. Copeland & Sons Ltd. These two pages, dating from *c.* 1880-90, are reproduced from a pattern book of 302 designs. The individual designs are on paper sheets which have been stitched to the cloth pages of the book. Such patterns would have been used for tiles or panels in furniture and fireplaces. In some cases designs were repeated in two record books, one version to be shown to the customer, the other to be retained as the factory production record.

pages 186–187

A timely reminder that the whole of English design for manufacture in the latter part of the nineteenth century was not imbued with the ideals of the Arts and Crafts Movement are these wooden mouldings offered in a trade catalogue of 1900 by Charrier & Marbut Carvings Ltd. These traditional designs for 'carved enrichments' were intended for 'builders and property developers.'

pages 188–189

Initially engaged in general commercial pottery, the firm of Thomas Twyford began to produce sanitaryware around 1850. By the time it was producing its 1883 'catalogue of earthenware sanitary goods', from which the reproductions on p. 188 are taken, the firm had been granted a royal warrant and had won many awards and medals; it also had agents in the United States, Germany, Austria, Switzerland, The Netherlands and Australia. The 1894 catalogue, from which the designs on p. 189 are taken, contains a number of variations on basic designs, including the engagingly named 'Deluge' flush lavatory.

pages 190–191

Archibald Knox (1864-1933) was probably one of the most prolific contributors of designs to Liberty's 'Cymric' and 'Tudric' ranges (see pp. 179 and 183) of metalwork. A relatively unsung master of the Arts and Crafts Movement in England, his work was exhibited with success on the Continent, notably in Germany. Indeed, these designs for his 'Forever, Never' clock have a

distinct affinity with those of the Darmstadt Jugendstil designers. The minute hand was intended to be in silver and that for the hour in mother-of-pearl.

pages 192–193

Like the wood mouldings illustrated on pp. 186-187, this page of ornamental masonry designs for windows and doorways from *The Illustrated Carpenter and Builder* of 17 April 1891 illustrates that the mainstream building and design industry was still very much beholden to historical references. Derived from classical models, the pediments and lintels and other features illustrated in this weekly tabloid are probably a much closer barometer of popular taste than the design aesthetic expressed in this sideboard (p. 193) from the firm of William Birch. This design may very well have been the original for pieces sold through Liberty's London shop.

page 194

Most commercial late Victorian design seems flaccid and unadventurous against the bold innovatory visions of

5
INTO ARTS *and* CRAFTS

Morris and De Morgan. Yet much of it is pleasant enough, as is this assembly of tile designs, showing the influence of the vision of the creative reformers of the latter part of the century. These designs are taken from a pattern book in the Victoria & Albert Museum, London: it has no introduction and bears no company name, although this may have been lost during later rebinding in the 1970s. The designs are printed one to a page in black but have been coloured by hand. The volume, probably intended for sales representatives, would have been printed in a small edition and disseminated among the manufacturers of such wares as fireplaces, wash-stands and other furniture.

page 195

Most closely associated with Edward Godwin (1833-86), the Aesthetic Movement was a powerful force in English art, literature, design and culture during the 1870s and 1880s. It was a self-conscious rejection of the values of the Victorian middle class in favour of an 'art for art's sake' approach to living. Interiors in the style tended to be relatively simple with a reliance on such

'aesthetic' colours as green and yellow, as in this example of 1878 by Walker & Sons for 8 Princes Gardens.

pages 196–201

Ornamental and tableware designs, probably for manufacture in silver, from the Liberty archive, in Westminster City Library; the heyday of the firm's silver venture ran from about 1900 to 1912, but many of these designs were still in production in the 1920s and 1930s. The 350-page pattern book from which these pages are reproduced is prefaced with a list of contents, including bowls, caddies, cruets, decanters, sugar tongs, tea sets and vases. The drawings are in pen and ink on ruled paper.

page 202

The Wedgwood factory continued the manufacture of what it termed 'majolica' until the latter part of the nineteenth century. This pattern for a 'Franklin Strawberry Set, brown ground' is recorded in the company archives (begun in 1760) as being from 1880.

page 203

As if to demonstrate the durability of the designs of William Morris, this pattern ('Fruit') in fact dates from the very early years of the company, although the production log from which this illustration is taken dates from 5 September 1910. This page, now separated from its binding, shows the three colourways of the pattern, along with the number of blocks (12) needed to print it. The aesthetics of Morris undoubtedly continued as a dominant influence on English design throughout the turn-of-the-century years of Arts and Crafts.

pages 204–205

The fireplace and chimneypiece had a peculiar fascination for Arts and Crafts designers, especially for those who tended to see the movement as a vehicle for reinterpreting the English vernacular. As a feature it dominated room settings and provided unique design opportunities. Ernest Gimson's undated sketch (p. 204) suggests some of the monumentality which characterized his furniture design. John Hungerford

Pollen's design (p. 205) for a fireplace at Blickling Hall seems to draw on a colder, grand-hall aspect of the English vernacular.

pages 206–207

The Silver Studio was one of the principal suppliers of textile designs to Liberty & Co. and many patterns which are thought of as being distinctly 'Liberty' in fact emanated from this group of designers. Notable among them was Harry Napper, the author of these two designs, who joined the studio *c.* 1893 and managed its production after the death of Arthur Silver in 1896. Like many Arts and Crafts designers, Napper turned his hand to other disciplines, including furniture and metalwork design.

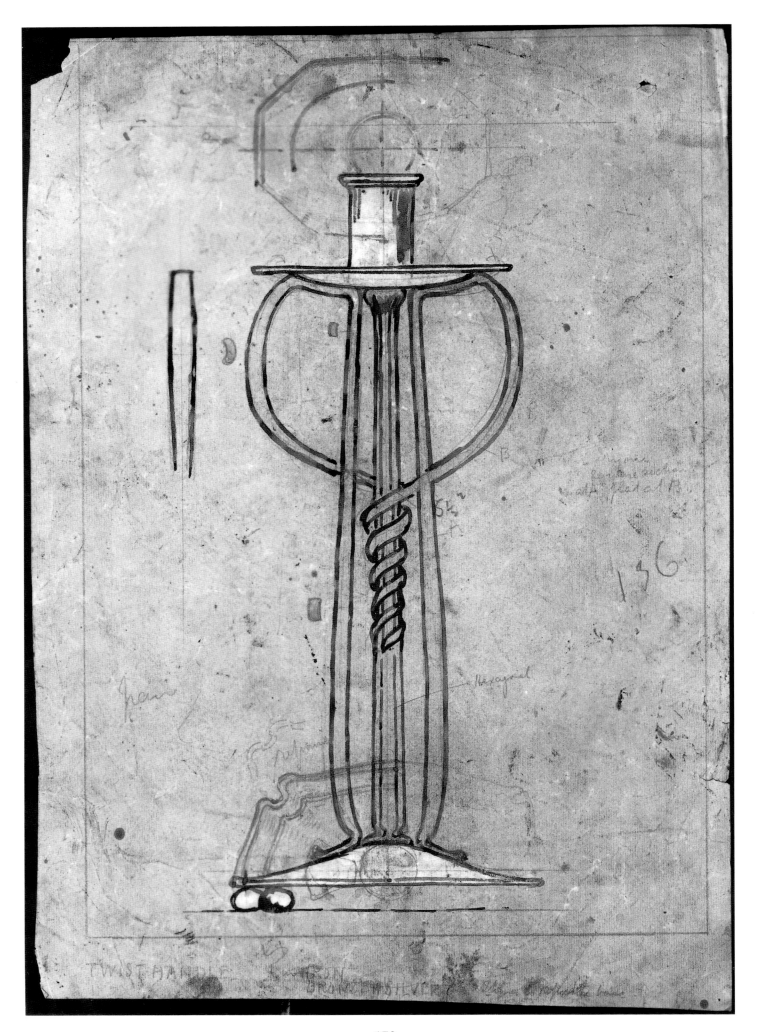

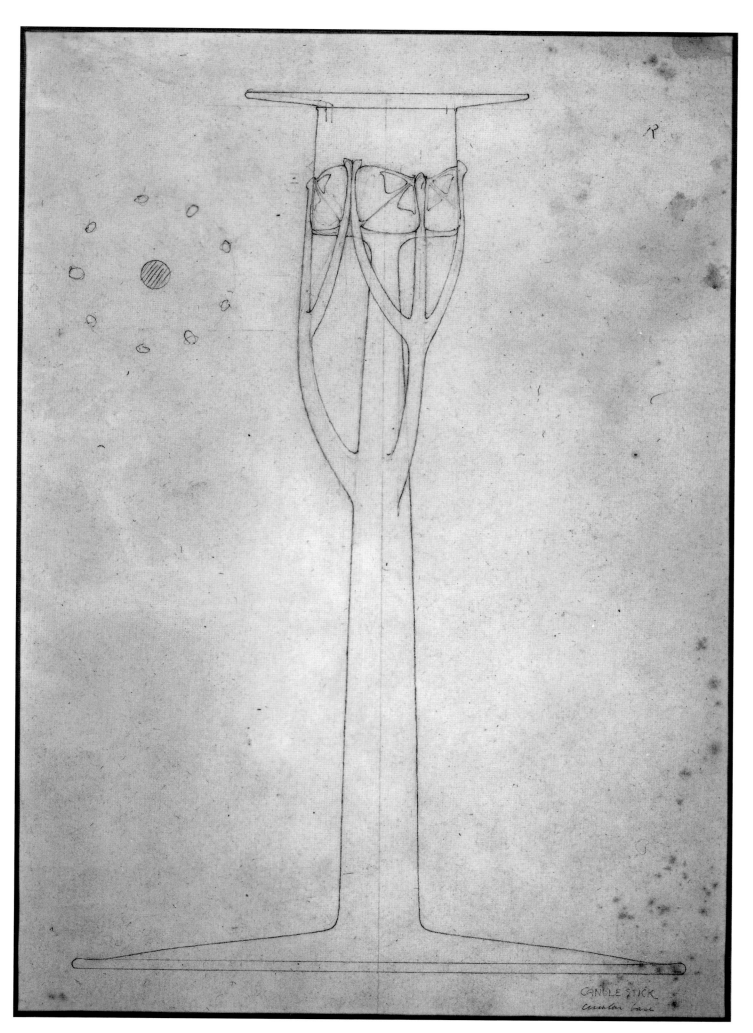

CANDLE STICK
circular base

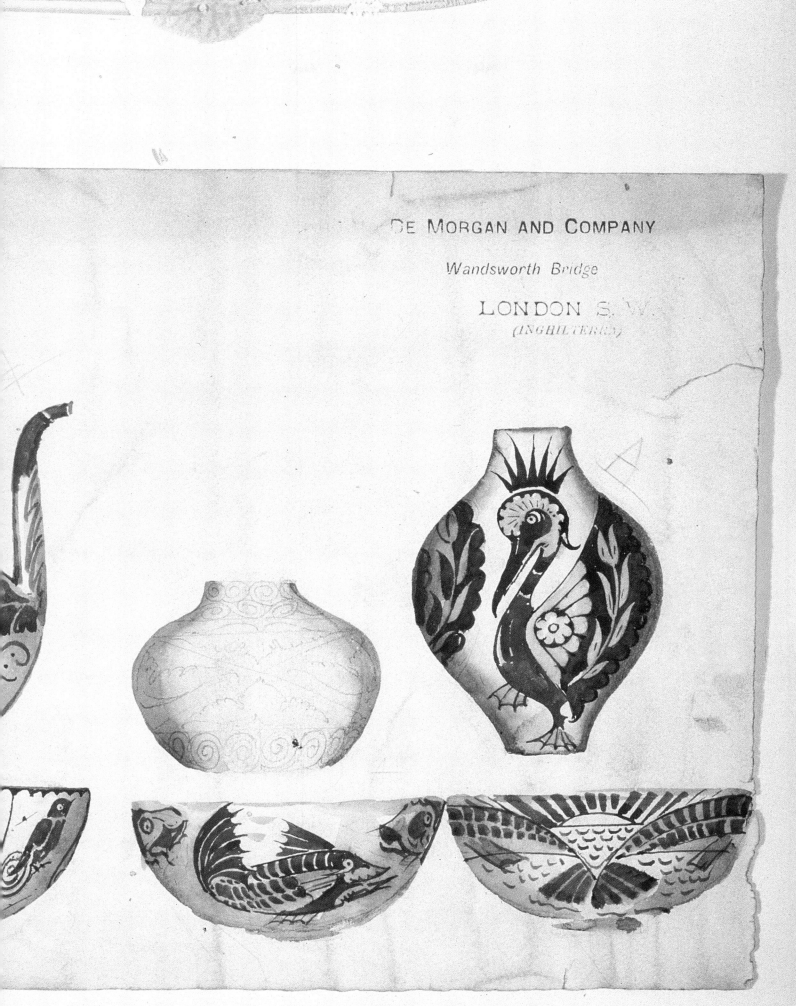

DE MORGAN AND COMPANY

Wandsworth Bridge

LONDON S. W.
(INGHILTERRA)

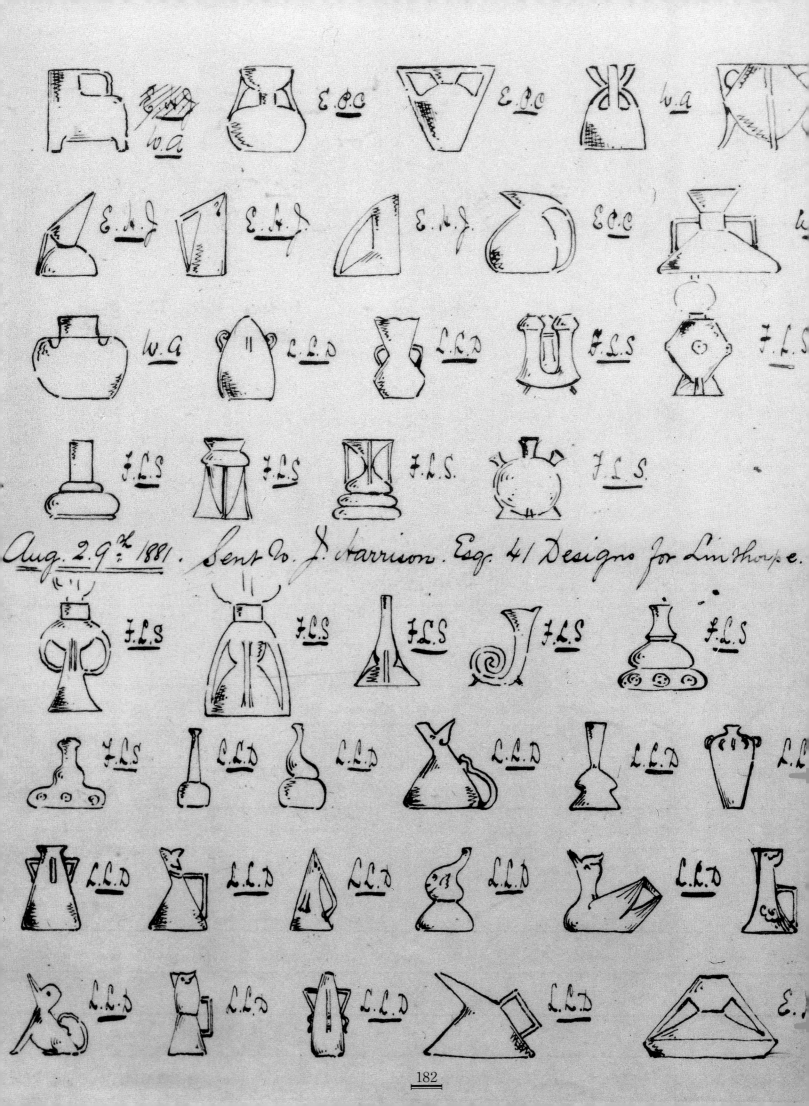

w.a

E.O.C

E.O.C

w.a

E.A.J

E.A.J

E.A.J

E.O.C

w.G

L.L.D

L.L.D

F.L.S

F.L.S

F.L.S

F.L.S

F.L.S

F.L.S

Aug. 29th 1881. Sent to J. Harrison. Esq. 41 Designs for Linthorpe.

F.L.S

F.L.S

F.L.S

F.L.S

F.L.S

L.L.D

L.L.D

L.L.D

L.L.D

L.L.D

L.L.D

L.L.D

L.L.D

L.L.D

L.L.D

L.L.D

L.L.D

L.L.D

E.

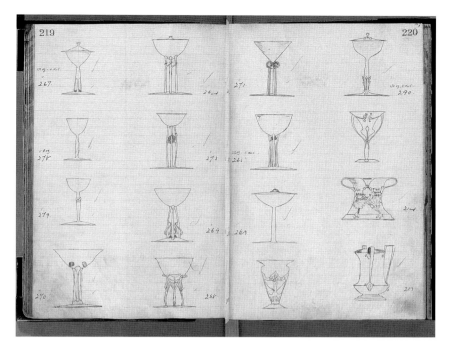

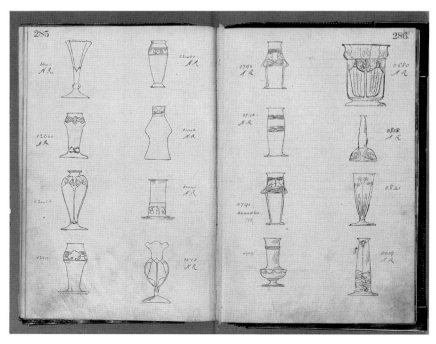

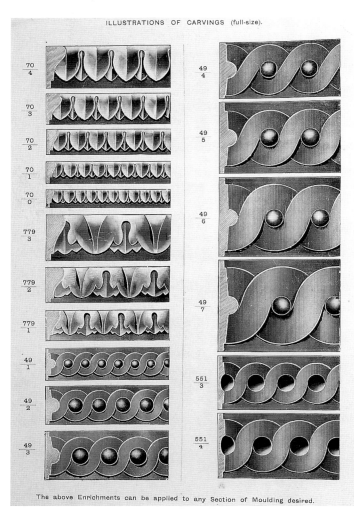

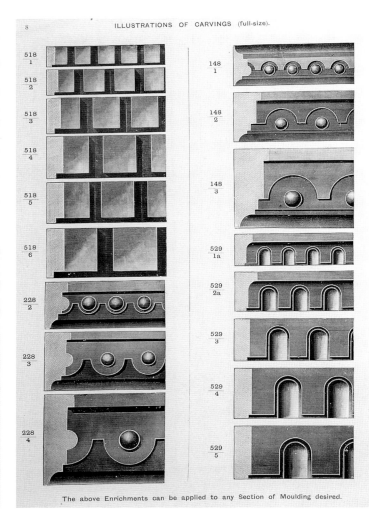

The above Enrichments can be applied to any Section of Moulding desired.

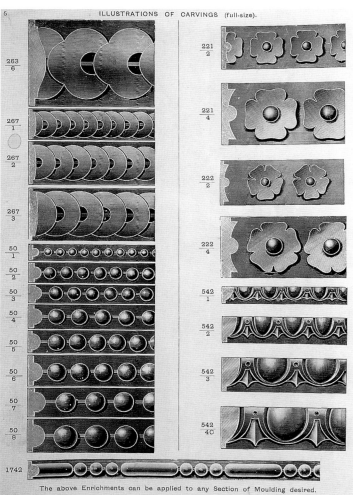

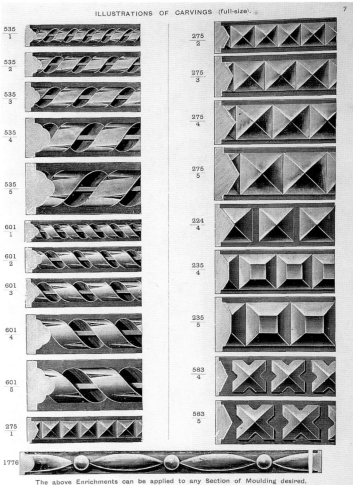

The above Enrichments can be applied to any Section of Moulding desired.

187

192

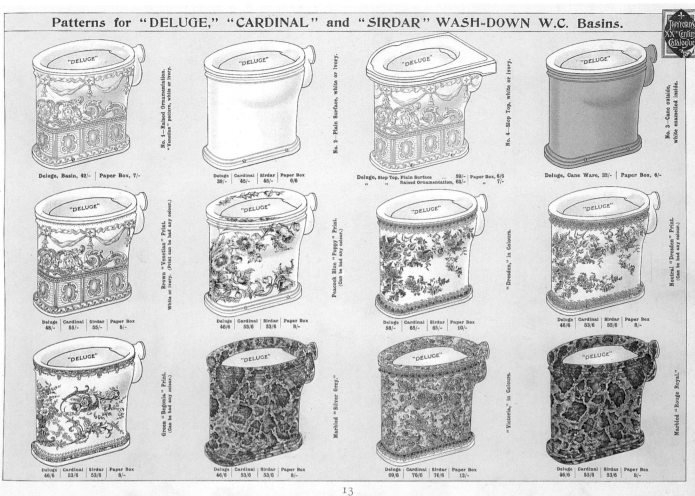

Patterns for "DELUGE," "CARDINAL" and "SIRDAR" WASH-DOWN W.C. Basins.

No. 1—Raised Ornamentation. "Venetian" pattern, white or Ivory.

No. 2—Plain Surface, white or Ivory.

No. 4—Slop Top, white or Ivory.

No. 3—Cane outside, white enamelled inside.

Deluge, Basin, 42/- | Paper Box, 7/-

| Deluge | Cardinal | Sirdar | Paper Box |
| 38/- | 45/- | 45/- | 6/6 |

| Deluge, Slop Top, Plain Surface | 59/- | Paper Box, 6/6 |
| " " Raised Ornamentation, | 63/- | " 7/- |

Deluge, Cane Ware, 32/- | Paper Box, 6/-

Brown "Venetian" Print. White or Ivory. (Print can be had any colour.)

| Deluge | Cardinal | Sirdar | Paper Box |
| 48/- | 55/- | 55/- | 8/- |

Peacock Blue "Poppy" Print. (Can be had any colour.)

| Deluge | Cardinal | Sirdar | Paper Box |
| 46/6 | 53/6 | 53/6 | 8/- |

"Dresden," in Colours.

| Deluge | Cardinal | Sirdar | Paper Box |
| 58/- | 65/- | 65/- | 10/- |

Neutral "Dresden" Print. (Can be had any colour.)

| Deluge | Cardinal | Sirdar | Paper Box |
| 46/6 | 53/6 | 53/6 | 8/- |

Green "Begonia" Print. (Can be had any colour.)

| Deluge | Cardinal | Sirdar | Paper Box |
| 46/6 | 53/6 | 53/6 | 8/- |

Marbled "Silver Grey."

| Deluge | Cardinal | Sirdar | Paper Box |
| 46/6 | 53/6 | 53/6 | 8/- |

"Victoria," in Colours.

| Deluge | Cardinal | Sirdar | Paper Box |
| 69/6 | 76/6 | 76/6 | 12/- |

Marbled "Rouge Royal."

| Deluge | Cardinal | Sirdar | Paper Box |
| 46/6 | 53/6 | 53/6 | 8/- |

13

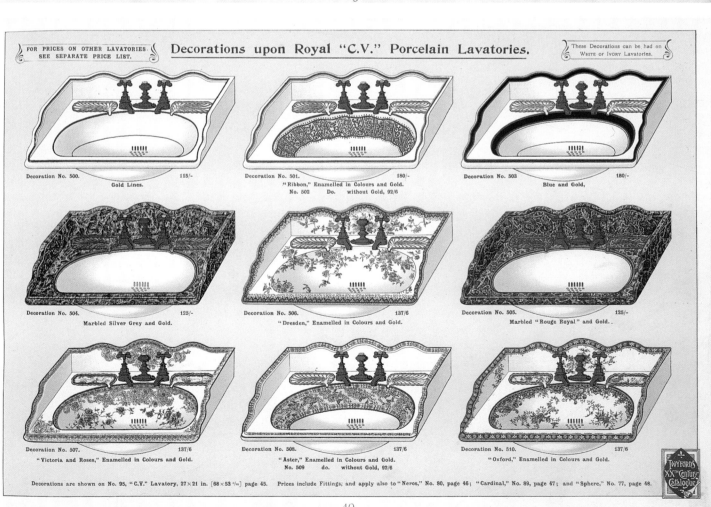

Decorations upon Royal "C.V." Porcelain Lavatories.

FOR PRICES ON OTHER LAVATORIES. SEE SEPARATE PRICE LIST.

These Decorations can be had on WHITE or IVORY Lavatories.

Decoration No. 500.   115/-
Gold Lines.

Decoration No. 501.   180/-
"Ribbon," Enamelled in Colours and Gold.
No. 502   Do.   without Gold, 92/6

Decoration No. 503   180/-
Blue and Gold,

Decoration No. 504.   125/-
Marbled Silver Grey and Gold.

Decoration No. 506.   137/6
"Dresden," Enamelled in Colours and Gold.

Decoration No. 505.   125/-
Marbled "Rouge Royal" and Gold.

Decoration No. 507.   137/6
"Victoria and Roses," Enamelled in Colours and Gold.

Decoration No. 508.   137/6
"Aster," Enamelled in Colours and Gold.
No. 509   do.   without Gold, 92/6

Decoration No. 510.   137/6
"Oxford," Enamelled in Colours and Gold.

Decorations are shown on No. 95, "C.Y." Lavatory, 27×21 in. [68×53 %/cm] page 45.   Prices include Fittings; and apply also to "Neros," No. 80, page 46; "Cardinal," No. 89, page 47; and "Sphere," No. 77, page 48.

49

No. 420.   71/6   Design No. 82.

No. 420.   71/6   Design No. 83.

No. 420.   71/6   Design No. 84.

No. 132,   52/6   Design No. 85.

No. 132,   52/6   Design No. 86.

No. 132,   51/6   Design No. 87.

No. 132,   51/6   Design No. 88.

No. 420.   71/6   Design No. 89.

No. 420.   71/6   Design No. 90.

No. 420.   71/6   Design No. 91.

These Designs are sent on White body as shewn, but can be had on Ivory body if preferred, at same prices.   For Prices on other Basins, see separate Price List.

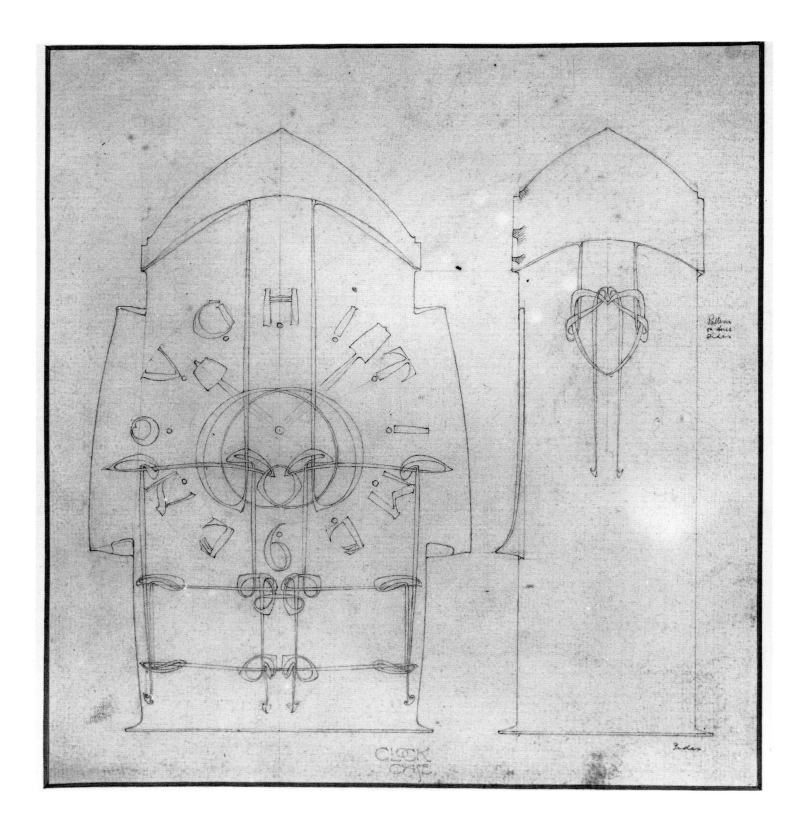

CLOCK CASE.

Pattern
on other
sides

sides

THE ILLUSTRATED CARPENTER AND BUILDER

JOINERS. DECORATORS. PAINTERS. PLUMBERS. GAS FITTERS. ARCHITECTS &C.

VOL. XXVIII.—No. 715.
Registered as a Newspaper.

FRIDAY, APRIL 17, 1891.

[PRICE ONE PENNY.

FIG. 9   FIG. 10   FIG. 11

FIG. 1   FIG. 2   FIG. 3   FIG. 4

FIG. 5   FIG. 6   FIG. 7   FIG. 8

SCALE 12 0 1 2 3 4 5 6 FEET

ORNAMENTAL MASONRY: MOULDINGS FOR WINDOWS AND DOORWAYS.

C.B.1906 15/14

№ 54

57

№ 75

№ 500

№ 63

№ A2   R ⅟₄ № 69700

№ F

№ A5

№ M

№ 81

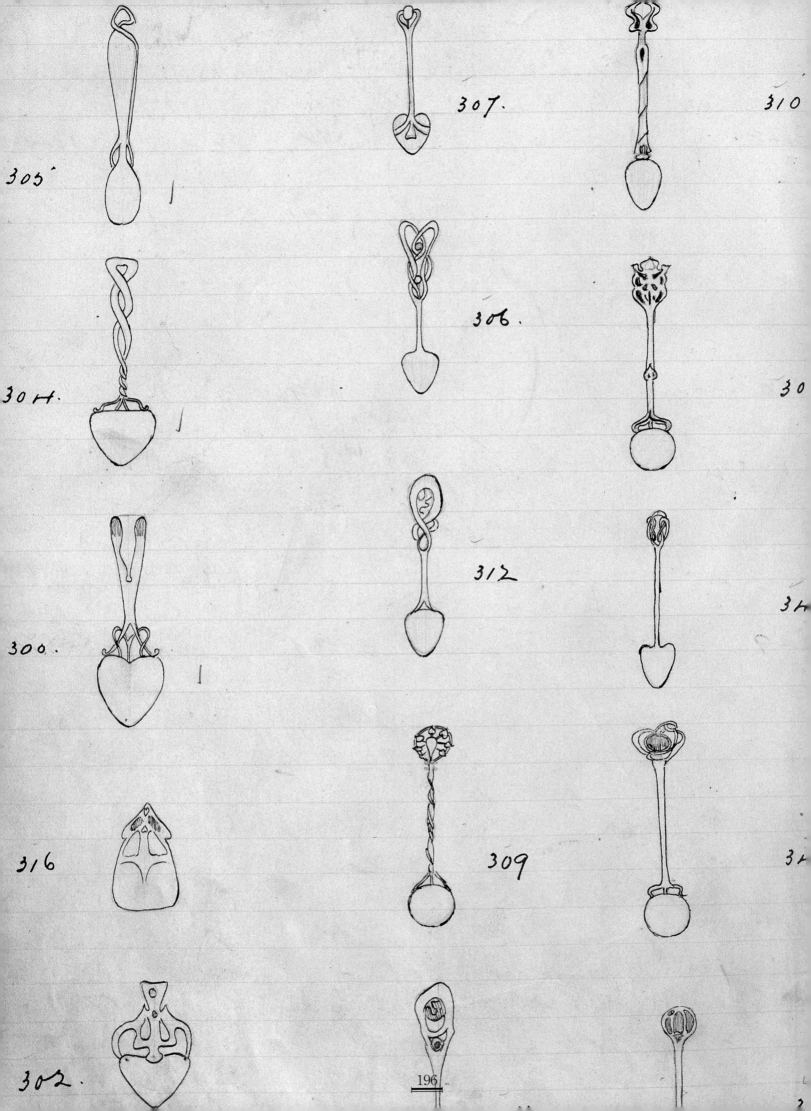

305.

307.

310

304.

306.

30

300.

312

3

316

309

3

302.

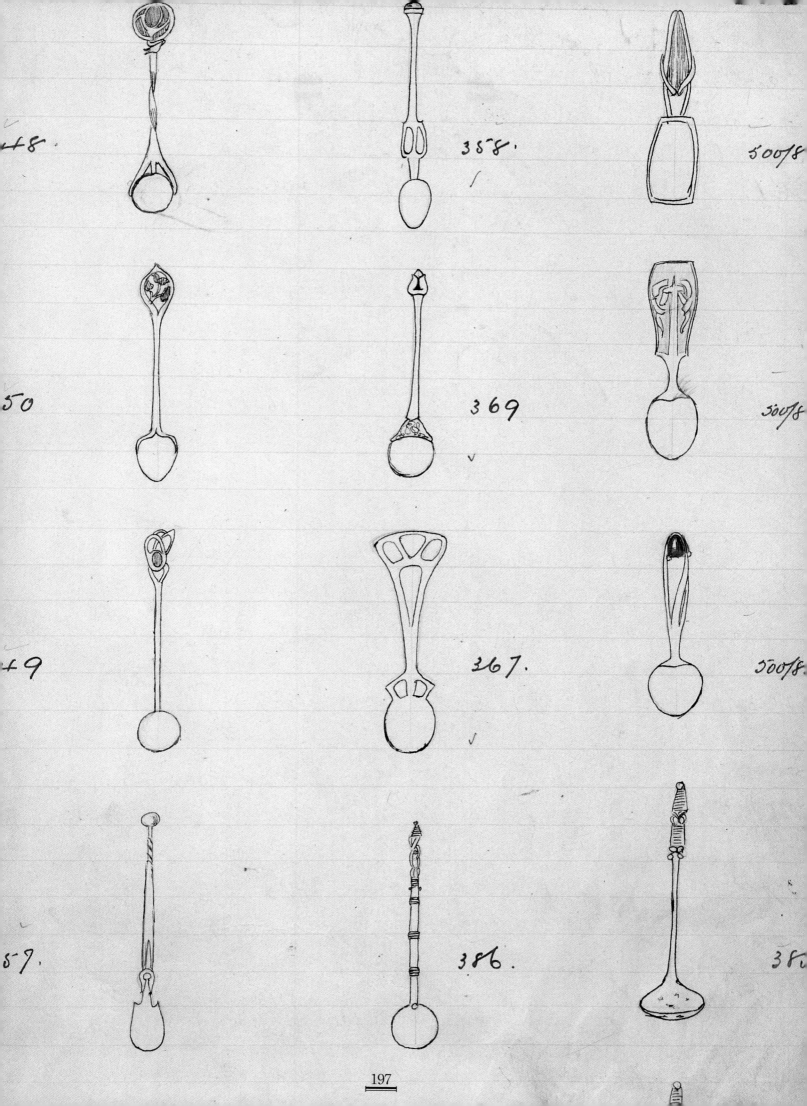

48.

358.

50018

50

369

50018

49

367.

50018

57.

386.

38

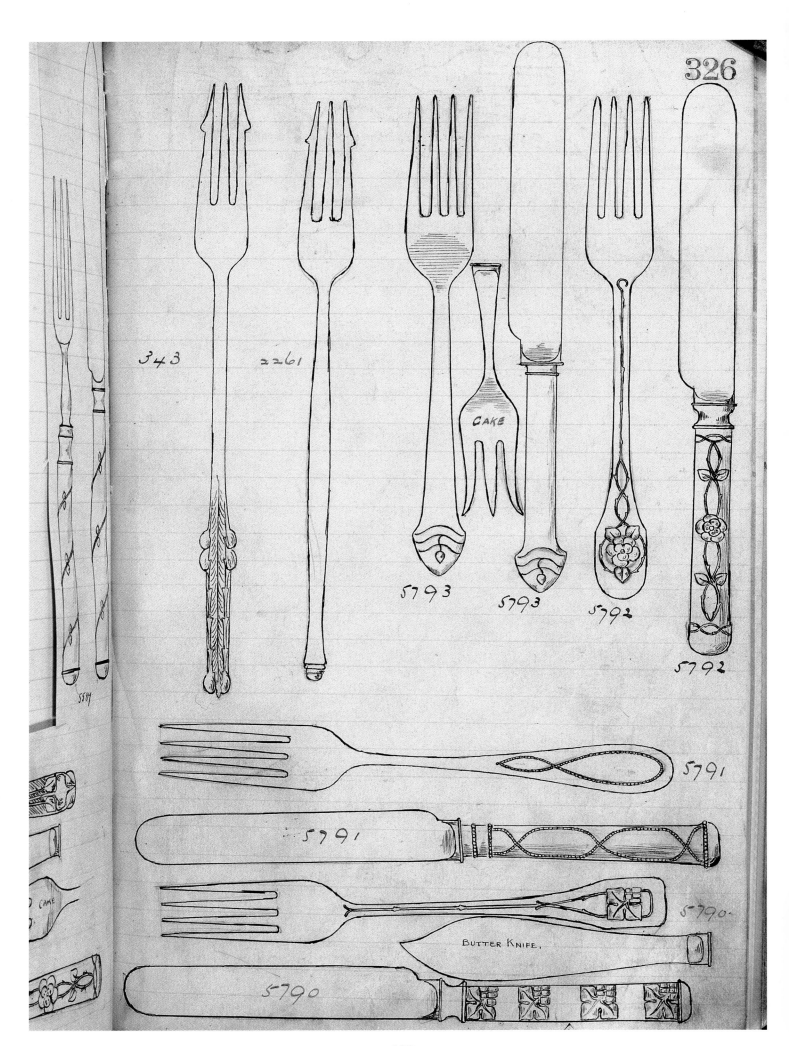

343

2261

CAKE

5793

5793

5792

5792

5791

5791

5790

BUTTER KNIFE.

5790

5584

CAKE

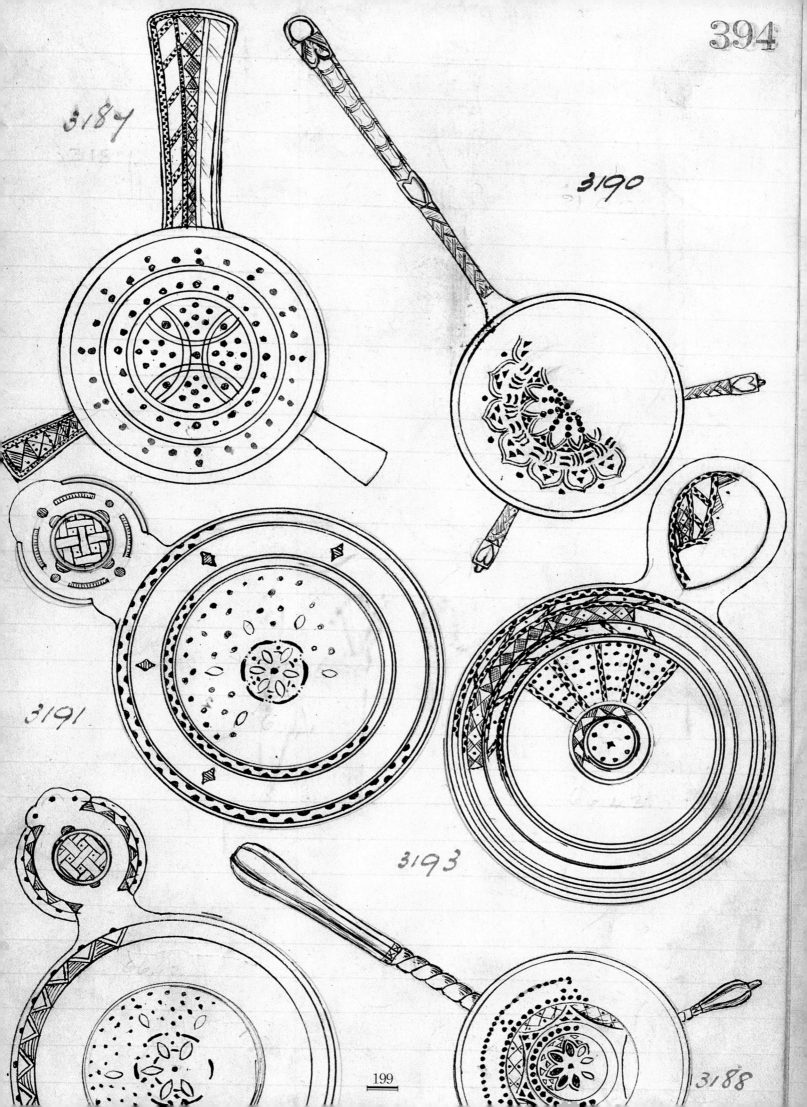

3187

3190

3191

3193

3188

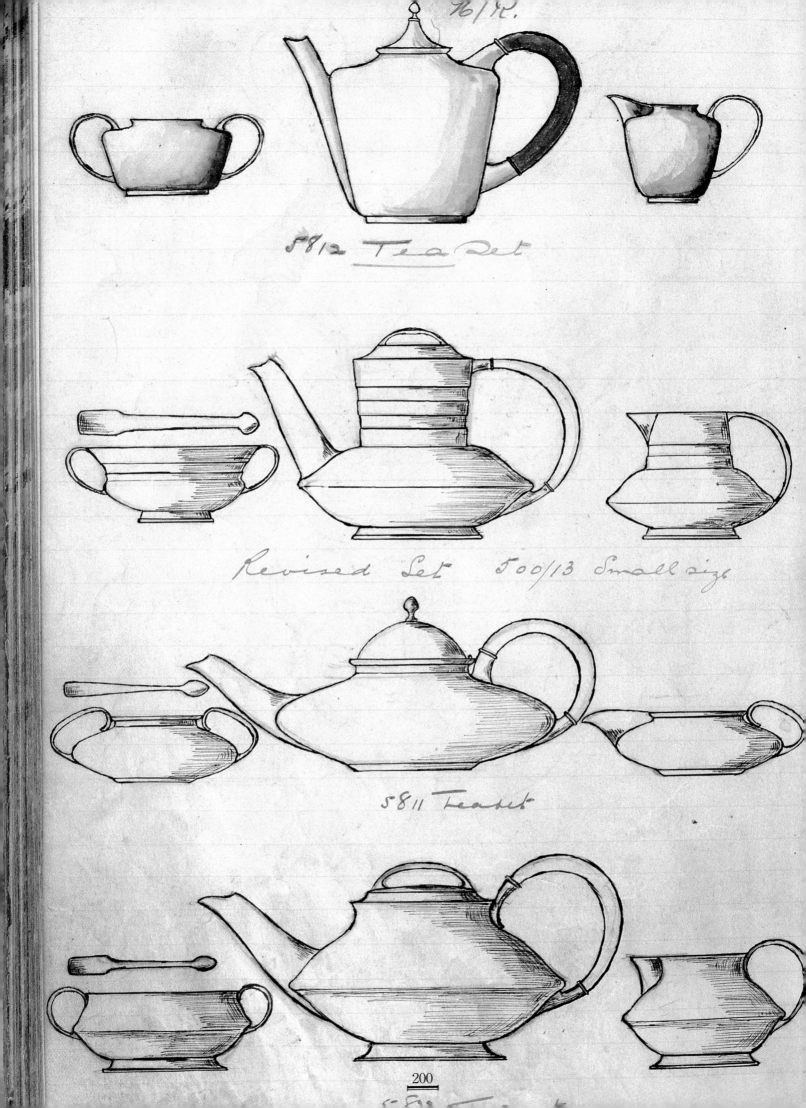

5812 Tea Set

Revised Set   500/13 Small size

5811 Teaset

5 8 2 1 Cream Sugar & Tongs

5815

4 3/8 Lip to Handle

Tur Sizes

5827

5814

Coffee Pot on page 418

No 2996. Franklin Strawberry brown ground see pattern

Flowers
White

Celeste

No 2997 Franklin Strawberry on celeste ground

Handles
No 2996

03594

Nº 03032.

SILVER STUDIO COLL.

raditionalism *to* MODERNISM

The very success of the Arts and Crafts

Movement led in the twentieth century to a relative decline in English design, mainly because it failed signally to address the problems of machine production and the new aesthetic associated with it. None of the major art schools provided training in design for mass manufacture. Even the Central School of Art, founded by W.R. Lethaby in 1896, which enjoyed a reputation throughout Europe for teaching progressive design theory, still drew heavily on the craft-orientated and anti-manufacturing thinking of the disciples of William Morris. The Design and Industries Association of 1915, whose founder members included Ambrose Heal, also retained many of the hallowed Arts and Crafts values, even though its avowed purpose was to improve the design of manufactured goods for domestic use.

In furniture design the legacy of the nineteenth-century reformers was continued by such as Ambrose Heal and Gordon Russell. Catalogues of the 'twenties and 'thirties show a selection of well-crafted but 'safe' pieces which now looked deeply conservative in comparison with production in Scandinavia and Germany and distinctly drab if set beside the magnificent creations exhibited at the 1925 Paris Exposition, dominated by Ruhlmann, Süe et Mare and Lalique. Liberty's turn-of-the-century catalogues show a similar continuation of Arts and Crafts styles in sturdy oak and mahogany pieces interspersed with ladder-back and slatted chairs resembling the productions of the Cotswold School.

Indeed, Gimson and the Barnsleys continued to exercise considerable influence over English furniture design, along with their Dutch associate Peter Waals, who continued the production of Cotswold craft furniture until 1937.

 n textile production Liberty's characteristic patterns of the late nineteenth century continued in production, but new design concentrated very much on a nostalgic English country style in the form of floral chintzes. But in a corner of Bloomsbury a more adventurous aesthetic was being applied to textiles and other articles of household use. The Omega Workshops (Artist Decorators) were founded by artists closely affiliated to the Bloomsbury Group, including Duncan Grant, Vanessa Bell, Wyndham Lewis and Edward Wadsworth, under the leadership of the art critic Roger Fry. Their gallery opened in Fitzroy Square in July 1913 to sell painted furniture, hand-dyed textiles, pottery and other items. In spite of a professed modernism and the application of abstract design, however, Omega always retained a slightly homespun air and its productions remained craft-based. But one of its artists, Wyndham Lewis (whose designs are reproduced on pp. 236 and 244–245), did develop a tougher, more aggressive style, much more suitable to modernist environments and interiors than the rather self-consciously charming colour schemes and patterns of Grant and Bell.

 nd modernism did eventually make itself known in British design. In ceramics the dominant British art tradition had always been that of the craft-based studio potter, exemplified by Bernard Leach and William Staite-Murray. But in commercial production, the 'twenties designs of Clarice Cliff and Susie Cooper showed a new boldness in colour and form which was distinctly modern.

 he kind of geometric, angular modernism of Cliff and early Cooper gradually came to be found in other types of design. Individual furniture designers working out of exclusive premises began to emerge to cater for the few, while the less privileged were learning the advantages of built-in, standardized furniture for a generation of smaller houses and flats. A less individual age of design had arrived.

page 208 It seems appropriate to begin this twentieth-century chapter with a 1926 design by C.F.A. Voysey (1857-1941). A versatile designer of houses and furniture, who looked back to Pugin and Morris as influences, Voysey nevertheless continued to design well into the twentieth century and is sometimes claimed as one of the first modernists. In addition to his three-dimensional work, he was a prolific designer of flat patterns for tiles, wallpapers, fabrics, rugs and carpets; this pattern was for a carpet by Tomkinson's of Kidderminster.

right F. Austin's furniture factory in Lea Bridge Road, London, 1936; a photograph taken for *The Cabinet Maker*.

6
TRADITIONALISM *t o* MODERNISM

pages 212–213

This modernist interior by Paul Nash (1889-1948) (see pp. 238-239) was first published in *The Studio* yearbook for 1930 after gaining second prize in a competition to design an apartment for Lord Benbow. The assessor's report, in its attempts to understand the modernist aesthetic, makes fascinating reading: 'The second prize has been awarded to a design which is made faintly ridiculous by the fact that the artist either misunderstood the purport of the remarks regarding Lord Benbow's sporting tastes, or deliberately surrendered to his sense of humour… At the same time, in the assessor's opinion this design shows a truer architectural quality than any other submitted. It is placed second because it is less successful than the winning design in exploiting the particular idiosyncrasies of Lord Benbow's plan. Taking very simple motifs, like the thin cylindrical light fittings and the square frames of picture and partition, it builds up by means of combination, repetition, and contrast a subtle fugue-like organization in which the planes of the walls play their part. The interplay of incident, the feeling for volume, the cunning punctuation provided by the dark bodies, is intellectually agreeable.'

page 217

Some of Voysey's later work (see p. 208) seems to run counter to the clean, bold lines of his turn-of-the-century furniture and architecture. This 'Ten Fruits' design from the Tomkinson Carpets archive, dated May 1926, was never actually put into manufacture and may have been originally intended as a wallpaper pattern. It is strikingly similar to a 1929 design for chintz, 'The House that Jack Built'.

pages 218–219

Like Voysey, Ernest Gimson (1864-1919) continued to produce designs in an Arts and Crafts idiom until well into the twentieth century. His partnership with the Barnsley brothers (both of whom lived on until 1926) appears to have dissolved in 1904, and from then on Gimson concentrated very much on design rather than on the practical aspects of making furniture. Many of the architectural sketches in the archives of the Cheltenham Art Gallery and Museums date from this period, and show a persistent affection for the English rustic vernacular, drawing on medieval models for the positioning of uprights and beams (p. 218) and even for overall layout (p. 219).

pages 220–221

Although Gimson stuck very much to his Arts and Crafts ideals in his twentieth-century work, a certain rectilinearity, more in keeping with the aesthetic of the new century, does appear in some of his later work. This bold, simple approach to furniture-making was continued by the Dutch cabinet-maker Peter Waals who went on to employ a number of Gimson's craftsmen after the death of Gimson in 1919. These undated sketches for 'Washstands & dressing tables with bright steel of brass handles. Chests-of-drawers' are executed in pencil and watercolour on tracing paper.

pages 222–223

One famous characteristic of Gimson's furniture design was his intense regard for the value and suitability of the varied woods and materials he used. Each had a distinct part to play in what were sometimes patterns and structures of great complexity. This cabinet (p. 222), for instance, is described as being in ebony (the 'brown' has been deleted) and English walnut with gilt gesso panels in black ebony; the stand is also in black ebony. This use of contrasting exotic woods, it has been suggested, anticipates the luxury furniture design of the French Art Deco masters in the 1920s. Even such an apparently simple design as that for a chair (p. 223) is deceptive; intended as the model for a set of six, it was to be made 'in ebony and burr elm on Honduras with stuffed leather seat'.

pages 224–225

The archive of the Whitefriars Glasshouse (James Powell & Sons) is a fascinating commentary on the creative process which leads to eventual manufacture. One of Harry Powell's notebooks dating from the turn of the century, from which these six pages are reproduced (p. 224) contains sketches and photographic records of designs and artefacts which could serve as inspiration for the making of glassware. These include a bottle from

1509, a silver-gilt chalice with enamel by Alexander Fisher, and a reproduction of an elephant carving from the choir stalls of Exeter Cathedral. One form entered in the book appears to be the likely inspiration for the pair of vase designs in the pattern book for 1903-10 (p. 225). This latter document is in fact a large ledger, possibly begun on 1 December 1903, although later amendments mention 1925-26. The designs, of both table and ornamental glass, are mainly executed in pencil, some with wash. Each one has a catalogue number and a letter to denote the type of glass. These two vase designs, which were intended for manufacture either in blue with sea-green 'tears' or in sea-green with blue 'tears', are similar to a less elongated version accompanied by the comment, 'Taken from a picture by Hugo van der Goes in the Uffizi Gallery.'

page 226

After the earnestness of Arts and Crafts, a note of colour and frivolity was brought to English design by the Omega Workshops. Founded in 1913 by the art critic Roger Fry in association with the artists Duncan Grant, Vanessa Bell, Wyndham Lewis and Henri Gaudier-Brezska, the workshop made painted furniture and ceramics and hand-dyed textiles. Unlike much of the production of the Arts and Crafts workshops, however, Omega artefacts were often shoddily made and are really only significant

because of their decoration. In the year following their opening, the workshops undertook the complete interior design of the Cadena Café at 59 Westbourne Grove, Bayswater, London, including the wall and ceiling decoration, furniture design, and even the design of the waitress's uniforms. Rugs to this design by Roger Fry were placed under each table. The Omega symbol appears in the original design but was omitted from the rugs which were actually placed in the café.

page 227

Described as being in 'the German modern style', this rug design from the Tomkinson archive does demonstrate that the modernist aesthetic had begun to influence English manufacture in the 1930s. Tomkinson's design director of the time, J.P. Bland, employed a staff of about forty, most of whom would have been engaged in turning out traditional designs. Nevertheless, their work was seen as being essentially 'art'; even as recently as 1969, the design staff still worked standing at easels.

pages 228–229

Tomkinson's carpet factory was originally established in Kidderminster, the heart of the English carpet-making region, in 1869, with its own design studio under the direction of a Mr. Cunningham. The company's design archive now

consists of over 10,000 original paintings on paper. Records also include a photographic log of every design and its specification. This 1930s design was produced by a member of the studio staff for manufacture as a high-quality stair carpet. The design is painted on two pieces of white cartridge paper measuring 36 inches by 30 inches and dated '23.3.39'. Calibrations marked at the edge of the design indicate the spool settings so that they could be loaded into the loom in the correct order.

page 230

From its foundation in the eighteenth century (see pp. 74-75, 148-149 and 203), the firm of Wedgwood has shown a willingness to adapt to changing circumstances. During the twentieth century, accordingly, it has been associated with some of the most innovative designers of ceramics, as well as continuing to manufacture its more traditional ware. Notable among the firm's rich and varied output for the first part of the twentieth century was the nursery ware of Susannah Margaretta (Daisy) Makeig-Jones (1881-1945), whose 'Golliwog' pattern is illustrated here. Daisy Makeig-Jones joined the Wedgwood factory, then based at Etruria, in 1909 and was given a permanent position there in 1911. She began to design tableware under the direction of resident artist James Hodgkins, her first lustre wares going into

production in 1915, continuing until 1931. Between 1916 and 1923 she produced a number of colourful nursery-ware patterns, including 'Chicken', 'Thumbelina', 'Cobble Bead and Zoo', 'Golliwog' and 'Yellow Stone Zoo'; she is perhaps best known for her 'Fairyland' and 'Ordinary' ranges of lustre ware. The 'Golliwog' pattern is entered in the factory records as number AK6580 and first recorded in May 1916. Its description reads, 'AK6580. Cream colour earthenware. Concave (shape). Golliwog printed in black underglaze, coloured underglaze in green, imperial violet, crimson, orange, brown, see-saw blue. Black line.'

page 231

These unattributed designs for ceramics are taken from albums dated c. 1912-20 now held by the Victoria & Albert Museum, London. Each design in the album is numbered and all are coloured by hand, but there is no mention of the designer's or manufacturer's name. The lack of the latter is strange and tantalizing, since the albums would have been used by the company as a record of designs available, most of which show floral and geometric decoration for plates, teapots, coffee pots, dishes and elegant jugs.

pages 232–233

The most eminent of the English lady potters of the first

part of the twentieth century, Clarice Cliff (1899-1972), started work in the lithography department at A.J. Wilkinson's earthenware factory in the town of Middleport in the Potteries in 1916. After four years she was transferred to the general decorating shop to work alongside Wilkinson's top designers, John Butler and Fred Ridgeway. By 1923 she was producing pieces bearing her own name - mainly figures of Indians or Arabs in a naïve style. The same naïveté can be seen in most of the sketches in this book, now lodged in the Hanley Library in Stoke-on-Trent. However, towards the back of the large-format scrapbook, which probably dates from the late 1920s, designs known as the 'Bizarre' range - first introduced in 1928 - begin to emerge. Though initially used as a colourful way of disguising inferior shapes, the range became more successful than anybody could have imagined and, by 1930, used Cliff's own shapes inspired by designs she had encountered in Paris.

pages 234-235

The reputation of Susie Cooper (1902-95) as an innovative designer now stands almost as high as that of Clarice Cliff; indeed, her many devotees would claim that she was the finer artist. These two pages, from one of two Cooper pattern books now lodged in the Wedgwood Museum archive, show earthenware entries E503-E506, dating from the 1930s. In an attempt to

establish her own style, Cooper set up her own pottery in the Chelsea Works, Moorland Road, Burslem, which she rented from Doulton & Co. from April 1930. She employed ten paintresses and was initially obliged to decorate blanks which she purchased from a variety of sources, including Doultons and Wood & Sons in Burslem where, in 1931, she moved the production and where she remained and indeed flourished until a fire in 1957. Susie Cooper Ltd., latterly a partner of R.H. & S.L. Plant, became a member of the Wedgwood group in March 1966, but undoubtedly her most creative period was during the 1930s.

pages 236-237

The association of Percy Wyndham Lewis (1884-1957) with the Omega Workshops was short-lived and he parted company with the rest of the group in 1914 to form his own Rebel Art Centre. This design of 1913 for a folding screen (p. 236) was one of the very few he produced under the Omega aegis. His style was altogether more aggressive and self-consciously modernist than the light, decorative designs of such as Duncan Grant (p. 237), whose pleasant, Post-Impressionist style was much more in keeping with the Omega ethos. Indeed, the break with Lewis was the result of a disagreement over the design for a Post-Impressionist room which Omega had been commissioned to contribute to

the *Daily Mail* Ideal Home Exhibition. The Grant design in watercolour is typical of the many he executed for Omega and was intended as a model for a domestic mural and door panels. It is not clear whether any eventual application would have been more precisely detailed.

pages 238-239

Best known as a painter, Paul Nash also designed glassware, tableware and domestic interiors (see pp. 212-213), including the famous bathroom for the dancer Tilly Losch in 1932. This design, however, is his only known foray into theatre sets; it was created for a one-act play, *The Truth About the Russian Dancers*, which J.M. Barrie had written specially for the ballerina Tamara Karsavina. The play, with music by Arnold Bax, was first performed on 15 March 1920 at the London Colosseum and revived six years later at the Savoy.

pages 240-241

These sketches for 'Moderne' light fittings are taken from a 460-page scrapbook of designs by A.C. Adamson, part of a bequest made by the designer to the National Art Library, Archive of Art and Design, held by the Victoria & Albert Museum, London. Adamson, whose designs show extraordinary variety of form within a generally Streamline Moderne idiom,

worked for the firm of Osler & Faraday from 1922, creating fittings for public buildings, churches and private houses.

pages 242-243

Omega pottery shapes, probably designed by Roger Fry; he was the only member of the Omega Workshops group to persevere with the design of new shapes rather than the decoration of existing 'blanks'. In 1914 he worked at Carter & Co.'s pottery in Dorset, where he made a prototype dinner service - plates, vases, and tea and coffee sets, so that moulds could be made, and larger quantities produced. In the Omega catalogue Fry proclaimed that pottery was 'essentially a form of sculpture', and intended that products made from the moulds should reproduce the irregularities of his originals.

pages 244-245

These four black-and-white designs for lampshades by Wyndham Lewis were lithographed in 1913. The products, part of an extensive collection of decorative furnishing objects, were probably among those shown by the Omega Workshop. Following a six-week exhibition on twentieth-century art held the next year at the Whitechapel Gallery and attended by 53,000 visitors, Roger Fry noted that the group had finally begun to show a small profit.

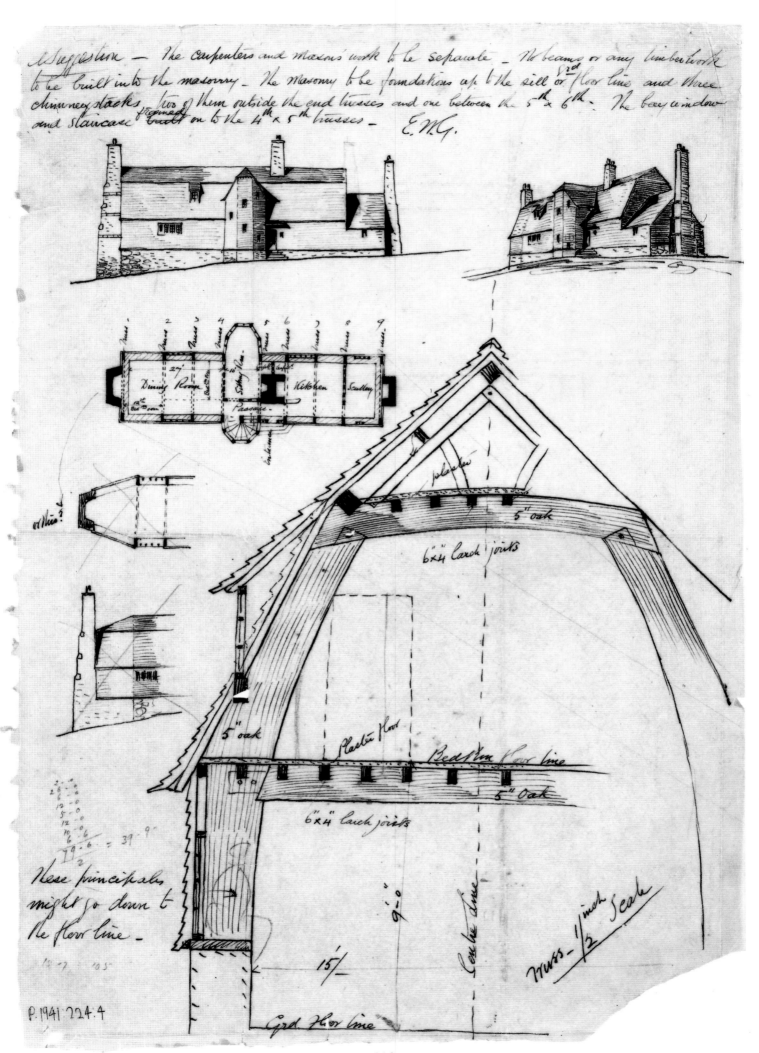

A Suggestion — The carpenters and masons' work to be separate — No beams or any timber work to be built into the masonry — The masonry to be foundations up to the sill or 3rd floor line and three chimney stacks, two of them outside the end trusses and one between the 5th & 6th. The bay window and staircase framed built on to the 4th & 5th trusses — E.W.G.

Dining Room

Sitting Room

Passage

Kitchen

Scullery

5" oak

6×4 Larch joists

plaster

5" oak

Plaster Floor

Bed Room Floor line

5" Oak

6×4 Larch joists

Centre Line

These principals might go down to the floor line —

Truss ⅟₂ inch Scale

Grd Floor line

15'

9"0

P.1941.224.4

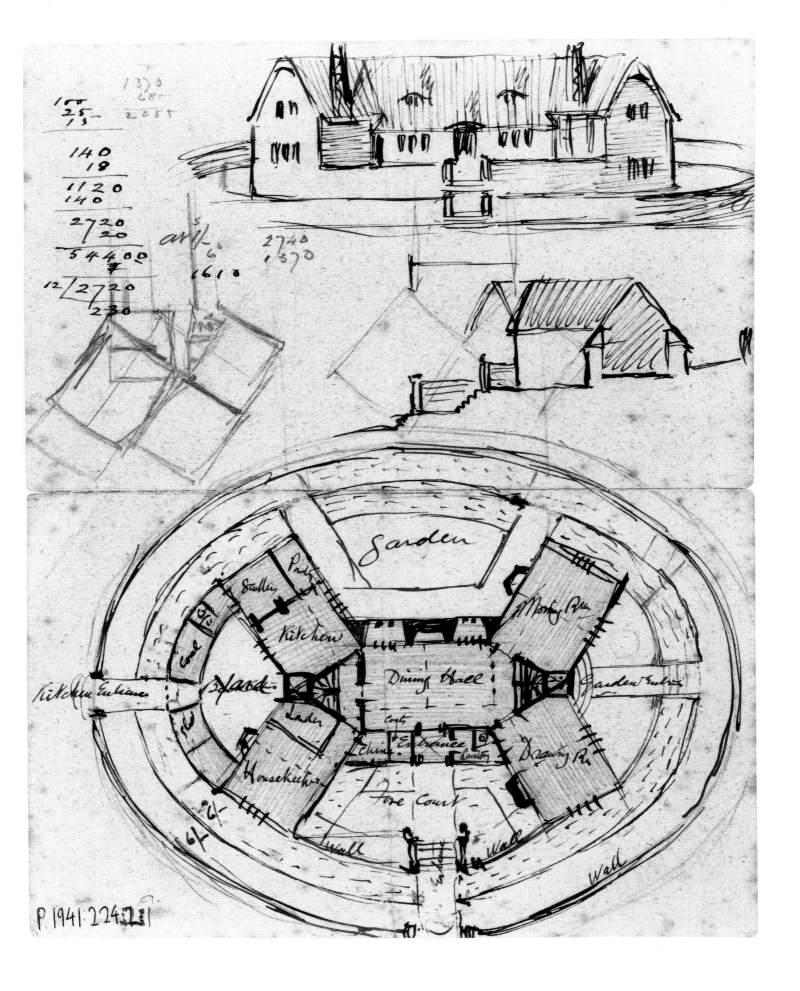

Washstands & Dressing Tables. Scale 1ft to 1 inch
with bright steel or brass handles –

Washstand or Dressing Table –
Price as drawn – 35/-
Without rails & drawer – 25/-

Wash stand – £4.
Without drawer & with shelf in top £3 –

Shelf –   Shelf –

Washstand £6-10 –

Washstand – £5-5-

Washs

Plan –

Chests of Drawers – with bright steel or brass Handles –
Scale 1½ ins to 1ft

£5.

Corner Washstand
£4.

Plan.

Washstand or Dressing Table — £6-15 — End —
Without drawers. £6.

Washstand £6-10

Plan.

Washstand or Dressing table £3-10
without cross braces. £2.

Cupd. with raised
panel.

£6-10.

£9
with 5 drawers & no cupd £8

Ernest W. Gimson

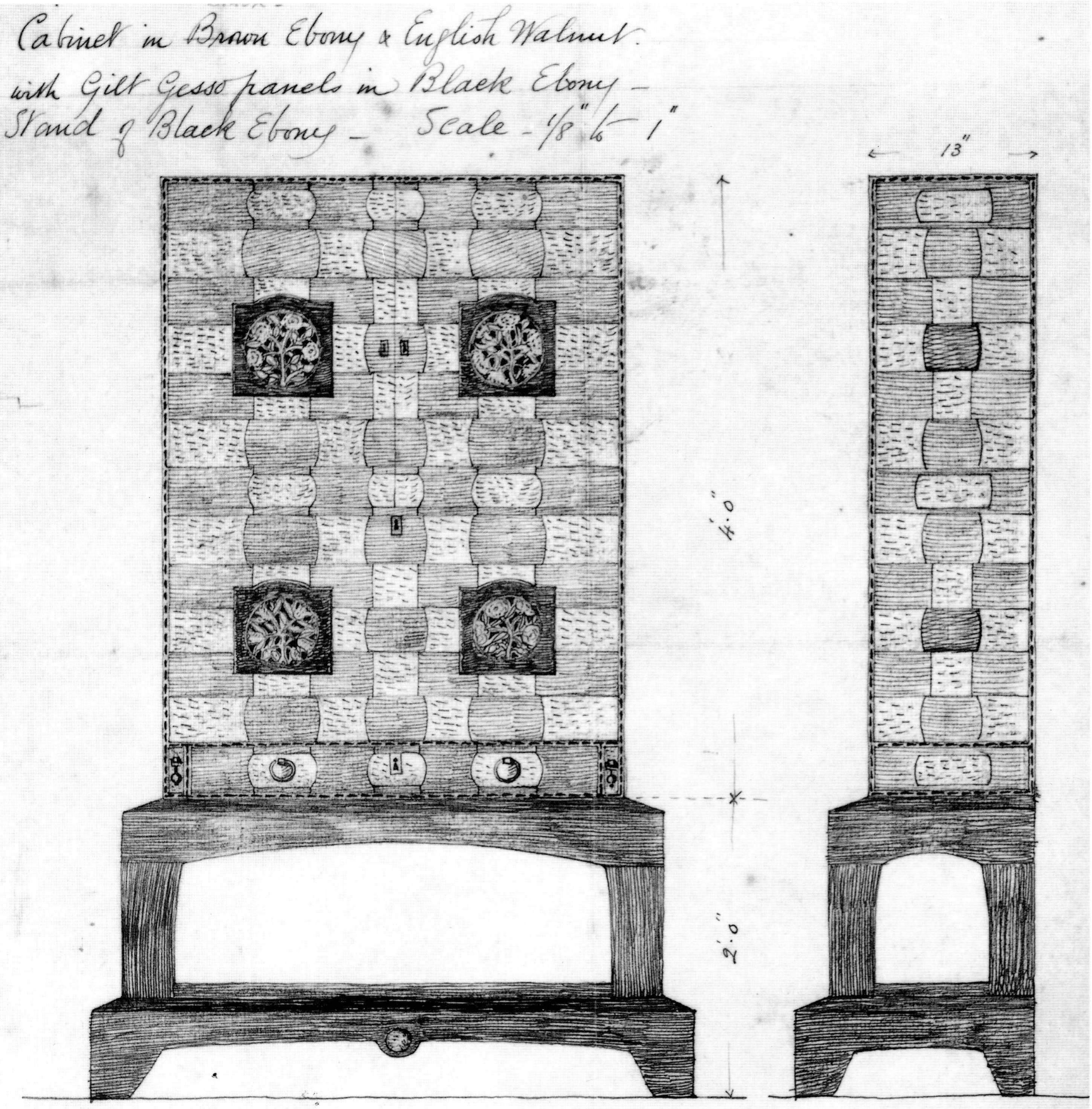

Cabinet in Brown Ebony & English Walnut.
with Gilt Gesso panels in Black Ebony —
Stand of Black Ebony — Scale - 1/8" to 1"

13"

4'0"

2'0"

Front —

Side —

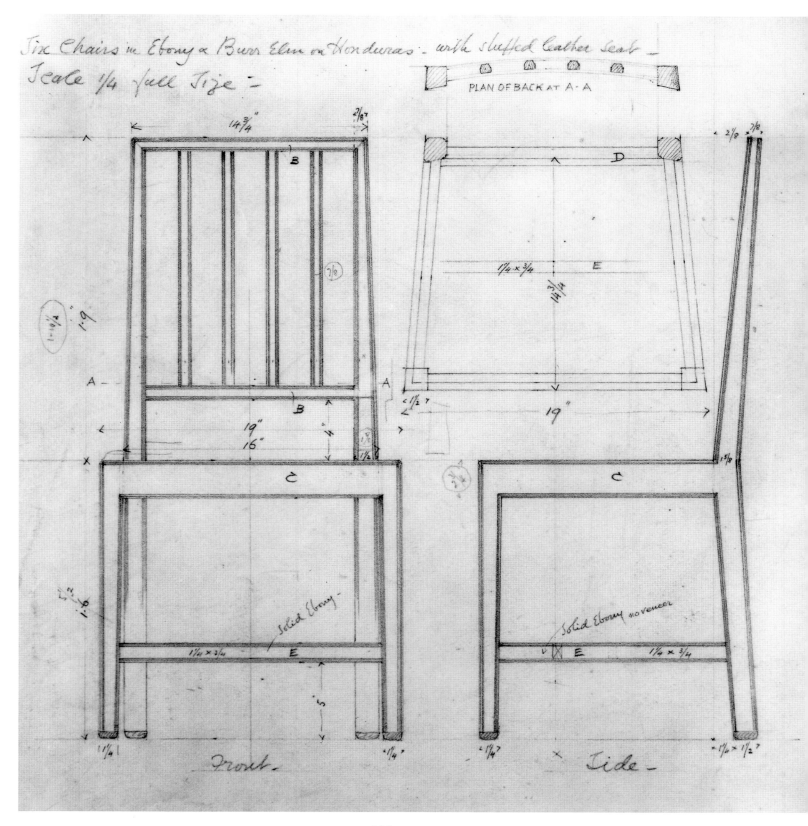

Six Chairs in Ebony & Burr Elm on Honduras. with stuffed Leather Seat.
Scale 1/4 full Size:—

PLAN OF BACK AT A·A

14¾" 2⅛"

B

⅞

19"

A—
B

19"
16"

C

1¼ × ¾   E

Solid Ebony.

1¼ × ¾   E

Front.

⅞   2⅛

D

1¼ × ¾   E

3/4
14/4

A

1½

19"

1⅝

Solid Ebony no veneer

E   1¼ × ¾

1¼   "¼"   "¼"   Side.   1/8 × 1½"

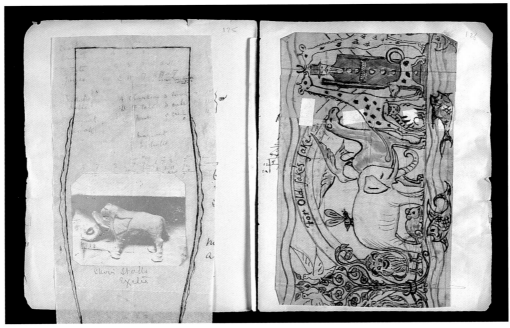

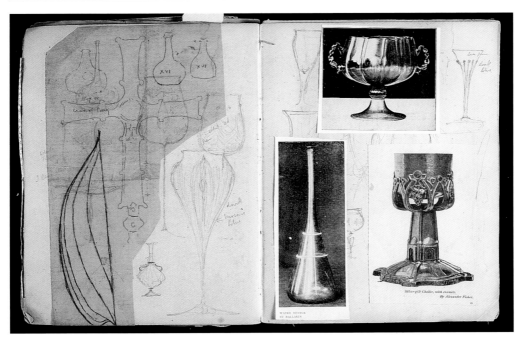

Flint with blue or sea green tears

1106
a 9/-
B 10/-
C 11/3

or

Sea green with blue tears

Coque
25/3/03

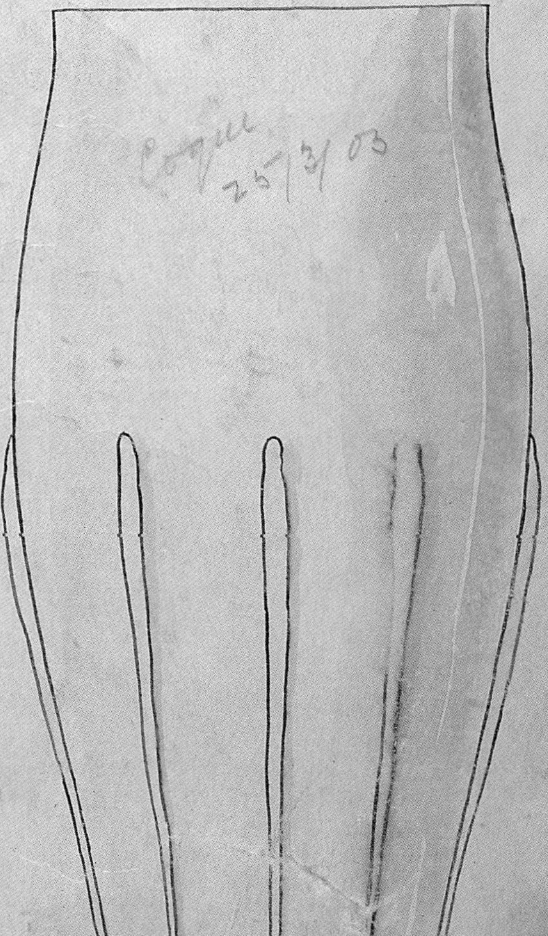

8 tears

1107
a 7/6   7/-   14
B 8/3   7/9   15/6
C 9/6   8/9   17/6

Coque
25/3/03

225

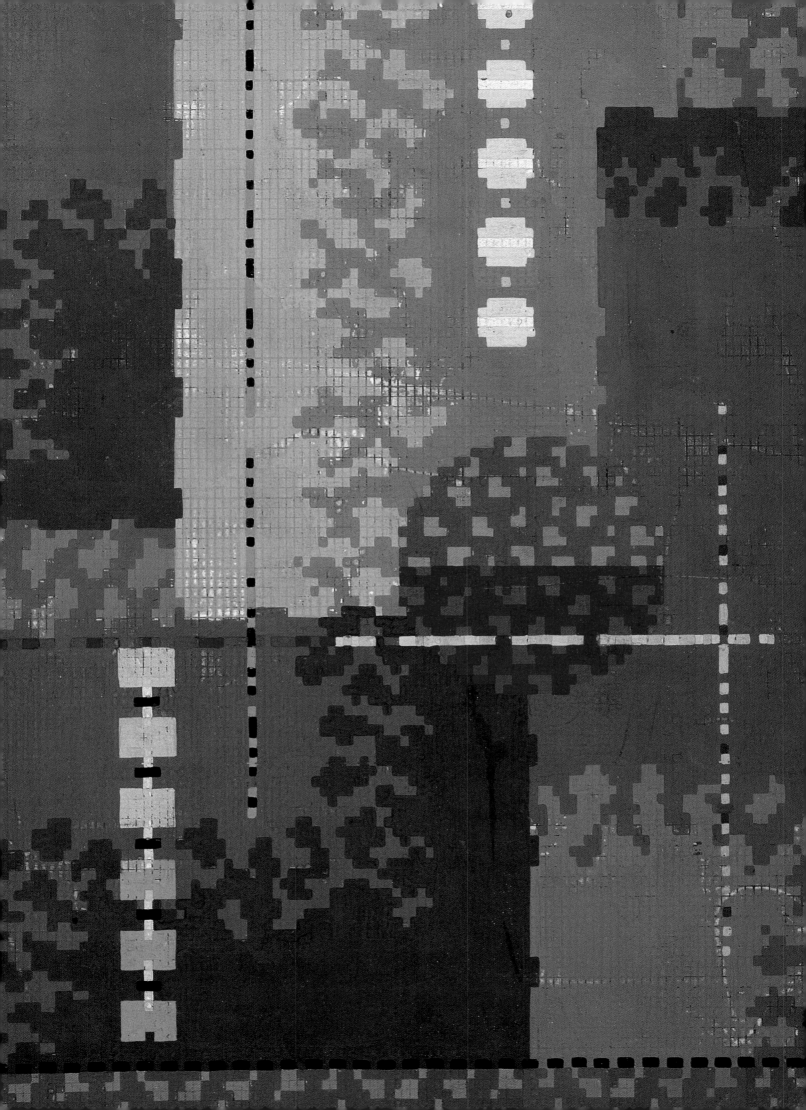

899

25/79/3

25/12/4

838

839

25/
1

897

25/79/1

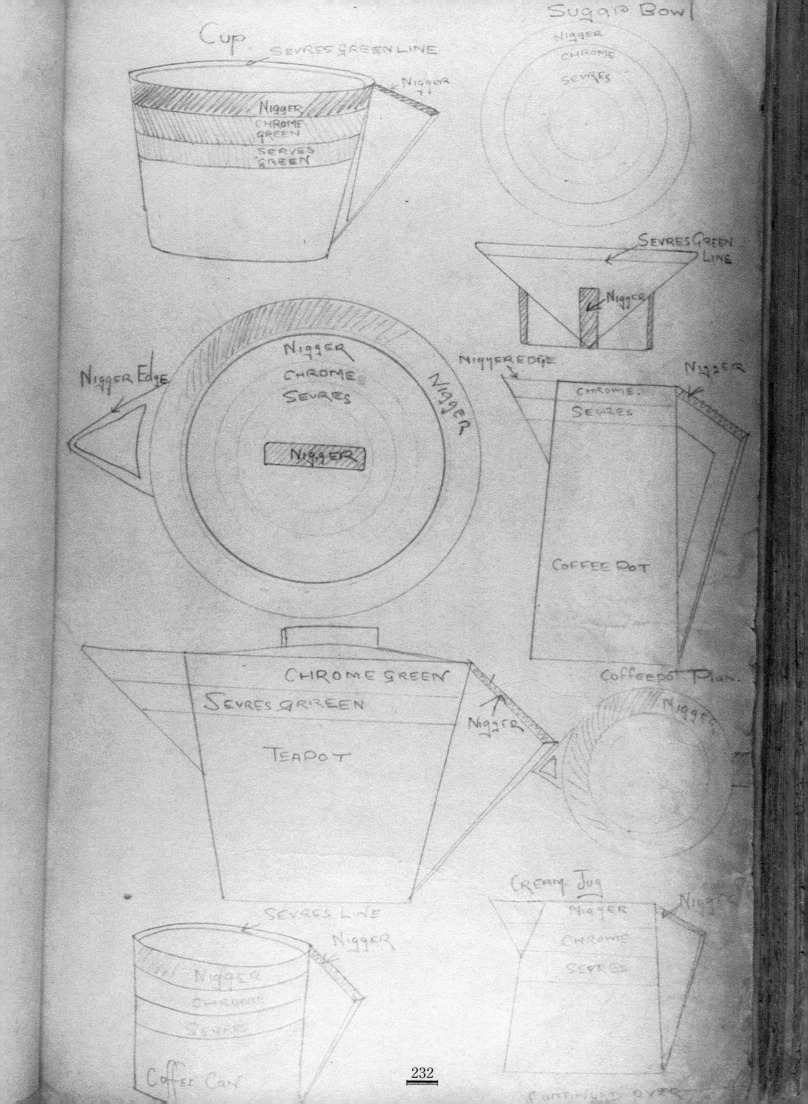

Cup

SEVRES GREEN LINE

Nigger

Nigger
CHROME
GREEN

SEVRES
GREEN

Sugar Bowl

Nigger
CHROME
SEVRES

SEVRES GREEN LINE

Nigger

Nigger Edge

Nigger
CHROME
SEVRES

Nigger

Nigger

NIGGER EDGE

CHROME.
SEVRES

COFFEE POT

CHROME GREEN

SEVRES GREEN

TEAPOT

Nigger

Coffeepot Plan.

Nigger

SEVRES LINE

Nigger

Cream Jug

Nigger

Nigger
CHROME
SEVRES

Nigger
CHROME
SEVRES

Coffee Can

CONTINUED OVER

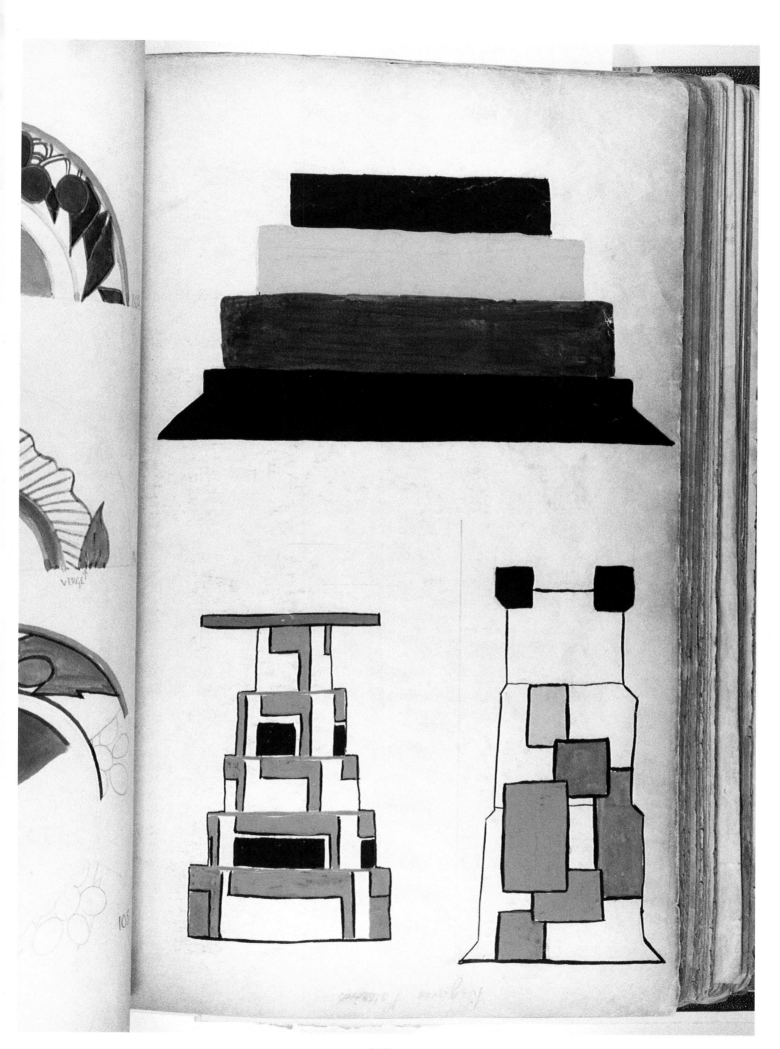

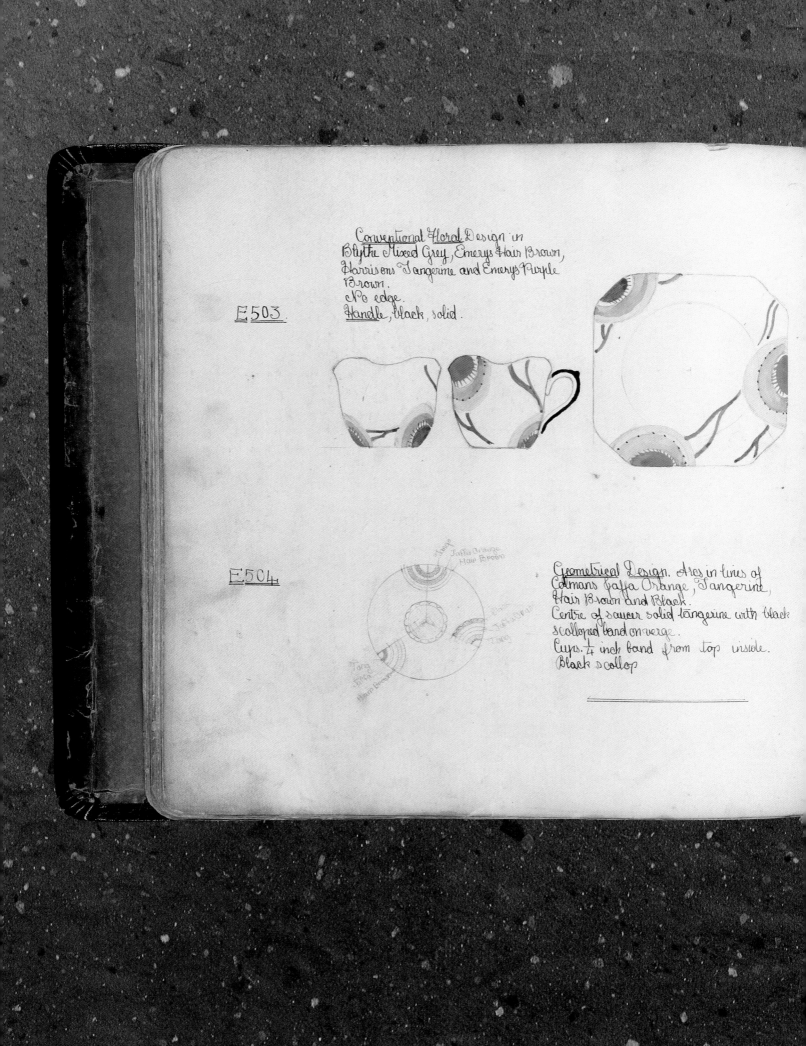

Conventional Floral Design in
Blythe Mixed Grey, Emerys Hair Brown,
Harrisons Tangerine and Emerys Purple
Brown.
No edge.
Handle, black, solid.

E 503.

E 504.

Geometrical Design. Arcs in lines of
Colmans Jaffa Orange, Tangerine,
Hair Brown and Black.
Centre of saucer solid tangerine with black
scalloped band on verge.
Cups. ¼ inch band from top inside.
Black scallop

Leaf Pattern in Light Mixed Green,
Blythe Blue, Emerys Apple Green,
Colmans Jaffa Orange, Purple Brown
and 860 Yellow.
Cup 4 leaves from top edge
interspersed with spray as on edge
of saucer. Inside cup and centre
of saucer solid Blue Green.
Handle half solid Purple Brown.

FRUIT SAUCER

Leaf Pattern in.
Blythe Blue, Jaffa Orange, 860 Yellow
Purple Brown, Light Mixed Green, Hair Brown and
Black.
Plate. Four leaves, spray in centre.
Saucer. Four leaves, solid Light Green in centre
Cup solid Light Green inside 4 leaves outside
Handle. Jaffa Orange, Half solid.

Paul Nash

V. A. M.

E.933-1927

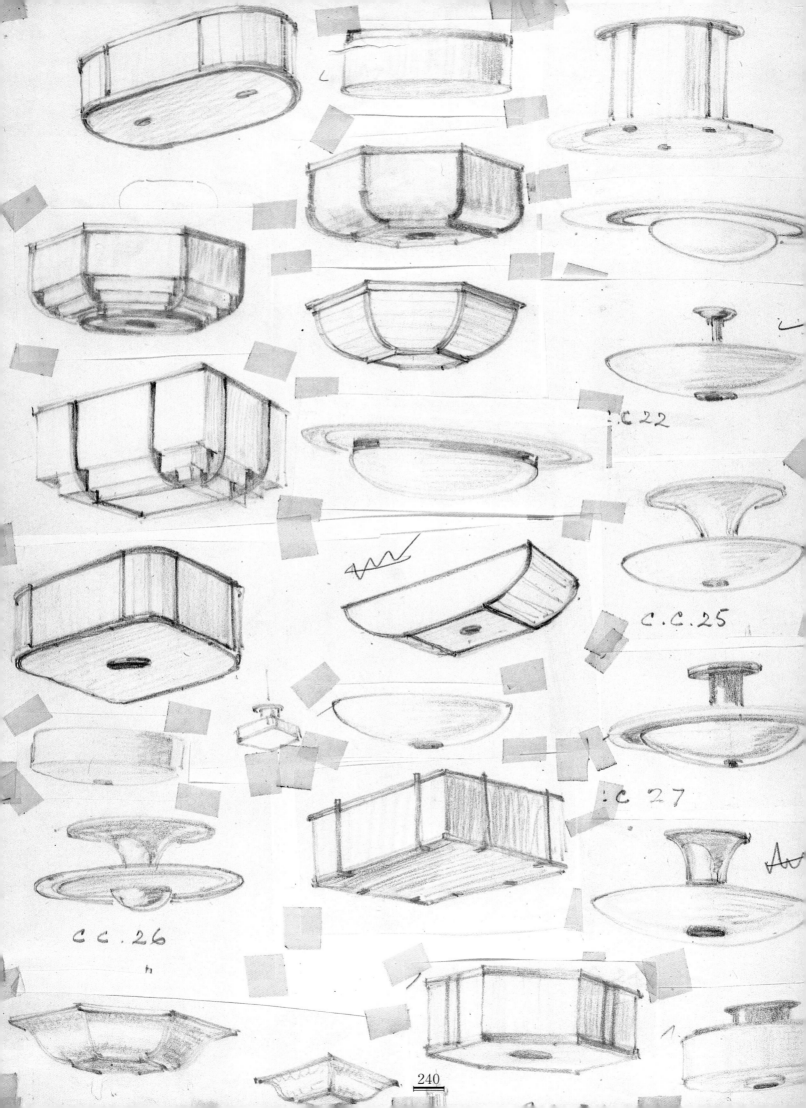

:C 22

C.C.25

:C 27

C.C.26

240

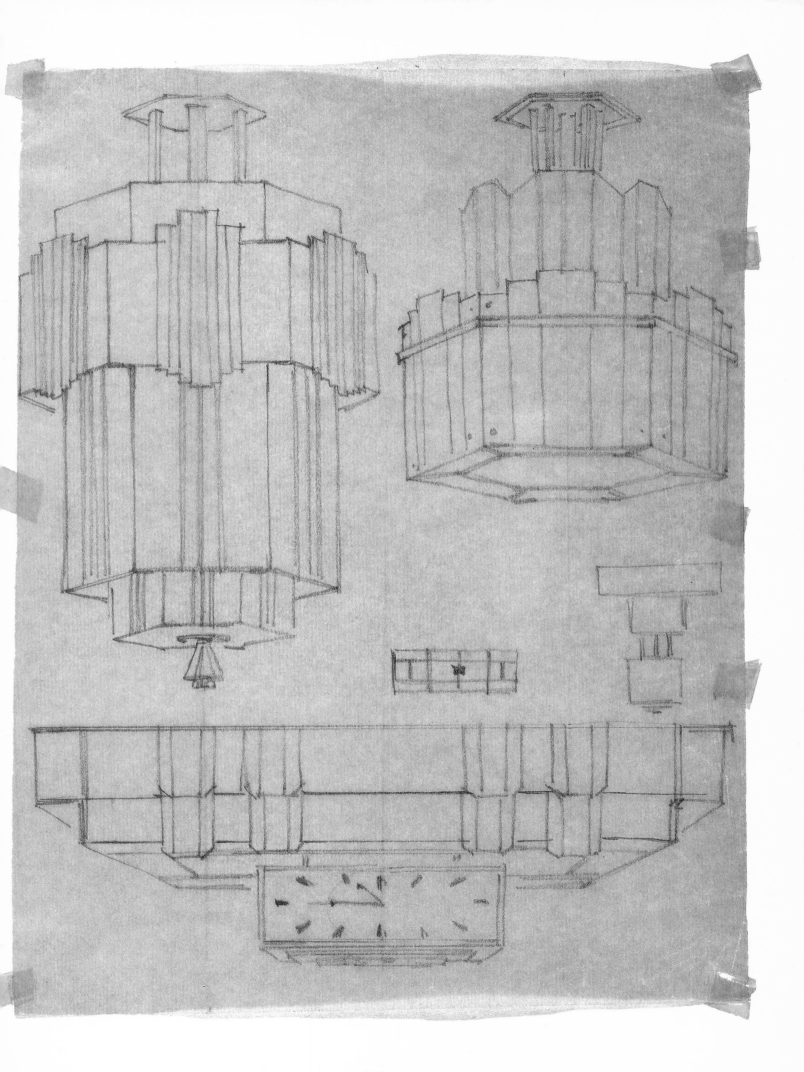

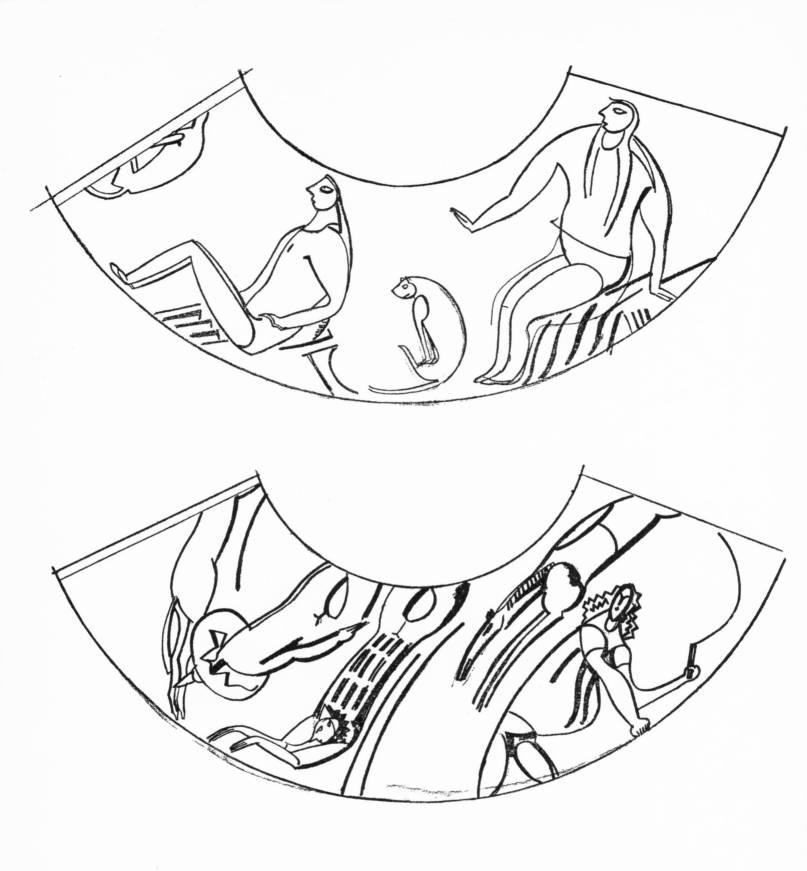

RESOURCE
Directory

ARCHIVES *and* MUSEUMS

Please note that access to archives and museums is often restricted. Readers are advised to telephone before visiting.

Artists' Papers Register
Henry Moore Institute, 74 The
Headrow, Leeds LS1
Tel: 0113 246 7467
A computerized register of papers
and primary sources relating to
artists and designers held in publicly
accessible collections.

**Birmingham Museum &
Art Gallery**
Chamberlain Square, Birmingham B3
Tel: 0121 235 2834
Metalwork archive, stained-glass
designs (including William Morris),
domestic glass archive, William de
Morgan ceramic designs and Bullock &
Bridgen furniture.

**Brighton Museum & Art Gallery;
Royal Pavilion**
Church Street, Brighton,
East Sussex BN1
Tel: 01273 292763
Early twentieth-century wallpaper
sample books and textile designs by
Bilbie and Laurence Scarfe.

Brinton's Carpets
P.O. Box 16, Exchange Street,
Kidderminster, Worcestershire DY10
Tel: 01562 820000
Early twentieth-century designs and
the Morton Sundour archive containing
material by most prominent nineteenth-
century designers.

British Museum
Great Russell Street, London WC1B
Tel: 0171 636 1555
Holds a number of drawings by Gibbs,
Wyatt and Paine, and Ambrose Heal's
collection of eighteenth- and nineteenth-
century trade cards.

**British Regional Furniture
Study Centre**
Wycombe Museum, Castle Hill House,
Priory Avenue, High Wycombe,
Buckinghamshire HP13

Tel: 01494 421899
Website: http://www.
buckscoll.ac.uk/furncen.htm
Collection of British and Irish regional
furniture and related archival material.

**Cheltenham Art Gallery
& Museums**
Clarence Street, Cheltenham,
Gloucestershire GL50
Tel: 01242 237431
Arts and Crafts designs for furniture
and artefacts, including a large number
by Gimson; watercolours of late
eighteenth-century, Regency and 1930s
interiors; extensive Gimson archive on
microfilm in adjacent library.

Christie's Images
1 Langley Lane, London SW8
Tel: 0171 582 1282
Old sales catalogues, including interior
design sales, sales of items by single
designers such as Dresser and Voysey,
and collection sales (e.g. Art Nouveau
and Art Deco).

**Crown House Collection of
Textile Documents**
Tom Lewis Studios, Crown House,
Bingswood Trading Estate, Whaley
Bridge, High Peak, Derbyshire SK23
Tel: 01663 735353
Archive of textile documents dating
from the 18th and 19th centuries.

Design Museum
28 Shad Thames, London SE1
Tel: 0171 403 6933
Archive of twentieth-century design,
including part of Heal's archive.

Fry Public Art Gallery
Bridge End Gardens, Castle Street,
Saffron Walden, Essex CB10
Tel: 01799 513779
Collection of designs by early
twentieth-century artist craftsmen,
in particular Edward Bawden and
John Aldridge (Bardfield Wallpaper
for Cole & Son), Marianne Staub
(Warner Fabrics) and Eric Ravilious
(Wedgwood).

Geffrye Museum
Kingsland Road, London E2
Tel: 0171 739 9893
Important furniture and interiors
collection; holds a large number of
sales catalogues covering the late 19th
century to the 1940s, which may be
consulted for private research purposes.

Gladstone Pottery Museum
Uttoxeter Road, Longton, Stoke-on-
Trent, Staffordshire ST3
Tel: 01782 319232

Houses a number of tile pattern
books and catalogues.

Guild of Handicraft Trust
The Old Silk Mill, Sheep Street,
Chipping Campden,
Gloucestershire GL55
Tel: 01386 841417
Holds a wide range of material
which may be consulted for study
purposes, including drawings and
photographs relating to the work of
the silversmith Sidney Reeve.

Ironbridge Gorge Museum Trust
The Wharf Edge, Iron Bridge, Telford,
Shropshire TF8
Tel: 01952 433522
Ironfounders' and floor-tile museum.

Kidderminster Library
Market Street, Kidderminster,
Worcestershire DY10
Tel: 01562 824500
Large collection of books on
flooring, carpets and textiles.

Knights Park Library
Kingston University
Knights Park, Kingston-upon-Thames,
Surrey KT1
Tel: 0181 547 2000
Large collection of trade catalogues
and illustrated company histories.

Lancashire Record Office
Bow Lane, Preston, Lancashire PR1
Tel: 01772 263039
Pattern drawings and designs of
Abbott & Co.

**Liverpool Museum Decorative
Art Department**
William Brown Street, Liverpool L3
Tel: 0151 478 4261
Tile panel designs by G.M. Forsyth
and papers relating to the work of
Joseph Tomkinson of the
Herculaneum Pottery.

London Library
14 St. James's Square, London SW1
Tel: 0171 930 7705
Houses books by important designers
such as Chippendale, Eastlake, Hope,
Pugin, Loudon and Sheraton. Access
for members only.

Manchester City Art Gallery
Mosley Street, Manchester M2
Tel: 0161 236 5244
Archives of Pilkington's Tile & Pottery
Co., Moyneux, Webb & Co. (glass) and
Whitefriars Glass Co.

Minton Archives, Royal Doulton
Minton House, London Road,
Stoke-on-Trent, Staffordshire ST4
Tel: 01782 292095
Comprise the Royal Doulton,
Royal Crown Derby, Royal Albert
and Minton porcelain archives.

Northumberland Record Office
Melton Park, North Gosforth,
Newcastle-upon-Tyne NE3
Tel: 0191 236 2680

Ceramics, interior and
architectural design.

**Rotherham Museum and
Arts Services**
Clifton Park, Clifton Lane, South
Yorkshire S65
Tel: 01709 823635
Own over 500 watercolour and pen-
and-ink drawings made for the
pattern books of George Wright &
Co. Foundries.

**Royal Institute of British
Architects**
21 Portman Square, London W1
Tel: 0171 580 5533 ext. 3627
Vast number of original designs
dating back to Inigo Jones; books on
architectural design and some trade
journals, such as *MacFarlane's
Castings*. Visiting charge.

Royal Worcester Porcelain
Severn Street, Worcester WR1
Tel: 01905 23221
Complete archive of the company's
designs, dating from 1850.

**John Rylands University
Library of Manchester**
Oxford Road, Manchester M13
Tel: 0161 275 3738
Textile and cotton archives.

Sanderson Design Archive
Arthur Sanderson & Sons,
100 Acres, Sanderson Road,
Uxbridge, Middlesex UB8
Tel: 01895 238244
Thousands of late nineteenth- and
early twentieth-century textile and
wallpaper designs, including many
by Jeffrey & Co., Morris & Co., Charles
Knowles and Sanderson. Visits by
arrangement with the archivist.

Silver Studio Collection
Museum of Domestic Architecture
and Design, Middlesex University,
Bounds Green Road, London N11
Tel: 0181 362 6614
Large collection of designs, wallpapers,
textiles and ephemera by the Silver
Studio and other prominent British
designers dating from 1870 to 1960;
houses a substantial archive relating to
English home decoration from the mid
19th to the mid 20th century.

Sir John Soane's Museum
13 Lincoln's Inn Fields,
London WC2A
Tel: 0171 405 2107
Home of the architect Soane
(1753–1837). Access to the museum's
research library and collections of
manuscripts and drawings (including a
large number by Adams) by
arrangement with the archivist.

Sotheby's Picture Library
34–35 New Bond Street,
London W1A
Tel: 0171 408 5383
Catalogues of items dating from the
18th century to the 1930s.

Spode
Church Street, Stoke-on-Trent,
Staffordshire ST4
Tel: 01782 744011
Spode's museum displays a unique
collection of ceramics, dating from
the company's beginnings in
1780. Its archive may be visited
by appointment.

Stapleton Collection
29 Westover Road, London SW18
Tel: 0181 877 3646
A huge photographic collection,
including decorative arts
designs, room settings and
architectural details.

Stead McAlpin Textiles
Cummersdale Print Work,
Carlisle CA2
Tel: 01228 525224 ext. 268
Important collection of over 20,000
original nineteenth-century documents,
including Voyseys, designs from
William Morris' studio and the archive
of the textile print works Bannister
Hall.

**Sunderland Museum and
Art Gallery**
Borough Road, Sunderland SR1
Tel: 0191 565 0723
Pattern books and designs for Jobling
art glass and flint glass, local
pottery designs by such artists as
Joseph Sewell and George Yearl.

**Temple Newsom House
Museum**
Temple Newsom Road, Leeds LS15
Tel: 0113 264 7321
Early wallpaper and flooring
collections.

**Tiles and Architectural
Ceramics Society**
Centre for Cultural and Education
Studies, Leeds Metropolitan University,
Calverley Street, Leeds LS1
Tel: 0113 283 2600
Provides information, publications,
conservation, tours and exhibitions.

**University of Glasgow Archives
and Business Records Centre**
13 Thurso Street, Glasgow G11
Tel: 0141 330 5515
Five main collections including the
archives of Wylie & Lockhead, a
major furniture manufacturer whose
catalogues date from the 1890s to the
1940s; houses a large deposit of textile
archives, including photographs of
Templeton Carpets dating from *c.* 1900.

Victoria & Albert Museum
Cromwell Road, London SW7
Tel: 0171 938 8500
Valuable collections covering all
aspects of interior design. Photographic
library contains material taken from the
archives of Anna-Maria Garthwaite and
John Leman, the principal designers of
eighteenth-century Spitalfields woven
silks; substantial Morris archive; very
good source of pre-industrial designs.

Warner Fabrics
Bradbourne Drive,
Tilbrook, Milton Keynes MK7
Tel: 01908 366900
Warner's fabric archive contains
designs which date back to the 17th
century and may be consulted by
researchers on application to the
archivist.

Wedgwood Museum
Barlaston, Stoke-on-Trent,
Staffordshire ST12
Tel: 01782 204141

Westminster City Archives
10 St Ann's Street,
London SW1
Tel: 0171 798 2180
Several large archives, notably
Liberty's and Gillow's, which may
be viewed by appointment.

Whitworth Museum
University of Manchester,
Oxford Road, Manchester M15
Tel: 0161 275 4865
National collection of wallpapers
dating from the mid 1880s onwards,
including designs by Voysey.

William Morris Gallery
Water House, Lloyd Park,
Forest Road, London E17
Tel: 0181 527 3782
Houses some William Morris and
related designs, and the archives
of the Century Guild.

Woodward Grosvenor
Stourvale Mills, Green Street,
Kidderminster, Worcestershire
DY10
Tel: 01562 820020
Archive comprises some 20,000
designs, which are soon to be
compiled on CD-ROM. Many are on
display in their archive showroom.

**Wycombe Local History and
Chair Museum**
Castle Hill House, Priory Avenue,
High Wycombe,
Buckinghamshire HP13
Tel: 01494 421895
Small but interesting museum focusing
on the local furniture industry. Holds
documents and archives relating to
individual companies and a
photographic archive; home to the
British Regional Furniture Study
Centre (see above).

ARCHITECTURAL
FEATURES *and*
SALVAGE

Antique Fireplace Warehouse
194–202 Battersea Park Road,
London SW11
Tel: 0171 627 1410
Two showrooms of original and one
showroom of reproduction fireplaces
and cast-iron inserts dating from the

Georgian, Regency and Victorian
periods.

Architectural Heritage
Taddington Manor, Taddington,
nr. Cutsdean, Cheltenham,
Gloucestershire GL54
Tel: 01386 584414
Expensive architectural antiques
from all periods, including
complete panelled rooms and
chimneypieces.

Architectural Salvage Centre
30–32 Stamford Road,
London N1
Tel: 0171 923 0783
Cast-iron fireplaces and radiators.

Architectural Salvage Register
Netley House, Gomshall,
Guildford, Surrey GU5
Tel: 01483 203221
Database of salvage dealers throughout
the country. For a registration fee,
they will search for pieces on a client's
behalf or for a buyer of items a client
wishes to sell.

Nigel Bartlett
63 St. Thomas Street, London SE1
Tel: 0171 378 7895
Antique chimneypieces dating from
the 17th to the late 19th century.

C.&C. Designs
2/18 Chelsea Harbour Design Centre,
London SW10
Tel: 0171 823 3040,
Workshops: 01328 855 396
Architectural joinery and bespoke
period furniture.

Clark & Fenn
Unit 19 Mitcham Industrial Estate,
Streatham Road, Mitcham,
Surrey CR4
Tel: 0181 685 5020
Specialists in fibrous plaster,
including cornices, dado rails, ceiling
centres, niches and brackets.

Copley Decor
Bedale Road, Leyburn,
North Yorkshire BDL8
Tel: 01969 623410
Produces a wide range of Georgian
and Edwardian decorative mouldings,
including ceiling roses, corbels, door
pediments, panel mouldings, cornices
and niches.

Crowther of Syon Lodge
Syon Lodge, Busch Corner, London
Road, Isleworth, Middlesex TW7
Tel: 0181 560 7978
Antique eighteenth- and nineteenth-
century chimneypieces, grates and
panelling.

Dorset Reclamation
Cow Drove, Bere Regis, Wareham,
Dorset BH20
Tel: 01929 472200
Victorian and Edwardian architectural
antiques, including chimneypieces,
panelling and flooring.

Drummonds
Hindhead, London Road,
Surrey GU26
Architectural antiques dating from the
early 16th century onwards, including
chimneypieces, doors and shutters;
period bathroom furniture.

Elgin & Hall
Adelphi House, Hunton, Bedale,
North Yorkshire DL8
Tel: 01677 450712
Elgin and Hall produce fireplaces
based on their own interpretations
of designs dating from the 18th
century to the present day.

Fens
46 Lots Road, London SW10
Tel: 0171 352 9883
Architectural antiques dating from
the Georgian, Victorian and Edwardian
eras, including fireplaces, doors,
shutters, bathroom fittings, banisters
and flooring; will search for items not
in stock; deals in and restores antique
furniture and reproduces bespoke
period furniture.

Robin Gage
Unit 7, Talina Centre,
23 Bagley's Lane, London SW6
Tel: 0171 610 6612
Reproduces bespoke eighteenth-century
club fenders.

Gallop & Rivers
Crickhowell, Powys, Wales NP8
Tel: 01873 811084
Georgian, Victorian and Edwardian
architectural antiques, especially
flooring and fireplaces.

**Havenplan Architectural
Emporium**
The Old Station, Station Road,
Killarmarsh, Sheffield S21
(close to exit 30 on the M1)
Tel: 0114 489972
Architectural antiques dating from all
periods, including doors, panelling,
decorative ironwork and brasswork
and 1920s sanitary furniture.

Hayles & Howe
25 Picton Street, Montpelier,
Bristol BS6
Tel: 01179 246673
Specialists in a wide range of
plasterwork, including panel
mouldings, ceiling roses, corbels, fire
surrounds, columns and capitals,
dating from the early 18th century to
the Art Deco period; undertake
conservation and restoration.

The House Hospital
68 Battersea High Street, London SW11
Tel: 0171 223 3179
Architectural antiques dating from
the late 18th century to the early
1940s, focusing especially on
staircases and fireplaces.

House of Steel
400 Caledonian Road, London N1
Tel: 0171 607 5889

Nineteenth-century architectural metalware; restores and reproduces steel furniture.

In Situ
Worsley Street, Manchester M15
Tel: 0161 839 2010
Architectural antiques encompassing period windows, radiators and sanitaryware.

G. Jackson
Unit 19, Mitcham Industrial Estate, Streatham Road, Mitcham, Surrey CR4
Tel: 0181 648 4343
Composition mouldings dating from the Adam period onwards.

LASSCo Flooring
41 Maltby Street, London SE1
Tel: 0171 237 4488
Dealers and contractors in old oak, Victorian pine, parquet, strip, block, flag and tile flooring.

LASSCo St. Michael
St. Michael's Church, Mark Street (off Paul Street), London EC2A
Tel: 0171 739 0448
Website: http://www.lassco.co.uk
The largest architectural salvage company in London. Specialists in fine architectural antiques, chimneypieces, panelled rooms and garden ornament.

Locker & Riley
Capital House, Hawk Hill, Battlesbridge, Essex SS11
Tel: 01268 574100
Reproduce fibrous plaster mouldings from any period.

London's Georgian Houses
291 Goswell Road, London EC1
Tel: 0171 833 8217
Recreate, fit and restore eighteenth- and nineteenth-century Georgian and Victorian woodwork.

London Plastercraft
314 Wandsworth Bridge Road, London SW6
Tel: 0171 736 5146
Website: http://www.plastercraft.uk
Interior and exterior mouldings dating from the Georgian period to the present day. Carries a large stock range, including corbels, cornices, columns, ceiling roses and fire surrounds. Catalogues available on request.

Marble Hill
70–72 Richmond Road, Twickenham, Middlesex TW1
Tel: 0181 892 1488
Reproduction Georgian and Victorian mantels in stone, pine and marble.

Oakleaf Reproductions
Ling Bob Mill, Main Street, Wilsden, Bradford, West Yorkshire BD15
Tel: 01535 272878
Reproduce seventeenth-, eighteenth- and nineteenth-century decorative mouldings in simulated wood, including oak beams, carved cornices, mirrors and wall panellings.

H.W. Poulter
279 Fulham Road, London SW10
Tel: 0171 352 7268
Antique fireplaces and associated metalwork dating from the 18th to the end of the 19th century.

Rainbow Fairweather
Unit 14, The Talina Centre, Bagleys Lane, London SW6
Tel: 0171 736 8693
Produces bespoke period mouldings.

Salvo
18 Ford Village, Berwick-upon-Tweed TD15
Tel: 01890 820333
Website: http://www.salvo.co.uk
Publishers of information on architectural salvage. For a fee, Salvo will send a Salvo Pack, including a county listing of businesses who buy and sell architectural antiques and reclaimed building materials, and one copy each of SalvoNews and the Salvo magazine.

Stevensons of Norwich
Roundtree Way, Norwich NR7
Tel: 01603 416676
Plasterwork specialists. Manufacture a standard range of mouldings dating predominantly from the Georgian and Victorian periods; undertake special project work and restoration.

Thomas & Wilson
454 Fulham Road, London SW6
Tel: 0171 381 1161
Manufacture a wide range of fibrous plaster mouldings; restoration and repair.

Tower Ceramics
91 Parkway, London NW1
Tel: 0171 485 7192
Reproduce plaster mouldings, including egg-and-dart, ceiling roses and cornices; reproduction tiles.

Townsends
108 Boundary Road, London NW8
Tel: 0171 372 4327
Townsends' glass workshop, restoring and reproducing stained and etched glass.

Townsends
81 Abbey Road, London NW8
Tel: 0171 624 4756
Eighteenth- and nineteenth-century fireplaces, and stained glass dating from the late 19th and early 20th centuries.

Troika
41 Clun Street, Sheffield, S4
Tel: 01142 753222
Reproduces mouldings dating from the 17th century onwards.

Christopher Tucker
P.O. Box 4028, Reading, Berkshire RG8
Tel: 0118 984 2393

Website: http://www.course-delivery.com/mirrors.nsf
Eighteenth- and nineteenth-century composition mouldings and decorative murals.

Walcot Reclamation
108 Walcot Street, Bath BA1
Tel: 01225 444404
Antique fireplaces, cast-iron radiators, sanitaryware and door furniture; reproduction fireplaces and door furniture.

Wilson Reclamation Services
Yew Tree Barn, Newton-in-Cartmel, Grange-over-Sands, Cumbria LA11
Tel: 01539 531498
Stock comprises oak panelling, Victorian and Edwardian lights and light fittings, doors and door furniture, cast-iron fireplaces, leaded-glass windows, window shutters and bathroom furniture and accessories; provides a restoration service for all wooden items; faithfully reproduces curtains and trimmings from original patterns.

BATHROOMS

Alscot Bathroom Co.
The Stable Yard, Alscot Park, Stratford-upon-Avon, Warwickshire CV37
Tel: 01789 450861
Original Victorian, Edwardian and Art Deco bathroooms.

Aston Matthews
141–147A Essex Road, London N1
Tel: 0171 226 7220
Designs based on Victorian, Edwardian and Art Deco bathroom furniture, including baths and basins, taps, sanitaryware and radiators.

Bath Shield
Blenheim Studio, London Road, Forest Row, Sussex RH18
Tel: 01342 823243
Restorers of bath enamel.

Burge & Gunson
13–27 High Street, Colliers Wood, London SW19
Tel: 0181 543 5166
Cast-iron baths, radiators and fittings dating from the Victorian period onwards.

Chadder & Co.
Blenheim Studio, London Road, Forest Row, Sussex RH18
Tel: 01342 823243
Sell restored and reproduction roll-top baths, basins and fittings.

Czech & Speake
39C Jermyn Street, London SW1
Tel: 0800 919728
Bathroom fixtures, fittings and sanitaryware influenced by Edwardian designs.

Drummonds
Hindhead, London Road, Surrey GU26
Antique bathrooms and architectural antiques.

Fens
46 Lots Road, London SW10
Tel: 0171 352 9883
Original bathroom fittings, architectural antiques, antique furniture and bespoke reproduction furniture.

Havenplan Architectural Emporium
The Old Station, Station Road, Killarmarsh, Sheffield S21 (close to exit 30 on the M1)
Tel: 0114 489972
1920s sanitary furniture and architectural antiques.

In Situ
Worsley Street, Manchester M15
Tel: 0161 839 2010
Original sanitaryware and architectural antiques.

LASSCo Radiators, Bathrooms and Kitchens
101 Brittania Walk, London N1
Tel: 0171 336 8221
Antique bathtubs and sinks, cast-iron radiators, Belfast sinks, teak worktops, towel-radiators and old taps.

Original Bathrooms
143–145 Kew Road, Richmond-upon-Thames, Surrey TW9
Tel: 0181 940 7554
Bathroom fixtures and fittings, tiles and marble dating from the Victorian, Edwardian and Art Deco periods.

Max Pike Bathrooms
4 Eccleston Street, London SW1
Tel: 0171 730 7216
Antique Victorian and Edwardian taps.

Pipe Dreams
72 Gloucester Road, London SW7
Tel: 0171 225 3978
Design, supply and install Victorian and Art Deco bathrooms.

Walcot Reclamation
108 Walcot Street, Bath BA1
Tel: 01225 444404
Bathroom furniture dating from the Victorian era onwards, and architectural antiques.

Water Monopoly
16–18 Lonsdale Road, London NW6
Tel: 0171 624 2636
Reproduction bathroom fittings and fixtures from c. 1850 to c. 1915.

Wilson Reclamation Services
Yew Tree Barn, Newton-in-Cartmel, Grange-over-Sands, Cumbria LA11
Tel: 01539 531498
Antique bathroom furniture and accessories, architectural antiques and bespoke period curtains.

CARPETS
and RUGS

David Black
96 Portland Road, London W11
Tel: 0171 727 2566
Stock includes Arts and Crafts carpets.

Brintons
P.O. Box 16, Exchange Street,
Kidderminster, Worcestershire DY10
Tel: 01562 820000
Reinterpret designs from Brintons'
archive and reproduce bespoke carpets
for a required minimum yardage.
Telephone for stockists.

Colefax & Fowler
39 Brook Street, London W1Y
Tel: 0171 493 2231
Produce carpets, fabrics and
wallpapers interpreted from eighteenth-
and nineteenth-century English and
French designs.

S. Franses
80 Jermyn Street, London SW1
Tel: 0171 976 1234
Antique carpets dating from the
17th to the late 19th century, and
tapestries dating from the 16th to
the mid 19th century; cleaning and
restoration service for carpets and
tapestries of all periods.

C. John
70 South Audley Street, London W1
Tel: 0171 493 5288
Antique carpets, rugs and tapestries
dating from the 17th to the 19th
century.

Robert Stephenson
1 Elystan Street, London SW3
Tel: 0171 225 2343
Antique decorative rugs, carpets
and tapestries dating from the 1870s
to the Second World War.

Stockwell
24 Harcourt Street, London W1H
Tel: 0171 224 8380
26 Krag Road, Preston, Connecticut
06365 (USA office)
Tel: 860 889 2880
Designers and suppliers of bespoke
carpets dating from the 18th century
to the present day.

Tomkinson's
P.O. Box 11, Duke Place,
Kidderminster,
Worcestershire DY10
Tel: 01562 820006
Reproduce carpets dating from the
mid 19th century onwards.

Woodward Grosvenor
Stourvale Mills, Green Street,
Kidderminster,
Worcestershire DY10
Tel: 01562 820020
Reproduces bespoke Wilton carpets
from its extensive archive of designs,
which date from 1790 onwards.

Zoffany
63 South Audley Street, London W1
Tel: 0171 495 2505
Produces carpets, woven and printed
fabrics and wallpapers; collections
include English eighteenth- and
nineteenth-century designs.

CERAMICS
and GLASS

Art Deco Originals
Halifax Antiques Centre, Queen's
Road Mill, on the junction of Queen's
Road and Gibbet Street, Halifax,
West Yorkshire HX1
Tel: 01422 347377 (daytime); 01274
882051 (evenings)
Website: http://
www.muir-hewitt.com/hewitt
Original Art Deco ceramics by
Clarice Cliff, Susie Cooper and
Shelley; furniture, mirrors, lamps
and chrome.

Bardith
901 Madison Avenue, New York,
New York 10021, USA
Tel: 212 737 3775
Wide range of antique tableware in
fine English china, including
Wedgwood, Spode, Derby, pearlware
and delftware; glass dishes, decanters
and glasses; light fixtures.

Beverley
30 Church Street, London NW8
Tel: 0171 262 1576
Antique ceramics and glass, including
designs by Clarice Cliff, Susie Cooper,
Shelley and Carlton.

Richard Dennis
144 Kensington Church Street,
London W8
Tel: 0171 727 2061
Antique and contemporary ceramics
dating from 1850 onwards. Richard
Dennis Publications (based at The Old
Chapel, Shepton Beauchamp, Ilminster,
Somerset TA19; Tel: 01460 242009)
produce a large number of books on
ceramics .

Thomas Goode
19 South Audley Street,
London W1Y
Tel: 0171 499 2823
Website:
http://www.thomasgoode.doc.com
Bespoke china and glass. Supplies
recreations from Thomas Goode's own
archive as well as from manufacturers
such as Royal Worcester.

Graham & Green
4–7 Elgin Crescent, London W11
Tel: 0171 727 4594
Reproduction china, glass, furniture
and fabrics from all periods.

Jonathan Horne
66C Kensington Church Street,
London W8
Tel: 0171 221 5658

Antique English pottery up to the
early 19th century.

Mercury
1 Ladbroke Road, London W11
Tel: 0171 727 5106
Eighteenth- and nineteenth-century
English ceramics.

Paul Reeves
32B Kensington Church Street,
London W8
Tel: 0171 937 1594
Original Gothic Revival, Arts and
Crafts and Mackintosh ceramics,
glass, textiles and furniture.

James Robinson
480 Park Avenue, New York, New York
10022, USA
Tel: 212 752 6166
Antique Georgian glassware and dessert,
tea and dinner services in fine china.

Royal Creamware
6 Redworth Way, Newton Aycliffe,
County Durham DL5
Tel: 01325 310477
Faithfully reproduces a wide range of
eighteenth-century British ceramics,
including tableware, lamps and
timepieces.

Royal Doulton & Minton
167 Piccadilly, London W1
Tel: 0171 493 9121
Reproduction Minton, Royal Crown
Derby and Royal Doulton china dating
from the 19th century.

Malvina Solomon
1021 Lexington Avenue, New York,
New York 10021, USA
Tel: 212 535 5200
Original English Arts and Crafts
pottery and late nineteenth-century
ceramic tiles.

Jean Sewell
3 Campden Street, London W8
Tel: 0171 727 3122
Antique English eighteenth- and
nineteenth-century porcelain and
pottery, including Derby and
Coalport.

Spode
Church Street, Stoke-on-Trent,
Staffordshire ST4
Tel: 01782 744011
Reproduces nineteenth- and twentieth-
century fine bone china, including blue
printed ware and personalized and
monogrammed tableware, using
traditional techniques and designs
from authentic engravings and moulds
preserved in the Spode archives. Spode
has a museum and visitor centre and an
archive which may be visited by
appointment.

Tiffany & Co.
727 Fifth Avenue, New York,
New York 10022, USA
Tel: 212 755 8000
English bone china, earthenware
designs by Susie Cooper.

Waterford Wedgwood
158 Regent Street, London W1
Tel: 0171 734 7262
Wedgwood reproductions
dating from the founding of the
company in 1759.

Mark J. West
39B High Street, Wimbledon Village,
London SW19
Tel: 0181 946 2811
Antique English and Continental
glassware, dating from the 18th
century to the Art Deco period.

William Yeoward
336 King's Road, London SW3
Tel: 0171 351 5454
Reproduction Georgian and
Regency crystal.

FLOOR *and*
WALL SURFACES

Castlenau Tiles
175 Church Road, London SW13
Tel: 0181 741 2452
Victorian-style floor tiles.

Steve Charles
42 Elcho Street, London SW11
Tel: 0171 228 5785
Early eighteenth-century hand-painted
reproduction ceramics and Victorian
floor tiles; restores period tiling.

Color 1 Ceramics
412 Richmond Road, Twickenham,
Middlesex TW1
Tel: 0181 891 0691
Stock tiles drawn from designs
dating from the late 19th century
to the 1930s.

Fired Earth
117–119 Fulham Road,
London SW3
Tel: 0171 589 0489
Wall tiles based on Arts and
Crafts designs; stocks a range of
heritage paints.

H.&R. Johnson
Highgate Tile Works,
Brownhills Road, Tunstall,
Stoke-on-Trent,
Staffordshire ST6
Tel: 01782 575575
Website: http://www.johnson-tiles.com
Manufacture Minton and Pugin
floor tiles and wall tiles from the
Minton/Hollins range; restoration
and refurbishment services.

Malvina Solomon
1021 Lexington Avenue, New York,
New York 10021, USA
Tel: 212 535 5200
Late nineteenth-century ceramic tiles
and Arts and Crafts pottery.

Tile Gallery
1 Royal Parade, 247 Dawes Road,
London SW6
Tel: 0171 385 8818

Stocks a wide range of tiles reproduced from designs created during the 18th and 19th centuries and the first half of the 20th, including Delft wall tiles, Victorian tesselated floor tiles and Art Deco wall tiles.

Tiles of Newport
Unit 3, The Talina Centre,
23A Bagley's Lane, London SW6
Tel: 0171 736 9323
Delft and Victorian tiles, limestones and marbles.

Walton Ceramics
21 Walton Street, London SW3
Tel: 0171 589 7386
Supply English tiles. Stock a small collection of Delft and Victorian tiles and reproduce bespoke hand-painted tiles.

Whichford Pottery
Whichford, nr. Shipston-on-Stour,
Warwickshire CV36
Tel: 01608 684416
Seventeenth- and eighteenth-century English Delft tiles.

FURNITURE

Norman Adams
8–10 Hans Road, London SW3
Tel: 0171 589 5266
Georgian furniture.

After Noah
121 Upper Street, London N1
Tel: 0171 359 4281
261 King's Road, Chelsea,
London SW3
Tel: 0171 351 2610
Antique furniture and housewares dating from the late 19th to the mid 20th century. Mail order service available at the same telephone number.

Apter-Fredericks
265–267 Fulham Road,
London SW3
Tel: 0171 352 2188
Eighteenth-century furniture, including tables, chairs, and chests-of-drawers.

Art Deco Originals
Halifax Antiques Centre,
Queen's Road Mill, on the junction of Queen's Road and Gibbet Street, Halifax, West Yorkshire HX1
Tel: 01422 347377 (daytime);
01274 882051 (evenings)
Website:
http://www.muir-hewitt.com/hewitt
Art Deco furniture, ceramics, mirrors, lamps and chrome.

Percy Bass Limited
184–188 Walton Street,
London SW3
Tel: 0171 589 4853
Faithfully copies sofa, chair and carpet designs and carries out re-upholstery, cleaning and restoration work; a drawing service for everything from floor plans to furniture is also available.

Beaumont & Fletcher
261 Fulham Road, London SW3
Tel: 0171 352 5594
Stock eighteenth- and nineteenth-century reproduction furniture, including upholstered furniture, wall lights, mirrors and accessories.

John Bly
27 Bury Street,
London SW1Y
Tel: 0171 930 1292
Georgian furniture.

Arthur Brett
103 Pimlico Road, London SW1W
Tel: 0171 730 7304
Eighteenth- and nineteenth-century furniture. Stocks a wide range of items including some upholstered furniture, dining tables and chairs, sideboards, bookcases and desks.

I.&J.L. Brown
636 King's Road, London SW6
Tel: 0171 736 4141
58 Commercial Road, Hereford HR1
Tel: 01432 358895
Focus on English country and French furniture dating from the 18th and 19th centuries. Range includes dining tables and chairs, dressers, desks, bureaux, armoires and linen presses.

C.&C. Designs
2/18 Chelsea Harbour Design Centre,
London SW10
Tel: 0171 823 3040;
Workshops: 01328 855396
Bespoke furniture of all periods and types, and architectural joinery.

Classic Chair Co.
Studio R, The Old Imperial Laundry, 71
Warriner Gardens, London SW11
Tel: 0171 622 4274
Reproduces bespoke English hand-painted furniture dating from the late 18th and early 19th centuries.

Codrington
Arch 80, Chelsea Bridge Business Centre, Queenstown Road, London SW8
Tel: 0171 498 9960
Reproduces bespoke furniture dating from any period.

Philip Colleck of London
830 Broadway, New York, New York
10003, USA
Tel: 212 505 2500
Queen Anne, Chippendale, Adam, Hepplewhite and Regency furniture and accessories.

Rupert Cavendish Antiques
610 King's Road, London SW6
Tel: 0171 731 7041
Empire and Art Deco furniture and *objets d'art*; specially commissioned Neoclassical furniture.

R.&D. Davidson
Romsey House, 51 Maltravers Street,
Arundel, West Sussex BN18
Tel: 01903 883141
Website: http://www.rddavidson.co.uk

Stock a wide range of furniture inspired by eighteenth- and nineteenth-century designs and Art Deco pieces; special commissions form an important part of R.&D. Davidson's activities.

The Dining Room Shop
62 White Hart Lane,
London SW13
Tel: 0181 878 1020
Antique dining-room furniture and tableware; reproduces period dining-room furniture to order.

D'eco
112 Windmill Road, Sunbury,
Middlesex TW16
Tel: 01932 779070
Hand-made furniture in the Art Deco style.

Dixon of Ipswich (exclusive furniture division of Tempus Stet. See below.)
Baird Close, Hadleigh Road Industrial Estate, Ipswich, Suffolk IP2
Tel: 01473 252121
Bespoke English reproduction furniture, including dining tables and chairs, dressing tables and console tables.

Martin J. Dodge
Southgate, Wincanton,
Somerset BA9
Tel: 01963 32388
Produces a standard range of fine English pieces from the 18th and 19th centuries, including designs by Chippendale, Gainsborough and Sheraton, and custom-made furniture.

Peter Farlow
189 Westbourne Grove,
London W11
Tel: 0171 229 8306
Gothic Revival, Arts and Crafts and Aesthetic period furniture; provides a specialist finishes decorating service.

Fens
46 Lots Road, London SW10
Tel: 0171 352 9883
Deals in and restores antique furniture; reproduces bespoke period furniture and stocks architectural antiques.

Fine Art Society
148 New Bond Street,
London W1Y
Tel: 0171 629 5116
Commercial gallery stocking nineteenth- and early twentieth-century furniture.

Christopher Gibbs
Dove Walk, 107A Pimlico Road,
London SW1
Tel: 0171 730 8200
Wide range of period furniture.

W.R. Harvey
86 Corn Street, Witney,
Oxfordshire OX8
Tel: 01993 706501
Furniture dating from the late 17th to the early 19th century.

Nicholas Haslam
12 Holbein Place, London SW1
Tel: 0171 730 8623
Eighteenth- and nineteenth-century tables and mirrors.

Heal's
196 Tottenham Court Road,
London W1
Tel: 0171 636 1666

**Christopher Hodsoll,
Incorporating Bennison**
89 & 91 Pimlico Road, London SW1
Tel: 0171 730 3370
Large collection of furniture, focusing especially on the late 18th and early 19th centuries.

Hotspur
14 Lowndes Street, London SW1X
Tel: 0171 235 1918
Georgian furniture.

Christopher Howe
93 Pimlico Road, London SW1
Tel: 0171 730 7987
Antique and reproduction country-house furniture dating from the Regency period to the present day.

The Iron Bed Co.
Terminus Road, Chichester,
West Sussex PO19
Tel: 01243 778999
Traditional and contemporary bedroom furniture and accessories. Mail order service available.

Jackson-Mitchell
5718 Kennett Pike, Centerville,
Delaware 19807, USA
Tel: 302 656 0110
Seventeenth-, eighteenth- and early nineteenth-century English formal and country furniture and associated *objets*.

Anthony James & Son
88 Fulham Road, London SW3
Tel: 0171 581 3807
Eighteenth- and nineteenth-century furniture, including dining tables, chairs, bookcases and tallboys.

Jeremy
29 Lowndes Street, London SW1X
Tel: 0171 823 2923
Eighteenth- and early nineteenth-century furniture and works of art.

S.&H. Jewell
26 Parker Street, London WC2B
Tel: 0171 405 8520
Antique and reproduction English furniture dating from the 19th and 20th centuries, with a strong emphasis on the turn of the century. Restoration service available.

The Lacquer Chest
75 Kensington Church Street,
London W8
Tel: 0171 937 1306
Antique English country-house furniture, ceramics, lighting and accessories dating from the early 18th to the mid 20th century.

Liberty
214 Regent Street, London W1
Tel: 0171 734 1234
Original furniture and fabrics dating
from the Arts and Crafts Movement
onwards.

Malvern Studios
56 Cowleigh Road, Malvern,
Worcestershire WR14
Tel: 01684 574913
Antique furniture, furniture restoration
and reproduction traditional lighting.

Thomas Messel
Bradley Court, Wotton-under-Edge,
Gloucestershire GL12
Tel: 01453 843220
Designs specially commissioned
furniture of all periods.

Newel Art Galleries
425 East 53rd Street, New York,
New York 10022
Tel: 212 758 1970
Antique furniture and associated
objets, including Adam pieces, Chinese
Chippendale and Brighton Pavilion -
style bamboo and lacquer pieces.

Parsons Table Co.
362 Fulham Road, London SW10
Tel: 0171 352 7444
Reproduction furniture dating from
the late 17th to the mid 19th century,
including tables, chests-of-drawers,
window seats, occasional tables,
bedside tables.

Pruskin
73 Kensington Church Street,
London W8
Tel: 0171 937 1994
Twentieth-century furniture and
carpets, including designs by
Bloomsbury and Omega, and
sometimes Mackintosh and Godwin.

Paul Reeves
32B Kensington Church Street,
London W8
Tel: 0171 937 1594
Gothic Revival, Arts and Crafts
and Mackintosh furniture, ceramics,
glass and textiles.

Geoffrey Stead
The Dower House, Chastleton, nr.
Moreton-in-Marsh, Gloucestershire
GL56
Tel: 01608 674364
Wide range of English eighteenth- and
nineteenth-century furniture.

Tatiana Tafur
134 Lots Road, London SW10
Tel: 0171 376 3115
Faithful reproductions of eighteenth-
century painted furniture.

Rankine Taylor
34 Dollar Street, Cirencester,
Gloucestershire GL7
Tel: 01285 652529
Furniture and rare associated *objets*
dating from the mid 17th to the mid
20th century.

Tempus Stet
Hereford House, Kennington Park,
Cranmer Road, London SW9
Tel: 0171 820 8666
Manufacturers and suppliers of a wide
range of eighteenth- and nineteenth-
century reproduction furniture,
including decorative pieces, console
tables and mirrors; period lighting and
curtain accessories; undertake special
projects worldwide.

William Tillman
30 St. James's Street, London SW1A
Tel: 0171 839 2500
Reproduces eighteenth-century dining-
room furniture.

Titchmarsh & Goodwin
Trinity Works, Back Hamlet,
Ipswich, Suffolk IP3
Tel: 01473 252158
Reproduction furniture dating from the
late 15th to the early 19th century, with
special emphasis on cabinets.

Wycombe Cane & Rush Works
Victoria Street, High Wycombe,
Buckinghamshire HP11
Tel: 01494 442429
French caning and traditional seating
specialists.

LIGHTING

Art Deco Originals
Halifax Antiques Centre, Queen's Road
Mill, on the junction of Queen's Road
and Gibbet Street, Halifax, West
Yorkshire HX1
Tel: 01422 347377 (daytime); 01274
882051 (evenings)
Website: http://
www.muir-hewitt.com/hewitt
Art Deco lamps, chrome, furniture,
ceramics and mirrors.

Bardith
901 Madison Avenue, New York,
New York 10021, USA
Tel: 212 737 3775
Brass and glass hanging light
fixtures; tableware.

Bella Figura
G5 Chelsea Harbour Design Centre,
London SW10
Tel: 0171 376 4564
Decoy Farm, Old Church Road, Melton,
Woodbridge, Suffolk IP13
Tel: 01394 461111
Manufacturers and suppliers of
seventeenth- and eighteenth-century
reproduction lamps.

Fergus Cochrane & Leigh Warren
570 King's Road, London SW6
Tel: 0171 736 9166
Lighting of all periods and all types.

M.E. Crick Chandeliers
166 Kensington Church Street,
London W8
Tel: 0171 229 1338
Chandeliers dating from the 18th, 19th
and early 20th centuries.

Denton Antiques
156 Kensington Church Street,
London W8
Tel: 0171 229 5866
Wide range of lighting, including
chandeliers, candelabra and
candlesticks.

Charles Edwards
582 King's Road, London SW6
Tel: 0171 736 8490
Antique and reproduction nineteenth-
century lighting and furniture.

The Facade
196 Westbourne Grove,
London W11
Tel: 0171 727 2159
Decorative lighting dating mainly
from the 20th century.

Forbes & Lomax
205A St. John's Hill,
London SW11
Tel: 0171 738 0202
Designer light switches, dimmers
and socket outlets, including their
unlacquered brass and
invisible ranges.

Fritz Fryer
12 Brookend Street, Ross-on-Wye,
Herefordshire HR9
Tel: 01989 567416
Victorian and Edwardian lighting.

Christopher Hyde
180 Wandsworth Bridge Road,
London SW6
Tel: 0171 731 8830
Reproduction lighting dating from the
Georgian period to the Edwardian;
manufactures bespoke lighting based
on original pieces, and undertakes
special project work with interior
designers and architects.

Anthony James & Son
88 Fulham Road, London SW3
Tel: 0171 581 3807
Lighting dating from the early 19th
century and furniture.

Jones Lighting
194 Westbourne Grove,
London W11
Tel: 0171 229 6866
Lighting dating from *c.* 1860
to *c.* 1960.

The Lacquer Chest
75 Kensington Church Street,
London W8
Tel: 0171 937 1306
Lighting, English country house
furniture, ceramics and *objets d'art*
dating from the early 18th to the mid
20th century.

Malvern Studios
56 Cowleigh Road, Malvern,
Worcestershire WR14
Tel: 01684 574913
Traditional lighting including
reproductions of Georgian, Victorian
and Edwardian designs; antique
furniture and restoration service.

McCEd
8 Holbein Place, London SW1
Tel: 0171 730 4025
Antique lighting suitable for the
country house.

McClenaghan
69, Pimlico Road, London SW1W
Tel: 0171 730 4187
Stocks a wide range of antique lighting.

McLoud
269 Wandsworth Bridge Road,
London SW6
Tel: 0171 371 7151
Lighting and light fittings based on
Gothic, Georgian and Victorian designs.

W. Sitch & Co.
48 Berwick Street, London W1
Tel: 0171 437 3776
Antique and reproduction lighting and
fittings, including chandeliers, wall
brackets and sconces; restoration service;
lacquerers, bronzers, gilders and platers.

Richard Taylor
91 Princedale Road, London W11
Tel: 0171 792 1808
Authentic recreations of eighteenth-
and nineteenth-century lighting,
glassware and crystalware.

Vaughan
23 Carnwath Road Industrial Estate,
London SW6
Tel: 0171 610 6544
Manufacturers and suppliers of 300
different lighting products based on
antique models, including table lamps,
floor lamps, sconces, chandeliers and
wall lanterns.

Christopher Wray Lighting
591–593 King's Road, London SW6
Tel: 0171 736 8434
Reproduces traditional lights in a wide
variety of styles including Regency
brass chandeliers, Art Nouveau bases
and Art Deco chrome and glass wall
brackets. Christopher Wray has 19
shops nationwide and produces a
catalogue of its products.

METALWORK

Antique Restorations
Brass Foundry Castings, Brasted
Forge, Brasted, Kent TN16
Tel: 01959 563863
Georgian, Regency, Victorian and
Edwardian door furniture; eighteenth-
and nineteenth-century furniture and
clocks. Mail order only.

A Touch of Brass
210 Fulham Road, London SW10
Tel: 0171 352 5495
Georgian, Regency and Victorian door
furniture, including knockers, knobs,
locks, escutcheons and finger plates.

J.D. Beardmore
3–4 Percy Street, London SW10
Tel: 0171 637 7041
Period brass door furniture.

R. Bleasdale
394 Caledonian Road,
London N1
Tel: 0171 609 0394
Victorian and Georgian cast iron.

John Churchill
The New Forge, Capton
Workshop, Capton, nr.
Dartmouth, Devon TQ6
Tel: 01803 712535
Blacksmith reproducing traditional
ironmongery, particularly door and
window furniture, dating from the
medieval period onwards.

Clayton Munroe
Kingston West Drive, Kingston,
Staverton, Totnes, Devon TQ9
Tel: 01803 762626
Unusual door furniture and cabinet
fittings dating from the 17th century
onwards. Mail order only.

Horton Brasses
P.O. Box 95, Nooks Hill Road,
Cromwell, Connecticut 06416, USA
Tel: 860 635 4400
Brass cabinet hardware in
Hepplewhite, Sheraton,
Queen Anne, Chippendale, and
Victorian styles. Mail order only.

Jim Lawrence
Scotland Hall Farm, Stoke-by-Nayland,
Colchester, Essex CO6
Tel: 01206 263459
Traditional ironwork.

Optimum Brasses
7 Castle Street, Bampton, Tiverton,
Devon EX16
Tel: 01398 331515
Faithfully reproduce eighteenth- and
nineteenth-century furniture hardware,
including handles, mouldings and feet.
Produce 26 catalogues of items in
addition to special commissions.

Period House Group
Main Street, Leavening, North
Yorkshire YO17
Tel: 01653 658554
Period door, cabinet and
window furniture.

H.E. Savill
9–12 St. Martin's Place, Scarborough,
North Yorkshire, YO11
Tel: 01723 373032
Cabinet fittings and door furniture
dating from the 16th to the early 20th
century.

J. Shiner
8 Windmill Street, London, W1P
Tel: 0171 636 0740
Regency, Victorian and Edwardian
furniture hardware.

Ghislaine Stewart
110 Fentiman Road, London SW8
Tel: 0171 820 9440
Modern interpretations of door
furniture, lamp bases and fireplaces
dating from the Renaissance to the
early 19th century.

Walcot Reclamation
108 Walcot Street, Bath BA1
Tel: 01225 444404
Antique door furniture, bathroom
furniture and architectural antiques.

TEXTILES

G.P.&J. Baker
P.O. Box 30, West End Road, High
Wycombe, Buckinghamshire HP11
Tel: 01494 467400 (Head Office.
Telephone for stockists)
Reproduce prints from G.P.&J. Baker's
own archive of designs, dating from the
early 18th to the mid 20th century.

Hilary Batstone
51 Kinnerton Street, London SW1
Tel: 0171 259 6070
Reproduce nineteenth-century curtains
in printed cottons and linens, damasks
and brocades.

Bennison Fabrics
16 Holbein Place, London SW1
Tel: 0171 730 8076
Faithfully reproduce printed fabrics
from Bennison's archive of antique
textiles, curtains and rugs dating from
the 18th and 19th centuries. Print to
order, carrying a small amount of stock.

Joanna Booth
247 King's Road, London SW3
Tel: 0171 352 8998
Seventeenth- and eighteenth-century
silks, velvets and tapestries.

Borderline
2/7 Chelsea Harbour Design Centre,
London SW10
Tel: 0171 823 3567
Archive prints dating from the early
19th to the mid 20th century.

Brunschwig & Fils
979 Third Avenue, New York, New
York 10022, USA
Tel: 212 838 7878
Woven fabrics, chintzes and wallpapers
from documentary designs, including
The Royal Pavilion at Brighton
Collection.

Colefax & Fowler
39 Brook Street, London W1Y
Tel: 0171 493 2231
Produce fabrics, wallpapers and carpets
interpreted from eighteenth- and
nineteenth-century English and French
designs.

Decorative Fabrics Gallery
278–280 Brompton Road, London SW3
Tel: 0171 589 4778
Stocks ranges from G.P.&J. Baker (see
above).

Gainsborough Silk Weaving
16 Coda Centre, 184 Munster Road,
London SW6
Tel: 0171 386 7153
Traditional handwoven silks and
archival wallpapers. Telephone for
stockists.

Linda Gumb
9 Camden Passage,
London N1
Tel: 0171 354 1184
Tapestries and textiles dating
from the late 17th to the 19th
century; interior design
consultation service.

Nicholas Herbert
118 Lots Road, London SW10
Tel: 0171 376 5596
Printed cottons faithfully
reproduced from archival designs
dating from the late 18th to the
mid 19th century.

Liberty
214 Regent Street,
London W1
Tel: 0171 734 1234
Fabrics (including William
Morris designs) and antique furniture
dating from the Arts and Crafts
Movement onwards.

Osborne & Little
304 King's Road,
London SW3
Tel: 0171 352 1456
Printed and woven fabrics and
wallpapers including the Liberty
collections dating from William
Morris to the present day.

Pavilion Textiles
Freshford Hall, Staples Hill,
Freshford, Bath BA3
Tel: 01225 722522
Suppliers of nineteenth- and early
twentieth-century document fabrics.

Ramm, Son & Crocker
G28–29 Chelsea Harbour Design
Centre, London SW10
Tel: 0171 352 0931
Specialize in the authentic
reproduction of handblock and
handscreen archive prints from
the 18th and 19th centuries. The
showroom displays a large collection
of documentary prints, weaves and
wallpapers.

Paul Reeves
32B Kensington Church Street,
London W8
Tel: 0171 937 1594
Gothic Revival, Arts and Crafts and
Mackintosh textiles, furniture,
ceramics and glass.

Sanderson
112–120 Brompton Road,
London SW3
Tel: 0171 584 3344
Late nineteenth-century fabrics
and wallpapers, especially designs
from the Morris archive; reproduces
designs from Sanderson's own
archive.

The Silk Gallery
G25 Chelsea Harbour
Design Centre, London SW10
Tel: 0171 351 1790
Reproduces woven and hand-printed

silks, including designs taken from
eighteenth- and nineteenth-century
documents.

Peter Smyth
42 Moreton Street,
London SW1
Tel: 0171 630 9898
Eighteenth- and nineteenth-century
upholstery fabrics, needlework,
hangings and tapestries.

Stothert & Miles
Calder Mount Showrooms, Calder
House Lane, Garstang, nr. Preston,
Lancashire PR3
Tel: 01995 605384
Archive prints dating from the
late 18th and early 19th centuries.

Titley & Marr
1/7 Chelsea Harbour Design Centre,
London SW10
Tel: 0171 351 2913
Have a wide range of English
nineteenth-century furnishing
fabrics, with particular emphasis on
chintzes.

Timney Fowler
388 King's Road, London SW3
Tel: 0171 352 2263
Black and white fabrics taken from
classical engravings, eighteenth-
century portraits and wallpapers.

Today Interiors
122 Fulham Road, London SW3
Tel: 0171 244 6661
Stock includes eighteenth- and
nineteenth-century fabrics and
wallpapers.

Warner Fabrics
G9 Chelsea Harbour Design Centre,
London SW10
Tel: 0171 376 7578
Produce fabrics and wallpapers
inspired by their archive of designs
dating back to 1669.

Watts of Westminster
2/9 Chelsea Harbour Design Centre,
London SW10
Tel: 0171 376 4486
Fabrics and wallpapers drawing on
material dating from the early 18th
to the early 20th century, including
designs by Pugin, Bodley, Sedding
and Voysey.

Wilson Reclamation Services
Yew Tree Barn, Newton-in-Cartmel,
Grange-over-Sands, Cumbria LA11
Tel: 01539 531498
Faithfully reproduces curtains and
trimmings from original patterns;
architectural antiques.

Zoffany
63 South Audley Street,
London W1
Tel: 0171 495 2505
Produces woven and printed fabrics,
carpets and wallpapers. Collections
include English eighteenth- and
nineteenth-century designs.

TRADITIONAL *and* HERITAGE PAINTS

Bolloms Paint Centre
71 Brushfield Street, London E1
Tel: 0171 375 0497
Makes up special paint matches for a client's particular requirements.

Cy-Près
14 Bells Close, Brigstock, Kettering, Northamptonshire NN14
Tel: 01536 373431
Paints, mortars and plasters for historic buildings. Mail order only.

Dulux Heritage
Tel: 01420 23024
Manufactures Georgian, Victorian and Edwardian and Art Deco colour ranges. Telephone for colour card and nearest stockist.

Peter Farlow
189 Westbourne Grove, London W11
Tel: 0171 229 8306
Specialist finishes decorating service; nineteenth-century furniture.

Farrow & Ball
Uddens Trading Estate, Wimborne, Dorset BH21 (factory, shop and free colour card)
Tel: 01202 876141
249 Fulham Road, London SW3 (showroom)
Tel: 0171 351 0273
Manufacture the National Trust colour range and colours drawn from their own archive.

Fired Earth
117–119 Fulham Road, London SW3
Tel: 0171 589 0489
Produces the Victoria & Albert Museum's three Traditional Paints ranges: The Historic Colours, The Pugin Colours and The William Morris Colours; wall tiles.

Green & Stone
259 King's Road, London SW3
Tel: 0171 352 0837
Supply pigments and 30–40 ranges of paints including the traditional Annie Sloane range.

Jocasta Innes Paint Magic
79 Shepperton Road, London N1
Tel: 0171 354 9696
Stocks a wide range of paints, including the Jocasta Innes Collection, a mix of 15 historic and contemporary colours; produces the William Morris Collection of stencils and stencil paints. Has shops in Marlow, Harrogate, Bath, Shrewsbury, Richmond (Surrey), Arundel, Guildford and Brighton.

Nutshell Natural
Hamlyn House, Mardle Way, Buckfastleigh, Devon TQ11
Tel: 01364 642892
Supplies a range of mineral pigments which can be mixed to produce heritage colours.

John Oliver
33 Pembridge Road, London W11
Tel: 0171 727 3735
Manufactures a range of paints, mostly based on heritage colours.

The Paint Centre
Unit 3, 1 Horton Close, West Drayton, Middlesex UB7
Tel: 01895 446232
Manufactures finishes to order.

Papers and Paints
4 Park Walk, London SW10
Tel: 0171 352 8626
Stock a very wide range of 'historic colours with precedent', including the Dulux Heritage colours and those drawn from the 1807 housepainter's colour card; books on historic colours and decoration are also available. Patrick Baty, a consultant in the use of colour 1660–1850, is obtainable at the same address.

Pine Brush Products
Stockingate, Coton Cranford, Staffordshire ST8
Tel: 01785 282799
The Old Post Office, Bradley, nr. Stafford (shop – open Saturdays only)
Tel: 01785 780908
Manufacture the Colourman paint range of 42 colours, which reproduce the effects of buttermilk paints of the 18th and 19th centuries.

Potmolen
27 Woodcock Industrial Estate, Warminster, Wiltshire BA12
Tel: 01985 213960
Traditional paints specialists.

Simpsons Paints
122 Broadley Street, London NW8
Tel: 0171 723 6657
Main London agent for Farrow & Ball, Sandersons, John Oliver, Paint Library and Dulux. Stock relevant tools, glazes and books.

WALLPAPERS

Baer & Ingram
273 Wandsworth Bridge Road, London SW6
Tel: 0171 736 6111
Victorian- and Edwardian-style wallpapers.

Alexander Beauchamp
2/12 Chelsea Harbour Design Centre, London SW10
Tel: 0171 376 4556
Designers, handprinters and manufacturers of fine wallpapers and fabrics. Designs are drawn from their extensive archive, which holds material dating from the late 17th to the mid 20th century.

Bradbury & Bradbury Wallpapers
P.O. Box 155, Benicia, California 94510, USA
Tel: 707 746 1900
Hand-printed wallpapers and borders in the Victorian style with designs by Morris, Dresser and Pugin. Mail order.

Brunschwig & Fils
979 Third Avenue, New York, New York 10022, USA
Tel: 212 838 7878
Wallpapers, woven fabrics and chintzes from documentary designs, including The Royal Pavilion Collection.

Cole & Son
G9 Chelsea Harbour Design Centre, London SW10
Tel: 0171 376 7578
Produce a number of wallpapers collections based on Cole's archive of designs, which date back to the 17th century; reproduce archive patterns to special order.

Colefax & Fowler
39 Brook Street, London W1Y
Tel: 0171 493 2231
Produce wallpapers, fabrics and carpets interpreted from eighteenth- and nineteenth-century designs.

Elizabeth Eaton
85 Bourne Street, London SW1
Tel: 0171 730 2262
Supplies wallpapers drawn from English historic designs of the 18th and 19th centuries.

Guy Evans
3/19–20 Chelsea Harbour Design Centre, London SW10
Tel: 0171 352 7118
Reproduces wallpapers, fabrics and trimmings dating from the 15th century to the present day.

Gainsborough Silk Weaving
16 Coda Centre, 184 Munster Road, London SW6
Tel: 0171 386 7153
Archival wallpapers and traditional handwoven silks.

Tom Lewis Studios
Crown House, Bingswood Trading Estate, Whaley Bridge, High Peak, Derbyshire SK23
Tel: 01663 735353
Offer a surface pattern design service to the wallpaper and home furnishings industry worldwide. Tom Lewis' designs are inspired by its archive of eighteenth- and nineteenth-century textile documents.

Osborne & Little
304 King's Road, London SW3
Tel: 0171 352 1456
Printed wallpapers and fabrics, including the Victoria & Albert Museum's Historic Collection.

Ramm, Son & Crocker
G28–29 Chelsea Harbour Design Centre, London SW10
Tel: 0171 352 0931
Specialize in the authentic reproduction of handblock and handscreen archive prints from the 18th and 19th centuries.

Sanderson
112–120 Brompton Road, London SW3
Tel: 0171 584 3344
Late nineteenth-century wallpapers and fabrics, especially designs from the Morris archive; reproduces designs from Sanderson's own archive.

Today Interiors
122 Fulham Road, London SW3
Tel: 0171 244 6661
Stock includes eighteenth- and nineteenth-century wallpapers.

Warner Fabrics
G9 Chelsea Harbour Design Centre, London SW10
Tel: 0171 376 7578
Produce wallpapers and fabrics inspired by their archive of designs dating back to 1669.

Watts of Westminster
2/9 Chelsea Harbour Design Centre, London SW10
Tel: 0171 376 4486 *(see Textiles)*.

Hamilton Weston
18 St. Mary's Grove, Richmond, Surrey TW9
Tel: 0181 940 4850
Specializes in period design, including wallpapers and fabrics, holding an extensive archive of designs dating from the 17th to the 19th century.

Zoffany
63 South Audley Street, London W1
Tel: 0171 495 2505 *(see Textiles)*.

Select
BIBLIOGRAPHY

Many of the volumes, records and documents from which the material reproduced in this book has been drawn are, by their very nature, unpublished and, in many cases, not immediately accessible. Indeed, the best possible bibliography for this book would be a complete listing of the archives and records held in public collections and by individual companies throughout England. The details of all such bodies are, however, given in the Resource Directory. The titles listed below are of those books which I would recommend for further reading.

Anscombe, Isabelle, *Omega and After: Bloomsbury and the Decorative Arts*, London, 1985

Atterbury, Paul (ed.), *A.W.N. Pugin: Master of Gothic Revival*, New York, 1995

Barrett, Helena and Phillips, John, *Suburban Style: The British Home 1840-1960*, London, 1987

Batkin, Maureen, *Wedgwood Ceramics 1846–1959*, London, 1982

Boynton, Lindsay (ed.), *Gillow Furniture Designs 1760–1800*, London, 1995

Calloway, Stephen, *The House of Liberty*, London, 1992

Catleugh, Jon, *William De Morgan Tiles*, Shepton Beauchamp, 1983

Cooper, Jeremy, *Victorian and Edwardian Interiors and Furniture*, London, 1987

Copeland, Robert, *Spode and Copeland Marks and Other Relevant Intelligence*, London, 1993

Durant, Stuart, *Christopher Dresser*, London, 1993

Evans, Wendy, Ross, Cathy and Werner, Alex, *Whitefriars Glass*, London, 1995

Forty, Adrian, *Objects of Desire: Design and Society 1750–1980*, London, 1986

Goodden, Susanna, *At the Sign of the Fourposter: The History of Heal's*, London, 1984

Griffin, Leonard and Meisel, Louis K., *Clarice Cliff: The Bizarre Affair*, London, 1988

Hoskins, Lesley (ed.), *The Papered Wall: The History and Techniques of Wallpaper*, London, 1994

MacCarthy, Fiona, *British Design Since 1880*, London, 1982

Meller, Susan and Elffers, Joost, *Textile Designs*, London, 1991

Parissien, Steven, *Adam Style*, London, 1992

Parissien, Steven, *Regency Style*, London, 1992

Parry, Linda, *Textiles of the Arts and Crafts Movement*, London, 1988

Parry, Linda, *William Morris Textiles*, London, 1983

Praz, Mario, *An Illustrated History of Interior Decoration From Pompeii to Art Nouveau*, London, 1964

Reilly, Robin, *Wedgwood: The New Illustrated Dictionary*, Woodbridge, 1995

Rothstein, Natalie, *Silk Designs of the Eighteenth Century*, London, 1990

The Silver Studio Collection: The London Design Studio 1880–1963, London, 1980

Slesin, Suzanne, Rozensztroch, Daniel and Cliff, Stafford, *Collecting Everyday Things: Kitchen Ceramics*, New York, 1997

Thornton, Peter, *Authentic Decor: The Domestic Interior 1620–1920*, London, 1984

Tilbrook, A.J., *The Designs of Archibald Knox for Liberty & Co.*, London, 1995

Youds, Bryn, *Susie Cooper: An Elegant Affair*, London, 1996

Picture
CREDITS

INDEX

Author's ACKNOWLEDGMENTS

My very grateful thanks is due to all those who have helped in the preparation of this book, especially the staff at the many museums and archives who took the time and trouble to reply to our letters; in particular, I would like to thank the staff of the various departments of the Victoria & Albert Museum, especially Isobel Sinden and Martin Durrant in the Picture Library.

Of the many companies who opened their archives to me, my particular thanks goes to Lynn Miller at the Wedgwood Museum, Paul Wood and Stella McIntyre at the Spode Museum Trust, Terry Woolliscroft at Caradon Bathrooms Ltd., Graham Darby and Richard G. Pugh-Cook at Tomkinson's Carpets Ltd., Peter Ravenhill and Yvonne Smith at Woodward Grosvenor & Co. Ltd., and Andrew Priest who photographed the Woodward Grosvenor archive material for us.

I am indebted to Philip De Bay for his enthusiastic support of this project, for the use of his photographic archive and for taking many more photographs for us, and to Kulbir Thandi, who took the photographs of the Spode Archive reproduced on the jacket and on the preliminary pages of this book, to Sara Waterson who did a remarkable job of picture and source research, and to John Scott for his continued assistance, support, patience and knowledge.

Finally, my thanks go to the designers of the past whose work accidentally or deliberately ended up in the nation's archives; this is a testament to their labours, but is only a sample of the riches which they created. The *Artists' Papers Register* at the Henry Moore Institute in Leeds is attempting the near-impossible in making a detailed listing of the holdings of over 1000 repositories in England and Scotland, including libraries, museums, galleries, universities, societies and institutions.

If, as a designer, your appetite is whetted by the contents of this book, go and search out the original archives for yourself. I have only been able to show a fraction of what is stored away, but if the illustrations in this book prove a source of inspiration to you, as I hope they will, then consider carefully before you consign your own designs to the attic or the incinerator rather than to a repository, where they may form part of a remarkable heritage in the future.

British Library Cataloguing-in-Publication Data
A catalogue record for this book is available from the British Library

ISBN 0-500-01883-9

Printed and bound in Singapore by C.S. Graphics